THE POLITICAL ECONOMY OF DEINDUSTRIALIZATION

Also by Ray Kiely and published by Agenda Publishing

The Conservative Challenge to Globalization: Anglo-American Perspectives

THE POLITICAL ECONOMY OF DEINDUSTRIALIZATION

Causes, Consequences, Implications

RAY KIELY

agenda
publishing

First published in 2024 by Agenda Publishing

Agenda Publishing Limited
PO Box 185
Newcastle upon Tyne
NE20 2DH
www.agendapub.com

ISBN 978-1-78821-756-9

British Library Cataloguing-in-Publication Data
A catalogue record for this book is available from the British Library

Typeset by Newgen UK
Printed and bound in the UK by TJ Books

CONTENTS

ACKNOWLEDGEMENTS

I began this book during the surreal and difficult period of the Covid-19 pandemic and the lockdowns that followed. Even lone researchers need support, and in such an environment, online professional support was particularly important and so many thanks to a number of colleagues – at Queen Mary University of London and beyond – who helped to keep it going, and supported initial ideas around it. These include Peter Brett, James Dunkerley, Alfredo Saad-Filho, Rick Saull, Ben Selwyn, Andrew Sumner, Matthew Watson and David Williams. Family also helped, especially Will and Ella Kiely, as did many friends too numerous to mention here (not least because I fear I might leave someone out). As always, music also helped, including Broadcast, De La Soul, Galaxie 500, Julia Holter, My Bloody Valentine, Spacemen 3, This is the Kit, Tricky, and the very much missed Low. A number of losses also occurred, and in the world of academia I should give special mention to Paul Kennedy of Manchester Metropolitan University and Leo Panitch of York University, Toronto. On a more personal level, I should mention one who I saw (and heard) many times but never formally met, and two who I knew very well, and the book is dedicated to the memories of Mimi Parker, Shani Joslin and Barry Kiely.

CHAPTER 1

INTRODUCTION

This is a book, as the title suggests, about the causes, consequences and perhaps above all, politics of deindustrialization. On the face of it, this is obvious because of the title, but actually we need to be clear about what this means, which is far from straightforward. This is in part because deindustrialization is not quite as well defined as some suggest, and indeed some media leave out any clear definition beyond bleak reports of rust-belt areas and run-down towns where employment in once secure manufacturing jobs has declined. Not unrelated, it is often assumed that deindustrialization is a phenomenon specific to the Global North and is a bad thing, an undesirable phenomenon. This position is not intrinsically incorrect or indeed correct, but it needs to be carefully argued and linked to wider implications, not least the aggregate effects on a particular national economy, as well as regional implications within that economy.

This in turn potentially leads us away from simply focusing on deindustrialization per se, part of which involves a focus on the politics of deindustrialization. As we shall see in the chapters that follow, most of the literature on deindustrialization is focused on the Global North, although this is changing, and most of it focuses on economic measurements. This is perfectly acceptable and much of this work looks at different ways of understanding the causes of deindustrialization. Although often briefly spelt out in the literature, understanding the causes of deindustrialization will have political implications – for example, if job losses in manufacturing in the US are caused by cheap manufacturing imports from the Global South, then this might, and indeed has given rise to protectionist pressures. So, in that sense we need to consider the links between the economic contentions about deindustrialization and the politics that might follow from these arguments. Moreover, politics are not simply derived from economics in any straightforward way, and even if the case is made that so-called industrial decline is a product of the rise of Southern manufacturing, this might resonate even if the evidence for it is not very strong. But this in turn may have deep political implications, as we shall see.

This book therefore focuses on the *politics* of deindustrialization. It does not neglect consideration of the economic arguments, but it looks at them with an eye to thinking through the political implications. The focus is on the politics of deindustrialization in two ways: (1) to show how bad economic ideas can lead to bad politics; and (2) to investigate the wider political fallout in response to broad socio-economic changes, of which deindustrialization is one part. This will be done in depth: in Chapter 6, which will consider contemporary geopolitics; Chapter 7, which examines contemporary populism; and Chapter 8, which looks at the politics of levelling up, right-wing populism, arguments around a universal basic income (UBI) and a Green New Deal. While these are explicitly considered at the end of the book, all of the chapters are written with an eye on how particular economic arguments might have political implications, and this is addressed in the first half of the book.

Before outlining further the structure of the book, and the basic cases made in the chapters that follow, we need to briefly define deindustrialization. The most basic definition is a decline in the proportion of the labour force in a country that works in the manufacturing sector, plus the mining and construction industries[1] (Rowthorn & Wells 1987: 5). This is usually considered a negative phenomenon among those writing in the classical tradition of political economy, and that is because of the special role that manufacturing can play in boosting the growth of a national economy (Kaldor 1967, 1978). In particular, the case has often been made that industrialization – compared to growth in agriculture and services – is likely to proceed more rapidly, as manufacturing in particular generates forward and backward linkages to the rest of the economy, and there is greater scope for capital accumulation, greater knowledge spill-overs to the rest of the economy, and so on. There is a strong link between manufacturing output growth and labour productivity, due to a deepening division of labour, specialization, learning by doing and the use of economies of scale (Kaldor 1978). Therefore, if a country wants to develop – in the sense of increase rates of growth but also possibly social development like education and health improvements – it must industrialize, especially in manufacturing (Kitching 1982; Kiely 1998). On the face of it then, deindustrialization could be seen as a negative phenomenon because it slows down growth, for which growth in the service sector cannot

1. Industrialization and deindustrialization thus refer to more than just the manufacturing sector, and include mining and construction industries. However, it is the manufacturing sector that is considered most important and significant in these debates, for reasons outlined in the text. This qualification is not made persistently throughout the book, but should be borne in mind in the references to both industrialization and deindustrialization.

compensate. This could be considered the classic case of negative deindustrialization, where declining shares of manufacturing employment coincide with falling growth, unemployment or at least underemployment, and so on (Rowthorn & Wells 1987: 5).

But there is another way of understanding deindustrialization, one that suggests that it can be a far more benign process. Neoclassical economists see no special role for industrialization, and therefore do not regard deindustrialization as intrinsically problematic. What is more important is the need for specialization, so that trade can help provide the basis for growth and ultimately convergence between the rich and poor world (Ohlin 1933). We might add that even those who do think that industrialization, and specifically manufacturing, is sectorally significant in terms of its capacity to generate growth, accept that at a certain point, countries begin to deindustrialize as increasing levels of manufacturing output can be achieved with comparatively fewer workers, precisely because manufacturing achieves more dynamic growth than other sectors. Thus, falling proportionate rates of manufacturing employment can coincide with increasing rates of output, which can be considered a case of positive deindustrialization (Rowthorn & Wells 1987: 5). The clear implication of this account is that deindustrialization does not matter, either in general or at a certain level of per capita income. The levels identified will be discussed in later chapters, but there are two issues that can be briefly highlighted here. First, there is an assumption that with specialization, the labour displaced from manufacturing will be absorbed by jobs offering better pay and conditions, and this has been questioned, including for economies in the Global North. Second, in terms of declining employment levels in manufacturing employment at relatively high per capita incomes, there does appear to be a growing tendency for deindustrialization to occur also at lower levels of per capita income, something referred to as "premature deindustrialization" (Rodrik 2016). If this is the case – and the evidence suggests it is – then this is a problem for various explanations around deindustrialization, and various political projects associated with the populist right. This in turn is important for while some have rightly called for treating such politics more seriously (Eatwell & Goodwin 2018; Goodwin 2023), often these calls simply want the populist turn and the demands of the right to be added to the "shopping list" of what is deemed "the political market". But if we are to take populist demands seriously, we also need to consider whether such demands can and should be delivered. As we shall see in Chapter 7, it is a short step from contextualization of the rise of the populist right, to apology for it.

The book deals with these issues initially by outlining in Part I, and in three chapters, different approaches to understanding deindustrialization. While each of them identifies a core position, and variations on that central approach, the focus is on the argument, and the evidence, but also the various politics that might arise out of these understandings. This is done in Chapters 2, 3 and 4. Chapter 2 examines in more depth the argument that deindustrialization does not matter, linking this to arguments around free trade and specialization, and the projection of an international division of labour based on a (relatively) deindustrialized Global North specializing in high-value services in a post-industrial knowledge economy, and a Global South that increasingly focuses on manufacturing (among other things). There are different versions of this argument, and include Third-Way approaches to globalization (Blair 2000; Giddens 2000), a post-manufacturing "global Britain" (Minford 2016) and some of the optimistic scenarios associated with the development of new technologies (also discussed in Chapter 4). We shall also highlight the problems of this approach alluded to above, namely the question of the nature of the new jobs in the service sector in the so-called advanced economies, and that of premature deindustrialization in the Global South.

Chapter 3 examines the question of whether or not the decline of manufacturing (employment) in the Global North is caused by the rise of manufacturing in (parts of) the Global South. The alleged causes vary and may reflect the rise of multinational companies investing more in manufacturing in the Global South or drawing on subcontractors through value chains in the latter. Slightly different, but not necessarily completely separate, it may reflect the rise of exports from the South and thus intensified import competition for the Northern economies. This may in turn reflect specific policies such as undervalued exchange rates in the South (and especially China), and various industrial policies designed to unpack and upgrade technologies in order to promote catch-up with the North. The politics of these explanations is far from straightforward, with some on the left identifying a new international division of labour that has led to unemployment and underemployment in the North, and the super-exploitation of workers in sweatshops in the South (Frobel *et al.* 1980; Frank 1984). Updated versions of this approach suggest that there is a global "race to the bottom" where labour standards are eroded in order to attract mobile capital (Burbach & Robinson 1999). But the right also sometimes draw on these kinds of arguments, and some decry national companies involved in foreign investment (Francis 1994). They also claim that the free movement of labour undermines wages and national identity and so are hostile to migration and multiculturalism. These kinds of arguments were made for example in the 1970s by some on the right (and indeed, left) in Britain (see Walker 1979), and today are made by the far right but also some conservatives otherwise committed to free trade (Francis 2004), and indeed some cultural conservatives of the left (Glasman 2020). We shall see in this chapter that these arguments face a number of problems. The import competition/ rising foreign investment/deployment of value chains as an explanation for deindustrialization in the Global North downplays the fact that at an aggregate level, manufacturing output remains high, and furthermore there is still the question of premature deindustrialization in the South. While this approach might work as an explanation for declining manufacturing employment in specific sectors, it does not work at the level of a national economy. Moreover, the migration argument focuses too narrowly on the supply of labour, and fails to note that migration can have beneficial economic effects as migrants are sources of demand for goods, and tend to be net contributors to government revenue, and indeed make positive contributions to ever-changing cultures. Nonetheless, while I reject zero-sum arguments about deindustrialization in the North and industrialization in the South, I shall also suggest that one example of industrialization in the South has far greater significance, especially in the realm of geopolitics, and that is the case of China. This is considered further in Chapters 5 and 6.

The fact that manufacturing employment may decline alongside aggregate increases in output is the main strength of the approach discussed in Chapter 4, namely that deindustrialization is a product of technological change. This argument can overlap with the one outlined in Chapter 2, and suggest that deindustrialization does not matter and jobs lost to manufacturing can be replaced by safer, cleaner and better paid jobs in the services sector, not only in the Global North but also in the Global South. This approach overlaps with what we might call a techno-optimism thesis, which suggests that humans are increasingly being liberated from boring, repetitive work, which can increasingly be carried out by new technologies, including artificial intelligence (AI) and robots (Pinker 2018; Ridley 2010). More pessimistic accounts point out that there is a real prospect that technological change might displace humans from the labour market, leading to an increase in the global population that is surplus to requirements (Davis 2004). While this has not generated massive unemployment in the Global North to date, it has coincided with relatively low increases in, and/or stagnant, wages, a worsening of employment conditions and security (such as healthcare access and pensions), and underemployment, as well as a massive informal sector in the Global South. All of this has happened alongside slower growth in the period from the 1970s through to the present, with particularly slow growth from 2008 onwards. All this suggests a somewhat downbeat assessment of the prospects for global labour.

This is addressed further in the second part of the book, which focuses on the wider context in which deindustrialization takes place and considers further the political implications. Chapter 5 further develops the critique of the technological change thesis of the previous chapter, and does so by moving the focus on to a consideration of the changes in global capitalism since the 1980s. The focus here is on the use of global value chains, and the selective rise of parts of the South in terms of manufacturing, but how this latter factor cannot be used as the main explanation for the deindustrialization of the North. The decline in living standards, stagnant wages and so on should instead be linked to the restructuring of capitalism, of which globalization is a significant part, and deindustrialization is a symptom. The chapter engages in depth with the work of Aaron Benanav (2020a), as does Chapter 4, and while I consider this to be perhaps the most sophisticated treatment of global deindustrialization, I also reject his arguments as to how this is part of a wider (50-year) crisis of global capitalism. Instead, I suggest that in many ways, this period represented – for a time at least – a triumph for that same capitalism, which in many ways is a more disturbing argument. However, the chapter also suggests that the fallout from the 2008 global financial crisis has given rise to a more prolonged crisis (since 2008, not 1973), exacerbated by Covid-19, reflected in the partial unpacking of globalization through trade and geopolitical tensions, interruptions to supply chains and of course the environmental crisis. These arguments are then developed further in the next chapter, which traces the shift from growing – and in some, though not all, respects, benign – interdependence to growing geopolitical tensions, with a particular emphasis on China and the US. Another manifestation of the fallout from the financial crisis – or what has been called the "polycrisis" (Tooze 2023a) – has been the resurgence of populism and this is considered in Chapter 7. Like the previous chapter, the treatment of the subject is far from exhaustive, and the focus is very much on how deindustrialization can help us to understand these issues, without making the wider – and wrong-headed – claim that it is the ultimate cause of these factors. The final substantive chapter looks at three suggested political alternatives, that of levelling up, universal basic income and the call for Green New Deals to deal with the environmental crisis and the jobs crisis. The chapter shows how each of these relate to the discussions in the previous chapter, and discuss both the viability and desirability of each, and how this help illuminate possible political futures.

This second half of the book brings together the arguments made throughout about the politics of – and it will become clear, *beyond* – deindustrialization, and the arguments are brought together in the book's short conclusion. While this is a book about deindustrialization, and it is one that examines the details and strengths and weaknesses around its causes, it is not one that necessarily adds to those economic arguments per se. Rather, it does review this literature and the data in some depth, but it is not for example, a definitive account, rather than a review of the debates around the so-called

"China shock" from around 2000 onwards. The book does take positions on the debates, but some are provisional and not as "conclusive" as some might desire. Rather, the positions taken are used to make explicit links to the politics of deindustrialization, both in terms of whether these positions rest on convincing economic arguments, but also – even if they do not – why such positions have arisen (but also why they may not "deliver"). There is plenty of quantitative data in the chapters to back up the arguments, but I have deliberately avoided tables in this book, but hopefully not at the cost of allowing the argument to flow. It should be clear, however, in the argument that follows that the book situates deindustrialization in a wider context of global capitalism, and while it rejects a great deal of Marxist dogma, the book does find some Marx-influenced accounts of capitalism useful (Chapter 5), without endorsing what passes for Marxist politics in the current age (Chapters 6 and 8). Any strict dichotomy of reform and revolution is rejected, as should be clear from the discussion in Chapter 8. It should also be clear that the book does endorse the idea of continued cores and peripheries in the international division of labour, while at the same time rejecting some of the methodological premises of world system theory (Chapter 3). In short, the book situates deindustrialization in the context of the uneven development of global capitalism, but also suggests that this is simply a context, and the politics that follow from it are uncertain, contingent and far from inevitable (Chapters 6–8).

PART I

EXPLAINING DEINDUSTRIALIZATION

CHAPTER 2

WHAT IS IT AND WHY IT MIGHT (NOT) MATTER

This chapter examines the argument that deindustrialization does not necessarily matter. There are a number of versions of this argument as we shall see, but ultimately the case rests on the contention that there is no need to be concerned if the proportion of the workforce employed in manufacturing falls, and in some respects, this decline should be welcomed. Sometimes the argument is made that there is nothing special about the manufacturing sector, and what is more important is specialization in competitive sectors, be they manufacturing or services, or even agriculture. But even some who argue that manufacturing does matter, go on to suggest that recent declines in manufacturing do not necessarily matter. This is because it shows both a healthy increase in productivity in manufacturing, and consequently less reliance on employing so many workers in that sector, and an upgrading in work to a post-industrial service economy, sometimes described as the knowledge economy. This account is usually applied specifically to the Global North, but this optimistic argument is often extended to the Global South, albeit to support specialization of manufacturing as part of a progressive process of development. The argument then is that the era of globalization has seen the rise of a new international division of labour, in which the North focuses on services, and the South on manufacturing. While much of this may initially be in low-value, labour-intensive work, the optimistic scenario presented is that countries of the South will eventually upgrade to higher-value manufacturing production, just as the North did so in the past.

This chapter examines these arguments and partly challenges them. It does so first by examining in depth the extent of deindustrialization in the Global North, something that is of great relevance for all of the chapters that follow. It then moves specifically to the argument that deindustrialization does not necessarily matter, by first looking again at positive and negative manifestations of the phenomenon. It then moves on to consider the argument for positive deindustrialization in more detail, and how this links to claims made for the rise of a post-industrial service economy in the North, and a new international division of labour in the era of globalization. This section briefly examines arguments made in the UK for positive deindustrialization by Third Way politicians in the 1990s and of advocates of Global Britain in the 2000s. The final section then provides a critique of this perspective, by focusing on the reality of jobs in the service sector in the North, and of jobs in the South, and indeed the rise of "premature deindustrialization" in the latter.

DEINDUSTRIALIZATION IN THE GLOBAL NORTH: THE EVIDENCE

In a pioneering account, Rowthorn and Coutts (2004: 1) usefully define – and contextualize – deindustrialization. They state that:

> In the course of economic development, virtually all countries follow a broadly similar trajectory. As development gets under way, the share of agriculture in national employment falls and there is a rapid increase in the share of manufacturing. This process is known as 'industrialization'. At a certain point, however, the share of manufactures stabilizes and then starts to fall back again. There is a corresponding increase in the share of services in national employment. By analogy with the preceding phase, this process is often described as 'deindustrialization'.

There are of course exceptions, which may be influenced by, for example, the presence of oil,[1] or favourable conditions for the development of tourism. Some economists have identified a "Dutch disease", in which the development of one sector can be so rapid that it is at the expense of other sectors, such as the discovery of natural gas in the Netherlands which also saw a consequent relative decline in manufacturing (*The Economist* 1977; Corden & Neary 1982). But broadly speaking, this is a reasonable description of more "normal" processes of industrialization and deindustrialization, although we shall come to see that to some extent this description needs considerable qualification. Furthermore, this account tells us little about particular policies and social processes linked to industrialization, and indeed the motives and interests that promoted it in different places (see Sutcliffe 1984; Kiely 1998).

1. This argument rests on a narrower definition of deindustrialization, which refers only to manufacturing.

Nonetheless, this remains a useful starting point for thinking about industrialization and deindustrialization.

In terms of falling employment shares, Rowthorn and Coutts (2004: 2) present evidence that shows clear evidence of deindustrialization from around 1960 to around 2000. Thus, for the period 1960–98, the proportion of the labour force employed in manufacturing fell from 35 to 18 per cent in the UK, from 26 to 16 per cent in the US, from 27 to 18 per cent in France, and from 36 (in 1965) to 25 per cent in Germany. The Organization for Economic Cooperation and Development (OECD) weighted average saw a decline from 27 per cent in 1960 to 18 per cent in 1999. More recent figures presented by Vu *et al.* (2020: 7) confirm this trend, based on a comparison of 1975 and 2015 figures. In those years, Austria saw a decline from 25 to 15 per cent; Canada from 21 to 10 per cent; France from 23 to 10 per cent; Germany from 35 to 18 per cent; Italy from 28 to 17 per cent; Japan from 27 to 17 per cent; and the UK from 30 to 8 per cent. The years from 2000 to 2014 saw a decline in the US from 14 to 10 per cent.

But it is not just in employment shares that manufacturing saw a decline, but also in the proportion of manufacturing to value added within particular developed economies. Once again for the years 1975–2015, there is clear evidence of decline: in Canada from 21 to 13 per cent; in France from 21 to 11 per cent; in Germany from 35 to 22 per cent; in Japan from 32 to 18 per cent; in the UK from 31 to 10 per cent; and in the US from 23 to 12 per cent (*ibid.*).

We need to treat these latter figures with some caution, however. This is because while they show a relative decline in the share of value added, this does not necessarily mean that there is solid evidence for an absolute decline in manufacturing output. This may well be the case in certain sectors, and this will be investigated in later chapters, but it is not necessarily true for manufacturing output as a whole. The arguments around this will be explored in detail in later chapters, but for now, we might make the following telling point, made by Rifkin (1995: 134): in 1980, the American company US Steel employed 120,000 workers; by 1990, just ten years later, the company required just 20,000 workers to produce a similar output.

TYPES OF DEINDUSTRIALIZATION

There is clear evidence that across the Global North there has been deindustrialization. However, this itself does not demonstrate that deindustrialization is an intrinsically negative phenomenon. While we shall see that most of the focus is on the negative consequences of deindustrialization, early commentators also suggested that there could be something described as positive deindustrialization, which was,

> the normal result of sustained economic growth in a fully employed, and already highly developed, economy. It occurs because productivity growth in the manufacturing sector is so rapid that, despite increasing output, employment in this sector is reduced, either absolutely or as a share of total employment. However, this does not lead to unemployment, because new jobs are created in the service sector on a scale sufficient to absorb any workers displaced from manufacturing. Paradoxically, this kind of deindustrialization is a symptom of economic success. (Rowthorn & Wells 1987: 5)

This then, is a case of "positive deindustrialization", in which manufacturing employment declines but manufacturing output increases because of higher productivity (Rowthorn & Ramaswamy 1999; Rowthorn & Coutts 2013; Tregenna 2009).

This argument will be considered in depth below, but its theoretical rationale can be linked to neoclassical arguments that different sectors in the economy do not matter and that there is nothing special about the manufacturing sector (see Herendorff *et al.* 2014). But ironically, a case can be made that deindustrialization does not matter for countries that have already experienced previously substantial manufacturing growth. This is associated with the famous inverted "U" of deindustrialization, whereby manufacturing employment grows up to a certain level of per capita GDP and declining levels of agricultural employment. But eventually, the share of manufacturing employment levels starts to fall and so deindustrialization – measured in terms of employment shares – kicks in. This level has been the subject of much debate and has included (at constant prices) estimates ranging from $10,000 to $21,000 (Palma 2005, 2008). What is interesting here, however, is that this "U" shape of rising and then falling levels of employment is not intrinsically problematic, and indeed could be said to reflect the special sectoral status of manufacturing in which higher rates of productivity, backward and forward linkages and the generation of economies of scale have led to higher output with less workers needed. The transition to a service economy is thus a product of the very success of earlier rounds of industrialization. Indeed, given that parts of the Global South are industrializing, this can be regarded as a win-win situation in which the poorer countries will themselves gain from the benefits of industrialization. These arguments about the new international division of labour are at the heart of the political programmes discussed below.

However, there is another way of thinking about deindustrialization, and this is one that focuses on it being a negative phenomenon. In this case, negative deindustrialization takes place where there is limited labour absorption of those that lose jobs in manufacturing, and growing unemployment or at least underemployment, and so it is "a product of economic failure and occurs when industry is in severe economic difficulties" (Rowthorn & Wells 1987: 5). This negative deindustrialization is closer to the spirit of the initial focus of studies of deindustrialization in the 1970s and 1980s, much of which focused on the British manufacturing decline (Singh 1977; Blackaby 1978). Even then, however, there were some that focused on deindustrialization in apparent manufacturing powerhouses like West Germany (Frobel *et al.* 1980). This negative deindustrialization thus also emphasizes declines in manufacturing employment in the Global North, but also points to negative effects over time, such as unemployment, underemployment, stagnant or slow wage increases, worsening labour conditions and so on. While it is unlikely that negative deindustrialization leads to something as stark as falling employment shares in manufacturing employment *and* falling output shares (although it did in Britain during 1980–82), it is possible for the former to occur alongside slower output growth than previously, as well as worse wage growth and work conditions. In the US from 1973 to 2007, manufacturing employment fell by 25 per cent but manufacturing output rose by 172 per cent, while in Britain in the same period manufacturing output rose by 16 per cent while manufacturing employment declined by 58 per cent (Rowthorn & Coutts 2013: 19).

What should be clear is that the debate over deindustrialization is far from straightforward, even over whether or not it is a negative or positive phenomenon. The next section considers the argument that it is a positive thing, at least for the Global North, with particular reference to trade theory and contemporary globalization and the current international division of labour.

POSITIVE DEINDUSTRIALIZATION, THE SERVICE ECONOMY AND GLOBALIZATION

Adam Smith ([1776] 1981) had argued for a division of labour in which specialization would increase the total aggregate output in an economy. This principle operated internationally so countries should not produce goods that they could purchase more cheaply from overseas. Ricardo developed this argument further through his theory of comparative advantage. Based on a two-country, two-product account of international trade, Ricardo argued that even in a situation where one country had an absolute advantage in both products, it still made sense for that country to specialize in production in the good in which it had a relative or comparative advantage. Thus, in his famous example, Portugal produces both cloth and wine with less labour than

England. However, Portugal is relatively more efficient at producing wine, and so should specialize in that particular product. If Portugal specialized in wine it would produce 200 barrels a week, and if it specialized in cloth it would produce 600 bolts of cloth. England's equivalent figures are 50 barrels of wine and 500 bolts of cloth. If both countries focus on producing both of these goods, based on half of the labour force concentrating on each good, then the figures would be 125 wine (100 Portugal, 25 England) and 550 cloth (300 Portugal, 250 England). Portugal has an absolute advantage in both; however, it has a lower opportunity cost in wine, in that it sacrifices 3 bolts of cloth to make 1 bottle of wine. Through trade, Portuguese winemakers will get more cloth from England for each bottle of wine sold to England, rather than through the purchase of Portuguese cloth for Portuguese wine. Through specialization, total output is increased to 700, with 200 barrels of wine from Portugal and 500 bolts of cloth from England. This rather neat case for free trade and the exercise of comparative advantage rested on a number of assumptions, including that capital can move swiftly from producing one product to another, and at the same time, this capital mobility operates at a national level but not internationally. A further assumption is made that trade takes place in the context of the full utilization of labour, or what we might today call full employment. This assumes that, like capital, labour will move relatively painlessly, rapidly and without cost, from employment in cloth to employment in wine, or vice versa. There are a number of problems with these assumptions. For instance, the Ricardian assumption, or "vice" (Schumpeter 1954) is that capital simply shifts from cloth to wine production, but the machinery necessary to produce one is very different from that needed in the other sector, and so the closure of wine-producing technology represents in effect lost capital. Furthermore, if Portugal has an absolute advantage in both products, then there is every incentive for capital to leave England and set up production of both cloth and wine in Portugal. For Ricardo ([1817] 2004: 290), this makes sense theoretically in terms of efficiency, but also for consumers in both countries that will purchase cheaper goods as a result. The problem with this argument is the failure to consider the effect on incomes in England if production did completely relocate to Portugal. In any case, Ricardo argued that such relocation was unlikely because of the uncertainty of investing in new countries with different laws, including those related to investment (*ibid.*: 136–7).

This would appear to render the theory redundant in the age of globalization and massive increases in the international movement of capital. However, in effect the theory has been adapted to take account of this mobility, to explain how specialization works in the international economy, and the fact that there is a clear international division of labour based on specialization. Labour-abundant economies essentially specialize in the production of labour-intensive goods, while capital-abundant economies produce high-margin goods and services. In this way, jobs lost to the Global South tend to be in labour-intensive sectors, but these will be compensated by increased specialization in more skilled and capital-intensive sectors (Krugman 1986; Grossman & Helpman 1991). So, with specialization, incomes would rise, and any short-term negatives, such as job losses in the US, would be compensated for by increased job creation in the US brought about through greater specialization and an expanded market, where incomes would rise as a result of its own specialization. Seen in this way, deindustrialization in the US or elsewhere does not matter, as it simply reflects efficiency gains from specialization.

How does this discussion relate to the case of deindustrialization? One way is to again emphasize that there is nothing special about manufacturing and the most important factor determining growth is specialization through competition. If countries specialize then they can exchange surplus goods, services or money for surpluses generated elsewhere through specialization. This fosters a win-win situation based on each developing through their respective comparative advantage. But we might also add that this scenario could on the face of it be championed even by those who give special status to manufacturing, because cases of positive deindustrialization in the richer countries have helped to lay the ground for the development of manufacturing in the Global South. Thus, just as already rich countries developed through manufacturing, so too can the poorer countries that increasingly (so the argument goes) specialize in manufacturing. This is a win-win even if we accept the special status of manufacturing.

These arguments have been influential since the 1990s, and in particular in relation to what we might call neoliberal and Third Way interpretations of globalization. Although there are different versions of this argument, all more or less agree with Ohmae's (1995) contention that in some respects mobile capital and so-called free markets have outgrown the relatively immobile nation state, and this has led to a reallocation of resources across the globe, part of which involves a tendency towards convergence between the rich Global North and the poorer Global South. While the Third Way social democracy of Bill Clinton and Tony Blair rejected Ohmae's contention that the state was in effect dying in the face of mobile capital, it adapted this contention and instead argued that in the face of mobile capital, states needed to respond accordingly. The key argument of the Third Way was that markets represent opportunities to which both individuals and states must respond (Blair & Schroeder 1999). While in the case of the former, this laid the ground for public sector and financial reforms to make individuals behave in (perceived) entrepreneurial ways, in terms of the state it was envisaged that globalization represented an opportunity for all. While sometimes this was presented as a necessity, there was also the key assumption that an enabling state was also desirable, not least because globalization was presented as an opportunity rather more than a constraint: globalization "by and large, has been a success. The problem is how to maximize its positive consequences while limiting its less fortunate effects" (Giddens 2000: 124; see also Hay & Watson 1999). This maximization of the positive in effect amounts to the promotion of market-friendly policies that embrace economic globalization. In the words, of former US Vice President Al Gore (1999): "In this fast moving, fast changing global economy – when the free flow of dollars and data are sources of economic and political strength, and whole new industries are born every day – governments must be lean, nimble, and creative or they will be left behind".

There is a role for the state in promoting the opportunities presented by globalization, and in particular there is a need to invest in the high-skilled, high-productivity, knowledge economy. This constitutes an investment in human capital, a concept that links Chicago School neoliberalism to the Third Way, via an economistic understanding of the idea of social capital, so that all social relations are understood in terms of their contribution to the economy (Becker 1976; see also Finlayson 2003; Kiely 2018: 153–6; Stedman-Jones 2018). In particular this meant promoting and expanding the new international division of labour in which the Global North specialized in the post-industrial knowledge economy, while the South built up its manufacturing base. Thus, according to UK prime minister Tony Blair in 2000: "Because 90% of new jobs will need skills with computers, there will be 6,000 centres round Britain, giving access to the internet and help with technology. Everyone will get an 80% discount on computer courses, the unemployed will get it for free" (Blair 2000). The issue here, as we shall see, was not the promotion of IT training, but the assumption that this heralded a new economy of highly skilled, high-productivity work. Equally significant is the assumption that poverty in the Global South and its associated problems "don't come from the global economy itself, or from the self-seeking behaviour on the part of the richer nations. They lie mainly in the societies themselves – in authoritarian government, corruption, conflict, over-regulation and the low level of emancipation of women" (Giddens 2000: 129). It is of course true that authoritarian government, corruption, the oppression of women and so on are undesirable in themselves, but it is quite another argument to suggest that these things have held back economic growth in some of the most successful "late developers" – South Korea, Taiwan and China – since 1945.

The second political project associated with the idea of a post-industrial service economy in the Global North and manufacturing in the South is associated with the idea of a post-Brexit "Global Britain". In many respects this is very different from the (selective) social liberalism and pro-EU stance of the British Third Way, but there are still some areas of overlap. There were many reasons as to why people in the UK voted to leave the European Union and some of these can be related – partly – to deindustrialization, as we shall see in later chapters. But here we focus on one particular Brexit project, and its wider implications. Some Eurosceptic Conservatives were hostile to the European Union because they considered it too inward looking, and too regionalist, and one that held back the potential of a revived Global Britain (Bennett 2016; Nelson 2016). Britain could revive its traditional global role which had been hindered when it joined the European Community in 1973 and re-establish closer relations with countries where it had stronger historical links (Roberts 2016). This above all meant closer ties with English-speaking peoples in an imagined Anglosphere of nations including the US, Canada, Australia and New Zealand (Bennett 2004). Although this Anglosphere was originally imagined in the late nineteenth century in response to competition from Europe, and potentially linked to Joseph Chamberlain's case for preferential treatment and thus some forms of protectionism (Bell 2016: 167–71; Kiely 2020: 80–85), the contemporary idea was that Britain would use its state power and system of alliances to promote a new era of genuinely global free trade, based on what Margaret Thatcher called "good Anglo-Saxon traditions" of commerce and culture (cited in Lloyd 2000).

Although this project does envisage free trade and market forces to be embedded in particular cultural traditions, there is also a strong assumption of spontaneity in its understanding of markets. As a result, the Economists for Brexit (2016) report contrasts an EU of harmonized rules which have the effect of artificially increasing prices, to one of unilateral free trade where all restrictions are lifted and Britain trades on the basis of World Trade Organization rules or even some notion of spontaneous global free trade. This understanding of trade without any institutional preconditions allows the report to suggest that any regulations constitute a restriction on truly authentic free trade, and so price differentials are simply mark-ups by monopolistic producers. In fact, these reflect differences in quality, proximity to the final market, safety standards, and in any case, it reflects above all a highly simplistic understanding of international trade. For the likes of the Economists for Brexit and lead author, Patrick Minford, they see "the harmonisation of regulations as a pernicious plot by vested interests to raise prices. But playing by a common set of rules is what has helped increase trade and competition in the Single Market" (Sampson *et al.* 2016). It is not a simplistic zero-sum game between trade on the one hand, and regulation on the other, but in fact the latter can be the basis on which trade happens at all, and indeed expands within a single market. Similarly, there is no zero-sum game between trade within the EU and trade beyond it, and indeed the much-hyped post-Brexit trade deals were largely insignificant in terms of impact on GDP and often simply replaced existing ones that existed between the EU and non-EU countries. None of them got anywhere near compensating for potential losses arising from the fact that in 2016, the year of the referendum, around 49 per cent of the value of Britain's exports were to the EU (Lis 2017). But what is of most relevance here is that Minford himself was quite candid about the impact of Brexit on British manufacturing, suggesting that it could all but wipe out large sections of it, such as the car industry (Reid 2019). Minford and the Economists for Brexit (2016) suggest that this could be more than compensated for by more jobs in the service sector, and the import of cheaper cars. This argument rests on precisely the questionable assumptions about trade and regulations already questioned above, and indeed some further odd ones about the nature of the car industry in a world of global value chains (see Chapter 3). But for now, we can emphasize that this is a scenario that envisages further positive deindustrialization, and an international division of labour based on highly paid service work in the Global North, and rising manufacturing in the South. It is these assumptions, which we now question in more depth.

A CRITIQUE: HIGH-PAID SERVICE WORK AND AN INDUSTRIALIZING GLOBAL SOUTH?

The argument so far then can be summarized as follows. Deindustrialization – measured in terms of the proportion of jobs in manufacturing and the contribution of manufacturing to GDP – has declined in the Global North, at least since the 1960s and 1970s. But in contrast to some early concerns about the negative effects of deindustrialization (Singh 1977), this is not a problem and indeed we can describe the process across the countries of the North – despite considerable differentiation – as a positive phenomenon. This is so for the North either because industrialization per se does not matter, and countries should specialize in any sector in which it has a comparative advantage, or because the very success of earlier industrialization has led to high productivity and output, and paved the way for a post-industrial service economy. Indeed, this is also likely to involve safer and cleaner jobs, and indeed more interesting and creative ones in the knowledge economy (Blair & Schroeder 1999). Moreover, this is also good news for the countries of the Global South as they specialize in goods in which they are most competitive, and indeed this can include manufacturing production, which is good news for those who believe manufacturing is the most important sector for reasons outlined above. This suggests then that the new international division of labour in which the Global North specializes in services and the South specializes in manufacturing is desirable for North and South alike. In this way globalization has promoted a win-win situation.

This section suggests that there are good reasons to be sceptical about such arguments. Although there are a number of factors that suggest a more "negative" take on deindustrialization, which are considered in depth in the chapters that follow, this section highlights two broad arguments. First, it questions the assumption that the shedding of manufacturing jobs has generally led to an upgrading in terms of employment for workers in the Global North. Second, it highlights the fact that, in contrast to many assumptions about the South in the new international division of labour, there has not been anything like a straightforward industrialization of the South as a whole, much that has taken place is quite shallow in nature, and indeed we might argue that much of the South has suffered from a stalled or even premature deindustrialization (Sumner 2020).

The first argument then, is that deindustrialization in the Global North is not a problem as it will lead to new, better jobs. However, the evidence for this contention is limited, and there is indeed much that suggests something closer to the opposite. At the height of the dot-com boom in 2000, highly skilled, high-tech workers constituted just 2 per cent of the labour force in the US (Henwood 2003: 71–8). According to Milberg and Winkler (2013: 9), from 1979 to 1999 as much as 63.4 per cent of those who changed jobs in the US labour market were re-employed with an average earnings loss of 13 per cent. By 2011, around 28 per cent of all US workers earned less than the official poverty-level wage of $11.06 per hour, and around 30 per cent of the workforce relied on public assistance (Moody 2017: 30). The period since 1973 has also seen a significant decline in employer-sponsored benefits such as healthcare and pension schemes, despite significant state subsidies. In 1979, 69 per cent of employees had some form of employer-provided healthcare benefits, but by 2010 this had fallen to 53 per cent (*ibid.*). By 2010, only 43 per cent of employees had employer-provided pensions, and secure defined benefit plans had fallen sharply from 29 per cent of all pensions in 1980 to 18 per cent in 2004 (*ibid.*). The impact of the turn to defined contribution plans, the value of which depend on financial investments, was felt in the period after 2008, when an average work-based savings account pension fell by an estimated 27 per cent. This meant that 56–61-year-olds who would have retired in 2013 saw median family savings fall from $35,929 in 2007 to around $17,000 in 2013 (*ibid.*: 31). At 24.8 per cent in 2017, the US had the highest proportion of its labour force earning less than two-thirds of the median wage (Coates 2018: 59). US household debt as a percentage of GDP rose from 11–12 per cent in the 1960s, to 51 per cent by 1980, and 69 per cent by 1997 (Langley 2008: 140), and by June 2008, aggregate (household, corporate and government) debt had reached a total of $51 trillion, compared to a GDP of $14 trillion (Lazzarato 2012: 112). In the first quarter of 2017, total household debt stood at $12.7 trillion, a figure higher than it was at the height of the global financial crisis (Coates 2018: 2).

When debates over deindustrialization took off in the 1970s and 1980s, much of this reflected the rise in unemployment in much of the Global North. Since then, unemployment levels have fallen, but this disguises some other significant factors. In the US, the labour market participation rate reached a ten-year low of 62.9 per cent in April 2017 (*ibid.*: 54). As we shall see in the next chapter, and in Chapter 7, this is an important context for understanding the rise of resentment among sections of the US working class, although the extent to which this accounted for the vote for Trump in the 2016 presidential election is far from straightforward.

These examples are taken solely from the US and there is considerable variation across countries. We return to the British example in Chapter 8, in the context of debates on "levelling up". Britain is probably closest to an example of negative deindustrialization, at least in the period 1980 to 1982, in that both manufacturing employment and output fell (see Chapter 8). Germany, on the other hand, is rightly seen as a country that has managed both deindustrialization and globalization more effectively than other countries, not least since reunification and its post-1991 aftermath (see Chapter 8). But even in Germany, there were similar, if less extreme trends to that of other countries. From the mid-1970s, a gap opened up between productivity and wage increases, and the value of real wages dropped, particularly for the non-unionized workforce (Nachtwey 2016: 111–13). One result was a sharp increase in inequality, with the top 10 per cent of wealth-holders increasing their share from 44 per cent in 1970 (West Germany) to 66 per cent by 2010 (*ibid.*: 116).

The other side of the equation is the argument that the new international division of labour is also good for the countries of the Global South, as they specialize in producing competitive goods, including in manufacturing. As we have seen, this approach can accommodate the view that manufacturing does matter, precisely because this new international division of labour is based in part on the rise of manufacturing in the South. We shall see in the next chapter that this is an assumption shared by those who take a much more critical view of this international division of labour. However, there is a problem for both of these perspectives, which is that industrialization in the South is not as great as is often suggested. Indeed, some have argued that deindustrialization is taking place in much of the South, and at lower levels of per capita income than took place in the North.

Rodrik (2016) has suggested that in this process of "premature deindustrialization" labour is moving into low-paid service work and a massive informal sector of urban marginality (Davis 2004; Sumner 2016). This account requires considerable analysis and is discussed in depth in the next chapter, but for now we can just identify the broad contentions and some of the evidence. Rodrik shows that in terms of shares of global manufacturing value added (MVA), and in terms of manufacturing value added's contribution to GDP, we have generally seen a decline in the period from 1970 to 2013 in Western Europe, but also in Latin America and the Caribbean, and sub-Saharan Africa. Meanwhile the shares in both have increased for non-China Asia, and China itself. China's share in global MVA (measured at 1.0) increased from zero in 1970 to 0.18 in 2013, while the share of MVA to its GDP increased from 0.09 in 1970 to 0.36 in 2013. Latin America's share in global MVA remained the same across the period at 0.06, while the share of MVA to its GDP declined from 0.20 to 0.16. Sub-Saharan Africa saw a static share in global MVA but a decline in MVA as a share in GDP (from 0.14 to 0.11). While the US's share of global MVA declined from 0.26 to 0.19, the contribution of MVA to its GDP remained the same (Rodrik 2016: table 1). In terms of output then, we do not see a sharp shift in terms of manufacturing to the South in general, and indeed some decline outside of Asia. This is deemed to be premature deindustrialization because, in contrast to the Global North, much of the South has reached peak manufacturing at an earlier point than the North. Stalled industrialization is where a rapid rise of employment and value added in manufacturing is followed by stagnation and relative decline. For instance, in a relatively successful "late industrializer" like Indonesia, there was a rapid rise in employment and value added from around 1980 to the late 1990s, followed by a period of stagnation from 2000 to 2005, and some decline after 2005, with the result that the employment and value-added shares in manufacturing in 2010 were similar to those in 1990 (Sumner 2020: 54). Manufacturing employment peaked in 1986 in Brazil, 2002 in India, 1970 in Colombia, 1980 in Mexico, 1971 in Peru, 1978 in Ghana and 1982 in Nigeria (Oks & Williams 2022). There are a number of possible reasons for these phenomena, which are discussed in the next chapter. What should be clear, however, is that since around 1960, agriculture's share of employment and GDP has fallen in the South as a whole, but growth in manufacturing shares is only really substantial in East Asia and not in the rest of the South (Sumner 2020: ch.3).

How do these issues relate to the trade theory discussed earlier in the chapter? What should be clear is that output, income and employment is not simply a product of specialization through trade and the exercise of comparative advantage. What is also important are the kinds of goods and services produced within a country. *The Atlas of Economic Complexity* (Hausmann *et al.* 2011; see also Keen 2017) suggests that it is *diversity* rather than *specialization* per se, which is important in determining success in international trade. Particularly important are *ubiquity* (how many countries export a particular product) and *diversity* (how many products a specific country exports). As Keen (2017) suggests, in a world of free trade and the exercise of comparative advantage one would expect flows based on low ubiquity and diversity. However, this is generally only true in the case of countries in the Global South, and not the richer countries of the North, which tend to produce and export a wider diversity of goods and those same goods tend to be produced in fewer countries. This diversity is in part a product of earlier processes of manufacturing, which have led to linkages, spill-overs, economies of scale, and higher productivity (the last of which has led to the employment of fewer workers, and in this sense, deindustrialization). In contrast, countries of the South are often dependent on export revenue from only a small number of products, many of which are produced in a large number of other (usually also developing) countries.

What this suggests then is that manufacturing does indeed matter, and it is for reasons such as these that many development economists after 1945 advocated industrialization in the newly independent "Third World". This was seen as necessary to overcome what were considered unequal terms of trade between higher-value industrial producers and lower-value primary goods producers, which faced a tendency for prices to fall more rapidly than industrial producers, above all because of intense competition between these "non-ubiquitous", non-diversifying specializers (Prebisch 1959). Seen in this way, specialization through the exercise of comparative advantage in effect recommended a policy of trading into poverty, or "immiserizing growth" (Mackintosh 2004). These countries are overwhelmingly in the Global South and certainly not the US. This assessment is of course compatible with the view that a new international division of labour in which manufacturing in the South has risen is desirable, but we have also seen that in fact much of the developing world is suffering from premature deindustrialization or at least stalled industrialization. We shall discuss this further in the next chapter where we demonstrate further that stalled industrialization does not lead to economies identified as ones being based on diversity.

Related to these points, while much has been made of the supposedly causal relationship between globalization-friendly policies, economic growth and poverty reduction since the 1990s (see World Bank 2002), in actual fact the picture is far more mixed than is often suggested. There are serious questions around how extreme poverty is measured, with many arguing that figures of living on \$1.90 or \$2.15 a day adjusted for purchasing power parity

(PPP) is too low, and that much of the reduction that has occurred is down to changes in one country, namely China. This does not of course mean that China should somehow be discarded from the measurements, but if we focus only on aggregates then China distorts the picture and we then do not necessarily see what else is happening in the world economy. Furthermore, while in some respects China has integrated into the world economy, it has not been as globalization-friendly as is often implied, an issue examined in later chapters. What we can say is that many of those who have a daily income above the "moderate" poverty line of $3.20 PPP (2011 measures) still live well below consumption levels associated with a permanent escape from poverty, measured at $13 a day PPP (World Bank 2019). Indeed in 2018, about one third of the population in the South lived below the $3.30 benchmark (and 20 per cent below $1.90), while about 20 per cent lived above $13 a day. Around 50 per cent lived in a precarious middle of somewhere between $3.20 and $13 a day, adjusted for PPP (Sumner 2020: 35). Indeed, contrary to optimistic accounts of progress (see, e.g., Pinker 2018), based on median consumption of the poor and developing country average annual growth rates from 1990 to 2012, it would take almost 60 years for the average poor person to reach "economic security" levels of living on over $10 a day PPP; and if we instead look at world annual average growth rates, the time lag rises to almost 130 years (Sumner 2016: 136). The effects of the Covid-19 pandemic, soaring energy prices, inflation, war and higher interest rates since 2020 has already put further pressure on indebted countries of the Global South and the poorest in those countries (World Bank 2023a; Wolf 2023; and see Chapter 5).

We can therefore conclude that while income growth has been important, "it has been slow and of a modest order, and many people remain, in spite of four decades of good economic growth, below the income line associated with a permanent escape from poverty ... Global poverty reduction since the Cold War has been mostly about moving people from below to somewhat above a low poverty line" (Sumner 2020: 35). This hardly conforms to a story of a win-win situation as outlined and critiqued in this chapter (still less does it confirm other arguments about the South, as we shall see in the next chapter). It instead suggests a scenario of limited high-wage service work in the North, and uneven and stalled industrialization and deindustrialization in the South.

CONCLUSION

This chapter has identified the key definitions and types of deindustrialization and related them to the historical significance of industrialization. The main focus of the chapter was to outline the case for positive deindustrialization, which was said to have taken place in the Global North as increased productivity led to greater output, and therefore less need for jobs in manufacturing. The argument that this was a positive phenomenon was then linked to the idea that the jobs displaced in manufacturing would be more than compensated for by new jobs in the service sector, including and perhaps above all, highly skilled and well-paid jobs in financial services and new technology. Furthermore, through appropriate policies of economic liberalization – in terms of investment, trade and finance – countries could grow rapidly through specialization in sectors in which they were most efficient and competitive. Whether or not this meant that there was something special about the manufacturing sector, this mattered less than the fact that the South was rising and potentially converging with the countries of the North, in part because of the rise of manufacturing in the poorer countries. We also showed how very different political projects – such as the Third Way in the 1990s and the vision of a Global Britain in 2016 and beyond – rested on these assumptions.

But it was also shown that these contentions were problematic. The replacement of manufacturing jobs by employment in higher paid jobs with greater security and benefits was far from universal, and in fact tended to be closer to the exception than the norm. We also showed how the much-noted rise of manufacturing in the South was uneven at best and stalled and premature at worst. While it is the case that parts of the South have risen, it is far from universal, as we shall see. None of these arguments demonstrates that deindustrialization is intrinsically negative, but they do show that it is far from intrinsically positive. For this reason, we can say that deindustrialization *does* matter, even if we have not yet established its causes or located the phenomenon in its wider socio-economic context. We undertake this task in the chapters that follow.

CHAPTER 3

DEINDUSTRIALIZATION AS A PRODUCT OF RELOCATION AND IMPORT COMPETITION

The focus of this chapter is firmly on the idea of negative deindustrialization, and so acceptance of the idea that deindustrialization in the Global North is a problem that requires explanation. The argument considered here is that deindustrialization in the countries of the North is indeed a problem, and it is one that has been caused by the rise of industrialization in the Global South. The precise mechanisms vary, from relocation of manufacturing from the North to the South, through fluctuations in exchange-rate valuations, to competition from cheaper imports from the South. These sub-explanations are not mutually exclusive however, and they all essentially agree that industrialization in the South has caused deindustrialization in the North. We shall see however that there are left- and right-wing versions of this argument and there is some disagreement – as well as overlap – about what should be done about this process.

This chapter considers this argument in detail. It starts by examining some earlier arguments, made from the 1970s onwards, concerning a new international division of labour, part of which was the rise of manufacturing in the Global South. The section considers some of these contentions, and problematizes the evidence made for them, at least as they were made in the 1970s and 1980s. Despite these problems, the second section shows how similar approaches developed in the context of debates around globalization, from the 1990s onwards. This second section shows how left-wing anti-globalization voices developed arguments which suggested that mobile capital encouraged a race to the bottom in terms of labour standards. But it also shows how right-wing anti-globalization thinking developed in this period as well, and these claims are considered in some detail, with particular reference to the Trump Republicans, both in the run-up to the 2016 election victory and beyond. Some comparison and contrast is made with the left-wing anti-globalization of the Democrats, trade unions and so on. The third section subjects these arguments to critical scrutiny, through an examination of data in both the Global North and South. Some tentative conclusions are drawn, which are considered further in the chapters that follow.

THE NEW INTERNATIONAL DIVISION OF LABOUR AND RACE TO THE BOTTOM

This section examines one approach in particular, developed in the 1970s, which suggested that a new international division of labour had emerged in which the so-called "Third World" was increasingly industrializing. At the same time, this was a major reason for both growing unemployment and deindustrialization in the so-called "developed", or "First World". This was a perspective influenced by Immanuel Wallerstein's (1980) world systems theory, which was sometimes seen as a neo-Marxist approach to understanding the international order. In particular, Wallerstein (1974) argued that the world was divided into three areas based on economic activity: the core, the periphery and the semi-periphery. Following on from and developing 1960s' underdevelopment theory (Frank 1966), Wallerstein argued that the core owed its privileged position in the world economy in part because it exploited the periphery. Although it was not altogether clear how this occurred, the argument appeared to be that a surplus was extracted from peripheral locations in order to develop core areas, leaving the periphery underdeveloped. Nonetheless, at times some room was given for peripheral areas so that they became semi-peripheries (Wallerstein 1974).

Whatever the value of concepts like core and periphery, the mechanisms by which a peripheral area might rise to semi-peripheral status were not made clear in Wallerstein's general theory. However, the theory of the new international division of labour was one application of Wallerstein-influenced ideas which did try to specify mechanisms whereby parts of the former periphery industrialized, and part of the "First World" core deindustrialized. This theory was associated with the work of Frobel, Henrichs and Kreye (1980). Interestingly, these were German writers and much of their empirical material was taken from West Germany, which was generally not seen as a country experiencing high rates of deindustrialization. Their focus was mainly (although not exclusively) on clothing and textiles, and their data does demonstrate an increase in the use of foreign subsidiaries by German companies in those sectors: from 8,000 workers in foreign subsidiaries in textiles in 1966 to 29,500 in 1974, and an increase from 15,000 to 31,000 workers in the garments sector for the same years (Frobel *et al.* 1980: 18). This amounted to an increase from 1.5 per cent to 7.5 per cent of the proportion of domestic workers in the textiles sector, and 3.7 to 10 per cent in garments (*ibid.*).

Frobel *et al.*'s argument was quite clear. Global capitalism entered a period of slowdown from the 1960s and into the early 1970s, and this was caused by a squeeze in profits on Western-dominated capital. A major reason for this crisis of profitability was that full employment and trade union power impacted on profits in the core countries as wages cut into profits. Aided by more efficient transportation and cheaper costs, sections of capital responded to this crisis by relocating capital investment from core to periphery. Frobel *et al.* (*ibid.*: 13) identified three preconditions for the development of a new international division of labour:

> Firstly, a practically inexhaustible reservoir of disposable labour ... Secondly, the division and subdivision of the production process [which] ... is now so advanced that most of these fragmented operations can be carried out with minimal levels of skill easily learnt within a very short time ... Thirdly, the development of transport and communication [which] ... has created the possibility, in many cases, of the complete or partial production of goods at any site in the world.

We saw in the last chapter that some theorists of globalization saw this new international division of labour in positive terms, with the Global North specializing in services and the Global South increasingly industrializing. But we also saw that some of the expectations associated with these apologetics – more secure, higher paid jobs in the North for instance – have not been fulfilled. Frobel *et al.* had a particularly pessimistic take on the argument that global capital had increasingly bypassed the state. On the face of it, the new international division of labour represented good news as some countries or locations rose from peripheral to semi-peripheral status, as they moved away from producing lower-value primary, unfinished goods, and upgraded to manufacturing goods. An optimistic interpretation of this argument was that this meant that the old colonial division of labour – in which the Global North specialized in manufacturing and "Third World" primary products – had been undermined. This was good news because it meant that the developing countries were no longer subject to unequal terms of trade with the developed world. This inequality was said to be the product of intense competition between comparatively many primary goods producers, as opposed to far fewer manufacturers, the effect of which was a tendency to drive prices down more quickly in the case of the former when compared to the latter (Prebisch 1959). Furthermore, manufacturing provided the basis for a more diversified economy which would mean that developing countries were not subject to rapid shifts in prices in sectors where they were so dependent for export earnings. Put in terms discussed in the last chapter, this involves a shift from an economy of excessive over-specialization to one based on economic diversity (Hausmann *et al.* 2011; Keen 2017).

However, Frobel *et al.*'s account did not share this optimism. More specifically, their pessimism was based on the idea that capital's hyper-mobility as compared to the immobility of nation states has downsides for labour in both core and (semi-)periphery. For the core areas, it has led to deindustrialization and unemployment, which certainly showed a marked increase in the 1970s. But crucially, and in contrast to Ohmae and other optimists (discussed in Chapter 2), this is not good news for the former peripheral areas either, because it involves the super-exploitation of workers in those locations, above all through the use of sweat-shop labour. This is not dissimilar to arguments about a global race to the bottom as we shall see in a moment. But specifically on Frobel *et al.*, the argument made in the 1970s was that new areas of manufacturing arose to take advantage of cheap labour in the "(semi-)periphery". The rise of the East Asian newly industrializing countries – South Korea, Taiwan, Singapore and to some extent Hong Kong – was explained in this way. Frobel and his colleagues suggested that in fact it was a negative development, because it led to unemployment and deindustrialization in the core countries of the Global North, and super-exploitation of cheap labour in the semi-peripheral countries of the South (Frobel *et al.* 1980: ch.13).

These arguments were not exclusive to the left, as we shall see, and some of the empirical material can be applied to right-wing versions of this argument. But there were important left-wing versions of this argument that went beyond neo-Marxism and world systems theory. For example, in Britain in the 1970s the Alternative Economic Strategy drew on some of these arguments (see Gamble 1994: 177). This policy initiative attempted to control the export of capital, and to introduce import controls that would protect national industries from import penetration and thus halt the tide of deindustrialization (Gamble 1994: 177; Cambridge Political Economy Group 1975). At the time the argument was made that this involved Britain leaving the European Community in order to set about "breaking the chains of the world economy" (quoted in Gamble 1994: 177; for a good critique see Tufecki 2020).

How convincing then, are these arguments, and specifically was deindustrialization in the 1970s caused by relocation of capital and import penetration? To answer this question, I shall first deal with the specifics of Frobel *et al.*'s contentions, and the basic timeframe in which they were writing, which was essentially the 1970s and 1980s. In questioning much of their arguments *when applied to that particular period*, I shall then suggest that this does not necessarily mean that their case is completely wrong, and it might be more relevant for understanding the period from the 1990s onwards, both generally and in particular in the case of China's rise. This in turn will lead to a consideration of newer versions of the theory of the new international division of labour, both from the left and perhaps more significant, the right. These might usefully be described as (left- and right-wing) anti-globalization.

Seemingly in favour of Frobel *et al.*'s arguments, in the late 1920s a few countries in Europe, together with the United States and Japan accounted for over 90 per cent of the world's industrial production, but this fell to around 60 per cent by the 1980s (Jenkins 1992: 16–17). The UK and the US together accounted for over half of the world's industrial production in 1948, but by the 1980s this had fallen to less than a third (*ibid.*: 17). However, we need to be careful in explaining these figures – the overall decline among core countries was largely explained by the growing share of the communist world, which increased from 8.4 per cent in 1948 to 25.4 per cent in 1984 (Gordon 1988: 31–5). Indeed, over that same period the "Third World's" share (as it was then known) declined very slightly, from 14 to 13.9 per cent (Gordon 1988: 31–5). It is therefore not surprising that the relative declines of the UK and US in terms of share in industrial production was partly explained by the rising share among other core countries, above all West Germany and Japan. Much of the case made by Frobel and his colleagues assumed a relocation of capital from core to periphery but in the period when they were writing their most influential work, the proportion of direct foreign investment from selected developed countries to the periphery actually fell: in the case of West Germany from 27 per cent in 1975 to 19 per cent in 1984; from 73 to 52 per cent in the case of Japan for the same years; and from 19 to 16 per cent for the UK (Jenkins 1992: 35).

In one respect of course proportions only tell part of the story, and the actual amounts are more important – and this is important for looking at the period since the 1990s as we shall see. But proportions are important for Frobel because it is assumed that there is a direct link between the industrialization of parts of the Global North and the deindustrialization of the South, as if there was a relatively straightforward zero-sum game between the two – something that can also be found in right-wing anti-globalization arguments, as we shall see. One further possible counter-argument is that it is not direct foreign investment per se that is the issue, as companies may draw on subcontracting agreements with local suppliers. However, in 1988, the Global North's consumption of imports from the South as a percentage of total consumption was as low as 2.83 per cent for the European Community, 3.42 per cent for the US and Canada, and 1.43 per cent for Japan (*ibid.*: 34). Even Frobel *et al.*'s (1980: 18) data on the clothing and textiles industry (see above) hardly demonstrate a wholesale relocation of jobs from West Germany to the Global South. Moreover, trade with the former "Third World" should again not be seen in simple zero-sum terms, and there is evidence that in the aggregate it creates rather than destroys jobs (Jenkins 1992: 34; see further below).

In fairness, the theory of the new international division of labour was not necessarily claiming that the whole of the Global South was industrializing, and that it might apply to only a few countries, such as South Korea and Taiwan. At a more abstract level, some Marxists (Charnock & Starosta 2016) suggest that the rise of the first tier of newly industrialized countries (NICs) was simply an expression of the changing conditions of global capital accumulation. The problem with the first argument was that it is not very convincing as an explanation of the rise of those countries, and the second uses Marxist abstractions as a substitute for any empirically grounded explanation for why these – specific – new areas of accumulation emerged. Thus, in the period under consideration, both South Korea and Taiwan carried out highly restrictive policies when it came to foreign investment, a fact which is also problematic for those neoliberal explanations that purport to explain the rise of these countries through their supposed adoption of market-friendly policies (World Bank 1993; for alternatives see Amsden 1989; Wade 1990). Thus, in the period from 1962 to 1979 direct foreign investment accounted for only 1.2 per cent of total domestic investment in South Korea and in the late 1970s, the share of foreign investment in its gross national product was less than half of that in Argentina, Brazil and Mexico (Edwards 1992: 115). The state also played a crucial role in adapting imported technologies to local conditions and generating new domestic technologies. In addition, central to the rise of both Taiwan and South Korea were government policies such as a nationalized banking system, state-directed credit to certain industries, subsidies and other forms of state protection and limits on the export of capital. Much of these policies were revised and even reversed in the 1980s and 1990s and equally these interventionist policies did not represent a magic bullet or model for other countries to follow. But it should be understood from even this cursory examination that any attempt to explain the rise of the first-tier East Asian NICs cannot be read off from changes in the core countries or explained away as the product of changing conditions of accumulation or the adoption of market-friendly policies (Kiely 1995, 1998).

It should be clear then that the first iteration of the theory of the new international division of labour was problematic. We should also note before moving on to the 1990s, that some of the assumptions and arguments associated with this theory were also taken up by sections of the far right in Europe. In Britain, for example, the National Front in the 1970s argued for import controls to protect British industry, a strategy which they believed required the country leaving the European Community (see Walker 1979). It also called for strict – and discriminatory –immigration controls, mainly because of their openly hostile racism, although this policy did influence sections of the Conservative Party and even the Labour Party, based on the argument that relatively open migration policies would have the effect of increasing the potential supply of labour and therefore keeping wages down. This argument was often made in the 1970s, and owed much to the notorious speeches of former Conservative MP Enoch Powell from 1968 onwards, although in his case it was combined with a commitment to the extension of neoliberal political economy, which he deemed to be impossible in the context of membership of the European Community (Powell 1971; Schofield 2013). Fascist parties were however far more protectionist in orientation (Macklin 2020), although historically they had argued that this should take place within the context of empire, which in the case of Oswald Mosley in the 1930s involved strict protection of the home market (thorough quotas rather than weaker tariffs), public works schemes, credit controls, closer trade with the Dominions, control of colonial markets through protection and suppression of any industry (see Skidelsky 1975). Fascists in power in both Italy and Germany in the 1920s and 1930s largely supported such schemes and placed much emphasis on a supposed "Jewish conspiracy" led by international finance that needed to be controlled. In Germany in particular, it was also envisaged that "self-sufficiency" could be achieved through a new empire in Eastern Europe, which would serve as a living space or *lebensraum* for Germans, and as a source of raw materials for German industry (Mazower 2008). Although the industrial policy envisaged by the Nazis involved considerable state intervention, it did not lead to wholesale nationalization and indeed, like Mussolini's Italy before it, was accompanied by comprehensive privatization programmes (Bel 2010). In the postcolonial era the focus of much fascism and authoritarian-right ideology is on ethno-nationalism, repatriation and immigration controls. We discuss right-wing populism further in Chapter 7, but the evidence for protectionism to protect domestic industry in the 1970s is clearly unconvincing. Furthermore, the arguments concerning migration and labour supply are also based on misinformation, as the argument that it leads to lower wages might apply in one specific sector (although it may well not), but in the aggregate, migration stimulates an economy – one needs to look at the increase in demand caused by labour and how this will stimulate economic activity (and increase tax revenue for the state) (Nickel & Salaheen 2015; Wadsworth 2017).

The 1970s debates on deindustrialization in the Global North often focused on competition from the South, either through relocation by multinational companies, cheap imports from developing countries, or migration into the richer world. This section has shown that most of these arguments were problematic, at least when applied to the 1970s and 1980s. However, these arguments never went away, and found a new context with the debates over globalization from the 1990s onwards.

ANTI-GLOBALIZATION OF BOTH LEFT AND RIGHT

We saw in the last section that when applied to the 1970s and 1980s, the arguments concerning a new international division of labour were at best exaggerated, and in many respects simply wrong. The evidence for wholesale relocation of capital from the Global North to the South was unconvincing, and the theory was equally – if not more – unconvincing as an explanation for the rise of the first-tier East Asian NICs. However, from the 1990s onwards, the data did suggest that parts of the developing world had grown economically, including in terms of manufacturing, and central to this argument was the rise of China. Thus, in 1970, 18.5 per cent of total exports from the developing world were manufactured goods; with the phenomenal rise of China since the early 1990s, this figure had increased to over 80 per cent by the end of the 1990s (UNCTAD 2002: 5). In 2021, China was the fourth largest source of foreign investment outflows, with a total value of $145 billion, behind the US ($403 billion), Germany ($152 billion) and Japan ($147 billion) (UNCTADStat 2022). In the period from 1993 to 2008, Chinese exports grew in real terms by about 500 per cent and by 2010, China had emerged as the world's biggest exporter (Steinfeld 2010: 71). In 1983, direct foreign investment amounted to $1.73 billion spread over 470 projects; by 2006, $193 billion of FDI found its way to 27,514 projects (*ibid.*: 72).

For Burbach and Robinson (1999), deindustrialization in the Global North and the industrialization of the South is indicative of a tendency towards convergence in which the latter is to some extent catching up with the former. For example, they contend that "[w]orldwide convergence, through the global restructuring of capitalism, means that the geographic breakdown of the world into north-south, core-periphery or First and Third worlds, while still significant, is diminishing in importance" (1999: 27–8). This is in part because the "particular spatial form of the uneven development of capitalism is being overcome by the globalization of capital and markets and the gradual equalization of accumulation conditions this entails" (Robinson 2004: 99). Kitching (2001: 267) argues for something similar when he states that "the free movement of productive capital, which is a hallmark of the globalization phase, allows the poor workers of the world to play their economic ace card (the low cost of their labour's production and reproduction). It does so by eliminating the capital stock advantage that enabled the richer workers of the world to compensate – in global competition for the higher cost of their labour". As far back as the 1980s, Nigel Harris (1987: 200–201) argued something similar when he suggested that:

> The conception of an interdependent, interacting, global value system cuts across the old view of a world consisting of nation states as well as one of groups of countries, more or less developed and centrally planned – the First, Third and Second Worlds. These notions bore some relationship to an older economy, one marked by the exchange of raw materials for manufactured goods. But the new world that has superseded it is far more complex and does not lend itself to the simple identification of First and Third World, haves and have nots, rich and poor, industrialized and non-industrialized.

What is distinctive about Kitching and Harris, however, is that they are celebrating the supposed diffusion of manufacturing across the globe. Frobel *et al.* and the race-to-the-bottom thesis accepts the argument about this alleged diffusion but draw very different conclusions. As we shall see in later chapters, there has been considerable resistance to the rise of China in the US, both from the Republican right and from organized labour. As early as 1994, Bernie Sanders, the left-wing Independent who was then a member of the House of Representatives, argued that "American workers cannot be, and must not be, asked to compete against the workers in China" (cited in Hung 2022: 17). This view was also central to organized labour's opposition to China joining the World Trade Organization. While it is sometimes associated with a view expressing solidarity with workers experiencing high rates of exploitation in sweat-shops, it faces the strategic dilemma of the impact factory closures might have in developing countries desperate for jobs. This of course does not mean that a blanket apology for sweat-shops should follow (indeed we argue below against the view that these provide a stepping-stone for upgrading in terms of work conditions, wages and poverty reduction) but it does demonstrate the difficulties strategies faced by those committed to international labour solidarity (Kabeer 2000: 382–3; Kiely 2003).

There is also a right-wing version of "anti-globalization". While the Conservative Brexit project was designed to promote sovereignty to extend a global Britain beyond the confines of the European single market, Trump represented an albeit ambiguous approach that in some respects endorsed the extension of protectionist principles in the United States. This overlapped with the protectionist wing of the Republican Party, which in recent years has been associated with "paleo-conservative" thinkers and activists such as Samuel Francis and Pat Buchanan (see Kiely 2020: ch.5). The argument they make is that the US is dominated by a cosmopolitan or "denationalized" elite that is separated from "ordinary" Americans[1] (Huntington 2004). This globalist elite has promoted mass migration and multiculturalism at home, and American expansion in the form of liberal wars of intervention and foreign investment, which in turn has led to unnecessary American deaths and deindustrialization (Francis 1994, 2004). Trump repeated these kinds of arguments and suggested that "China is robbing us blind in trade deficits and stealing our jobs" (cited in Lamp 2018: 6), and the 2017 Trade Policy Agenda claimed that the US had lost 5 million manufacturing jobs since China joined the WTO in 2001 (Office of the US Trade Representative 2017). Trump adviser Peter Navarro called for increased rates of protection that would facilitate an increase in the proportion of the labour force engaged in manufacturing, from around 10 per cent in 2016 to 20 per cent in the foreseeable future (Navarro & Autry 2011). In his inaugural speech in 2017, Trump (2017) asserted that "We must protect our borders from the ravages of other countries making our products, stealing our companies and destroying our jobs. Protection will lead to greater prosperity and strength".

An additional version of the argument made against China in particular was that it had deliberately undervalued its currency in order to make its exports cheaper and therefore more competitive. In 1994, the government devalued the currency from RMB 5.8 to the US dollar to 8.7, and a year later fixed it at 8.3. This was maintained until 2005, and by then China had a trade surplus of 6.2 per cent of GDP (Klein & Pettis 2020: 109). In 1988, the US had passed a law, the Omnibus Foreign Trade and Competitiveness Act, which argued that a currency's value is supposed to increase alongside any significant rise in exports to the US. If a country's central bank intervenes to halt appreciation of the currency (usually by purchasing foreign currency in exchange for domestic currency), then this is considered to be an export subsidy and so the US can technically reciprocate by placing extra duties on imports. There was a great deal of talk about China as a currency manipulator from the 1990s, which intensified in the 2000s and especially in the 2010s. This was part of an anti-China coalition which included some companies threatened by cheap imports and organized labour. In terms of currency manipulation, we should note that in the period from 2000 to the 2008 global financial crisis, the difference between China's wage levels and those of its neighbours was still considerably greater than could be explained by an undervalued currency. As Hung (2009: 7) pointed out, in the period from 2000 to around 2010, even if its currency appreciated by 20–30 per cent relative to the dollar, Chinese

1. A British version of this argument can be found in Goodwin (2023).

wages would still have been significantly lower. We shall consider this in more detail in Chapters 5 and 6, but we should immediately note that much of this was resisted by other US companies which benefited from outsourcing, but in the 2010s this intensified, in particular during the Trump administration.

EVIDENCE AND CRITIQUE

This section, along with the opening section in the next chapter, provides a critique of the relocation thesis and its offshoots. It starts by focusing on the US, both generally and in relation to the claims and realities of the Trump administration, before moving on to a wider critique, drawing on evidence from the rest of the developed capitalist world and indeed the developing world. The evidence presented so far points to manufacturing job losses and the rise of manufacturing exports from parts of the South, especially China. We might add some specifics here about the US, which has become more trade dependent, with trade accounting for around 5 per cent of GDP in the period from 1950 to 1975, but more recently has accounted for around 15 per cent of GDP (Guilford 2016). The North American Free Trade Agreement was signed in 1994, and from then, the US moved from having a trade surplus with Mexico to a trade deficit, which was around $60 billion in 2016 (Erken & Tulen 2017). The US ran a $350 billion deficit with China in 2016, while for Germany the figure was a substantial but smaller $80 billion (*ibid.*). In clothing, while the US accounted for 1.3 per cent of exports in 2014, US companies accounted for 46 per cent of the total global profit share (Starrs 2015: 15–16). According to Credit Suisse's Global Wealth Report of 2015, the US accounts for 46 per cent of the world's millionaires, which reflects the fact that many of these make their money through overseas investment (*ibid.*: 20). For Trumpian conservatives, this reflects the rise of a post-American corporate elite. The resurgence of manufacturing is seen as part of the solution to these problems, and Trump made much of the fact that while in 1994 the percentage of the workforce in manufacturing stood at 15 per cent, by 2016 the figure was just 10 per cent (see Benanav 2016).

Job displacement in the US was the subject of an influential paper by Kletzer (2001) that examined the impact in low, medium and high competitive importing industries in the US. As noted in Chapter 2, a significant proportion of workers – as much as 63.4 per cent from 1979 to 1999 – were re-employed with an average earnings loss of 13 per cent (Milberg & Winkler 2013: 9). But it is one thing to point to evidence of this kind, and quite another to demonstrate that job losses are simply caused by manufacturing imports. While it may be true that some job losses might be caused by trade *per se*, we have to account for the far greater proportion of job losses *not* accounted for by these factors. Rowthorn and Coutts (2013: 10) suggest that the employment share of manufacturing in 23 developed countries fell by 8.7 percentage points, but an estimated 80 per cent of this was due to productivity growth and 20 per cent trade with low-wage economies. Indeed, in the period from 1982 to 2007, when deindustrialization in terms of employment was hugely significant, US manufacturing *output* increased by 131 per cent, which was faster than overall GDP growth (Moody 2017: 10). The sharpest falls in manufacturing employment occurred in periods of recession (1980–82, when 2.5 million manufacturing jobs were lost, 1990–92, when 869,000 manufacturing jobs were lost, and 2007–10 when 2 million manufacturing jobs were lost), which were also periods which saw significant falls in imports (Moody 2017: 12). Now of course these falls in imports did not cause falls in employment, and both reflected recessions, but equally it is mistaken to assume that falls in employment are caused by increases in imports, even if this might hold in specific sectors of the economy. For manufacturing *output* in the US, apart from exceptions such as the period following the 2008 crash, there has been a consistently upward trend. There have been some sectoral declines, but in terms of output, these have been more than compensated for by rises elsewhere, and this is discussed in the next chapter. Hicks and Devaraj (2017) estimate that in the period from 2000 to 2010, 88 per cent of job losses were accounted for by productivity increases rather than trade deals. Similarly, and contrary to Trumpian rhetoric, there is little correlation – let alone causation – between trade deficits and job losses. In the seven years following the implementation of the NAFTA agreement, when trade deficits averaged 1.8 per cent of GDP per annum, 22 million new jobs were created (Rose 2018: 1). In the mid-1980s, trade deficits were high and so was unemployment, but from 1987 to 2002 trade deficits increased but the unemployment rate fell, and during 2006–09, as deficits fell, unemployment increased (Rose 2018: 4). In the period 2000–15, the value of imports grew to a value of 15 per cent of GDP, while export values rose to 11 per cent, and in this period, China emerged as a major manufacturing exporter. Also in this period, manufacturing employment fell from around 19 million in 2001 to 12 million by 2009. Some have argued that the trade deficit with China was a principal reason for this fall in employment numbers (Scott 2017), and Acemoglu *et al.* (2016) have suggested the numbers amount to 2.6 million job losses caused by Chinese industrialization. Other studies have suggested that the number of job losses in manufacturing from 2000 to 2007 amounted to 0.55 million, which is about 16 per cent of manufacturing job losses in this period (Caliendo *et al.* 2019). However, these figures leave aside the positive employment effects of exporting sectors, and Feenstra and Sasahara (2018) suggest that the net effect – which considers gains as well as losses – is close to zero. Moreover, as Rose (2018: 8) argues, if we break this down into sectors then any correlation is difficult to find. In 2015, the only manufacturing sector that ran a trade surplus was "other transportation" (which includes aircraft manufacturing and railway and boat construction) but these sectors still saw large falls in employment. Meanwhile, the automobile and automobile parts sector ran high deficits but retained a significant number of workers. Some have questioned the positive employment effects (Autor *et al.* 2016), and we can accept that there may well have been significant US job losses in a relatively short period of time from around 2001 to 2007, in what some have called the "China shock" (*ibid.*). In this respect, we can accept that while Frobel *et al.* somewhat jumped the gun in the 1970s, their analysis may be of more (although still limited) relevance for the period from the 1990s with the rise of global value chains and specifically China's role in these production networks. But even the highest estimate (2.6 million), which leaves out the (highly unlikely) scenario of no jobs in export sectors, cannot account for anything like the 7 million job losses in US manufacturing from 2001 to 2009.

So, while we can accept the reality of deindustrialization, and indeed the failure of displaced jobs to be replaced by higher value ones, it is far less clear that trade per se is responsible for all, or even most of these problems. While we might identify job displacement in some sectors, across the whole economy it is far from clear that deindustrialization has occurred because of a wholesale relocation to the developing world. Trump's claim that "We are reclaiming our heritage as a manufacturing nation again … We are going to bring back our jobs" should be seen in this light (cited in Lamp 2018: 7). Indeed, despite his usual overblown rhetoric, the Trump presidency hardly saw a renaissance in manufacturing jobs, even before the impact of the Covid-19 pandemic is factored into the equation. The so-called "blue-collar boom" of 2016–19 saw gains of around 500,000 manufacturing jobs, an average of 166,000 jobs a year. But this was no different from the pre-Trump period of 2010–19, and included the closure of 1,800 factories in the 2016–18 period, an increase in the trade deficit in manufacturing goods, and was of course followed by massive job losses in manufacturing (Scott 2020: 2). Key swing Rust Belt states such as Pennsylvania, Michigan, Ohio and Wisconsin saw significant job losses in manufacturing in 2019, totalling around 16,000 people, and much of the new manufacturing jobs were low paid, around 20 per cent less than the national average, and thus reliant on federal assistance (Trafecante 2020). Trump's record on trade deficits also did not match his rhetoric. The US goods and services trade deficit increased to $679 billion in 2020, compared to $481 billion in 2016, although Trump was successful in bringing down the bilateral trade deficit with China, when higher tariffs were imposed on more than $350 billion worth of Chinese goods (Palmer 2021). The trade gap with China was $311 billion in 2020, compared to the record high of $419 billion in 2018. However, trade deficits increased with other countries as US companies turned to other foreign suppliers (such as Vietnam, Thailand, Taiwan and South Korea). Imports from China also grew sharply in the second half of 2020 (Palmer 2021), although this in part reflected an initial rapid recovery from Covid by China in that year. Trump's record on manufacturing jobs and trade deficits was thus far from impressive, even when the impact of Covid-19 is factored in, and this suggests again that "bringing back" manufacturing jobs is more complicated than he assumed.

What about the industrialization of the so-called semi-periphery? If one accepts the arguments from the left – a race to the bottom – and the right – stolen jobs by the South – then one would expect a significant rise in manufacturing jobs there. However, in the period since NAFTA was signed, while it is true that US manufacturing jobs as a proportion of all US jobs has fallen, this is also true of Mexico, where over the same period the proportion fell from 20 to 15 per cent (Benanav 2016). Job losses in US manufacturing are thus hardly being "stolen" by Mexican workers. Furthermore, the decline of manufacturing long pre-dates free-trade agreements like NAFTA. Manufacturing accounted for around 30 per cent of non-farm jobs in 1950, and around 25 per cent by 1970. The figure for 2016 of slightly less than 10 per cent suggests an acceleration since 1970, and indeed the period from 2000 to 2010 saw a sharp decline in manufacturing employment, but long-term manufacturing employment decline has also occurred in manufacturing powerhouses like Germany, even when allowing for the effects of reunification (DeLong 2017a).

We saw above, however, that in some respects China might be different: manufacturing employment has expanded over the past 30 years. Autor *et al.* (2016) and Acemoglu *et al.* (2016) refer to a "China shock" (see also Acemoglu *et al.* 2016). This accords with the argument that job losses might be a product of relocation or trade competition in some sectors (Wood 2017), of which China is a major factor. In the period from 1991 to 2001, US imports from China increased from 0.6 per cent of the US market for manufacturing goods to 2.3 per cent, and by 2007, after the "China shock", the figure was 5.8 per cent (DeLong 2017a). Indeed, it could be argued that while the panic over NAFTA was actually exaggerated, China's rise is much more significant, and we shall develop this argument further in Chapters 5 and 6.

On the other hand, the evidence is still clear that trade alone cannot account for all of the employment losses that have taken place since China's rise, as argued above. This is because of long-run trends in manufacturing employment, and the jobs created in export sectors. Moreover, trade figures in the context of the rise of global value chains (see below), can present a distorted picture and the "Made in China" label is often misleading. For instance, as Dedrick *et al.* (2010) show, firms located in China contributed little to the 2006 iPod model, and accounted for less than 5 per cent of the final retail price, while US firms captured over half the retail price ($75 to Apple, $80 to retail, much of which was Apple stores, and $8 to companies that made iPod parts). What this means is not only that there are hierarchies within value chains, but also that trade statistics can be misleading. As "imports and exports don't actually reflect the value added within a country. If Japan and Korea ship complex, expensive iPhone parts to China, and a Chinese worker slaps them together and ships them on to American consumers, the whole value of the iPhone get counted as a Chinese export to the US even though the amount of economic value added in China was miniscule" (Smith 2022).

But it is still the case that China's rise cannot be explained without considerable reference to its role in global value chains, and while jobs losses from 2001 to 2007 in the US were not largely the result of competition from China (see above), the short-term impact within particular sectors was significant. For these reasons, China's industrialization has led to growing protectionist pressures, from companies and labour affected by imports. But more important, it has led to calls for protectionism for geopolitical reasons, and we discuss this further in Chapters 5 and 6.

Nonetheless, it is far too simplistic to assume or assert a zero-sum game between Chinese imports on the one hand, and US (or EU) job losses on the other, and this brings us back to the discussion around stalled industrialization and premature deindustrialization, briefly outlined in Chapter 2. As we saw, there is significant debate over whether or not specific economic sectors are more important than others. Above all, there is a debate as to whether or not industrialization is the primary driver of growth, due to its association with higher productivity, the generation of economies of scale, linkages to the rest of the economy, and so on. In the postwar period, as former colonies won their independence, most new nations accepted the view that in order to develop you must industrialize. In addition to the arguments about productivity, scale and linkages, was the Prebsich–Singer thesis (Prebsich 1959; Singer 1950), which – as we saw above and in the previous chapter – argued that there was a long-run tendency for the terms of trade to decline for primary goods producers, as against the manufacturing sector. While it was true that the price of manufacturing products would cheapen over time, this tendency was all the greater for primary goods producers in a situation of free trade. There were a number of reasons why this was the case, but all could be more or less traced back to the argument that competition was particularly intense in the primary goods sector because there were so many producers compared to those in the manufacturing sector. This meant that prices were likely to decline even more rapidly in the primary good sector. Furthermore, specialization in primary goods did not generate the linkages that developed out of manufacturing and so in the context of over-specialization and lack of diversity (see Chapter 2), laid the basis for trading into poverty.

This argument did not mean a rejection of trade and the promotion of economic autarky, but it did provide the rationale for the dominant industrialization strategy from the 1950s to the 1980s, namely import-substitution industrialization (ISI) (see Kiely 1998). This strategy argued for selective protectionist policies by developing countries, in order to build up industries in at least some sectors and reduce dependence on the import of manufactured goods from the developed world. In this way, the old colonial division of labour would be displaced, and the newly independent countries would begin to catch up with the Global North and build new nations. This involved different, although not mutually exclusive protectionist policies, such as tariffs and subsidies, and in more extreme cases the use of selected import controls through licences.

This policy of developing infant industries was hardly new, and indeed in some respects had been followed by already developed countries in the early stages of their industrialization processes (Chang 2002). On the other hand, the success of ISI policies was mixed at best and often involved creating new dependence on the import of capital goods from the North, and the protection of industries that were far from efficient. For some leftists, this fostered a new dependency which "replaced" the old one associated with the colonial division of labour (Sunkel 1966; Amin 1976). The critique that ISI was inefficient was taken up in particular by neoliberals, who increasingly came to dominate international institutions like the IMF in the 1970s and 1980s, despite previously criticizing them as irredeemably Keynesian and developmentalist institutions (see Toye 1987; Mirowski 2013; Bauer 1971). The 1982 debt crisis, which originated in Latin America, laid the basis for the partial roll-out of neoliberal reforms across much of the Global South. The rationale for this included the argument that much of the South could not meet their debt/interest payment obligations because they had adopted bad policies, which above all included the ISI strategy which in effect protected economic sectors from competition, and which therefore were inefficient and often corrupt (for example, it encouraged unproductive bribes to government ministers in order to gain access to import licences; see Kruger 1974). The argument was also made that this contrasted sharply with the efficiencies of the booming East Asian economies, which carried out export-oriented industrialization (EOI) policies that forced different sectors to compete in the world economy (Lal 1983; World Bank 1993). However, this last assertion was particularly questionable as it rested on a far too rigid dichotomy between ISI and EOI, and in fact the first-tier East Asian NICs carried out protectionist policies, including subsidies, credit to selected industries, nationalized banking, limits on the movement of capital and so on – arguments that also undermined the contentions of Frobel and his colleagues, as we have seen (see Amsden 1989; Wade 1990; Kiely 1998; Chang 2002).

Nonetheless, pro-free-market neoliberal reforms became increasingly common in the 1980s and 1990s. Furthermore, as we saw in Chapter 2, neoliberals rejected the idea that industrialization was a more important sector than any other, and what mattered was economic specialization regardless of sector. However, as neoliberal reforms were rolled out, it also became apparent that at least parts of the developing world were increasing their manufacturing base, as should be clear from the discussion above. For neoliberals and other globalization "optimists" this was because developing countries increasingly abandoned their protectionist policies, which included (in some – but far from all – cases) limits on foreign investment. As we saw in Chapter 2, this account was at the heart of the optimistic perspective on globalization, which rejected Frobel *et al.*'s pessimistic take on deindustrialization in the North and super-exploitation in the South, and instead argued that we were witnessing important tendencies towards convergence between the Global North and South. Industrialization per se may not matter, but even if it did, it was occurring and involved genuinely efficient manufacturing in contrast to the inefficiencies of protected industries that were a product of ISI. In this way, development was taking place through industrialization, and this in turn was a product of globalization-friendly policies (Ohmae 1994).

This of course brings us back to the debate between the optimists and pessimists around globalization, with the former emphasizing growing North–South convergence and the latter a race to the bottom. Despite their differences, in some respects there are some shared assumptions between these positions, with both emphasizing capital and "free markets" outgrowing the nation state, and both in effect suggesting some kind of North–South convergence, albeit with the former asserting a levelling-up process and the latter one of levelling down for global labour.

The rest of this section challenges both these versions of "levelling" positions, and instead suggests an alternative perspective based on uneven development, including limited and stalled industrialization, and premature deindustrialization. The post-independence case for industrialization was associated with nation building and the promotion of development, which as we have seen involved the promotion of ISI policies. However, we also saw that from the 1980s, developing countries largely retreated from such policies (with some notable exceptions as we shall see) and moved towards more economically liberal policies. At the same time, multinational companies began to shift their corporate strategies, and aided by lower transportation costs and the use of information and communications technologies to coordinate investment decisions, increasingly drew on subcontracting arrangements including in the Global South, and direct foreign investment. Central to this has been the rise of what has been called global commodity chains (Gereffi & Korzeniewicz 1994; Gereffi 2018), global value chains (Werner *et al.* 2014) and global production networks (Dicken 2014). There are technical differences between them but for our purposes we can highlight that for all three the production process occurs in "at least two stages conducted in different countries" (World Bank 2020: 265). The World Bank estimates that by 2008, around 52 per cent of world trade occurred through these chains or networks, and while there has been a relative decline since then, the figure was still around 48 per cent in 2015 (*ibid.*). Initially much of the commodity chain approach was influenced by Wallerstein's world systems theory, which as we have seen focused on the division of the world into core, semi-peripheral and peripheral regions (Hopkins & Wallerstein 1986). As we also saw above, Frobel and his colleagues attempted to apply this approach to what they perceived to be a new international division of labour in the 1970s, and in the 1990s, Gereffi & Korzeniewicz (1994) applied it to multinational company restructuring and its impact on the Global South. Global value chain analysis was similar to the global commodity chain approach but was more policy oriented and attempted to examine ways in which developing countries could find ways to upgrade within these chains. While not always focused on manufacturing (see Daviron & Ponte 2005; Selwyn 2012), much of the focus was on the ways in which these chains could – or could not – provide mechanisms for promoting industrial development in the Global South (Kaplinsky 2005; Dicken 2014).

Ironically then, while Frobel and his colleagues' discussion of the new international division of labour was quite problematic as an analysis of changes in the 1970s, it could be argued that it has become more relevant from the 1990s onwards, in an age of global fragmentation of production. At the same time, the weaknesses of their approach are still evident in this era. As we saw in Chapter 2, Rodrik (2016) shows that outside of Asia, there has been a decline in manufacturing value added in developing countries since 1970. Furthermore, much of this decline has taken place since the 1990s, at precisely the time when debates around globalization and the global fragmentation of production started. Drawing on data from the three most detailed studies of industrialization – the Gronigen Growth and Development Centre 20-sector database (2015 version), the UNIDO INDSTAT-2 dataset (2019 version) and the UNSD National Accounts Main Aggregates Database (December 2018 version)[2] – Sumner (2020: ch.3) shows a lower peak of employment shares for developing and former developing countries (taken as a whole) in both the categories "all" and "formal" manufacturing, and at a lower GDP per capita than the peak for developed countries. While there was a clear upward curve for manufacturing employment before 1990, this in effect plateaued in the post-1990 period (*ibid.*: 59–62). While the picture is less clear in terms of manufacturing value added, there is still a peak that has been reached in the formal manufacturing sectors, and Rodrik's longer-term data also tells a story of stalled and premature deindustrialization.

On the face of it then, we seem to have a paradoxical situation of a dispersal of manufacturing accompanied by limited advances in terms of employment and value-added growth. As Sumner (*ibid.*: 75) explains:

> the emergence of a GVC world has changed the very meaning of economic development from 'deep' industrialization to 'shallow' industrialization in the sense that the building of entire industries or even entire products is no longer even the goal for developing countries. Furthermore, the emergence of a GVC world has changed the nature of economic development from one of potentially unbounded industrialization to stunted industrialization.

Put simply, the global fragmentation of production has not "equalized the conditions of accumulation" in terms of levelling up or levelling down, and has instead seen the continuation of a hierarchical international division of labour. An earlier study to those cited above gives some clue as to what is happening in terms of a so-called new international division of labour. In a 2005 study of 46 developing countries at different stages of industrial development, Shafaeddin (2005a, 2005b) suggested that around 40 per cent (20 out of 46) of these countries have experienced rapid export expansion, and 11 of these countries have had high output growth. Of these 20 success stories, two had moderate output growth and seven had low output growth. The next 20 countries had moderate export growth and the bottom six had low levels of export growth. Fifty per cent of the sample actually experienced a level of deindustrialization, which could not be attributed to industrial maturity and diversification into services, but rather "forced diversification", based on the decline of some industries. Where new industries had emerged,

2. The Gronigen Growth and Development centre is available at https://www.rug.nl/ggdc/structuralchange/previous-sector-database/10-sector-2014?lang=en; UNIDO INDSTAT is United Nations Industrial Development Organization Industrial Statistics, available at https://stat.unido.org/; and UNSD is United Nations Statistics Division, whose National Accounts Database is available at https://unstats.un.org/unsd/snaama.

these were often in resource-based or labour-intensive sectors, and where on paper, developing countries did see a considerable increase in participation in medium- to high-skill/technology/scale sectors, this was actually misleading as "for the most part developing countries' involvement in skill and technology intensive products is confined to the labour intensive parts, frequently just assembly, of vertically integrated production systems", with the result that "while developing countries are becoming increasingly similar to major industrial countries in the structure of their exports, this is not the case for the structure of their manufacturing value added" (Kozul-Wright & Rayment 2004: 11–12).

The World Bank's 2020 *World Development Report* explicitly focused on global value chains and their role in promoting development in the Global South. The general tone of the report was upbeat, arguing that specialization within these chains reflects "different comparative advantages not only in different sectors, but also in different stages of production within sectors" (World Bank 2020: 69). Participation is such chains will lead to growth and poverty reduction, and insofar as poverty continues, this was said to be a product of insufficient economic liberalization (*ibid.*: 36). The general thrust of the argument in the report was that "GVCs boost incomes, create better jobs and reduce poverty" (*ibid.*: 3). However, as Selwyn and Leyden (2022: 176) point out, much of the evidence in the report suggests otherwise. This includes some glaring omissions on labour conditions within factories (*ibid.*: 187–8), but most relevant for our purposes is the report's discussion of upgrading (World Bank 2022: 22). The Bank identifies four tiers within a value chain: (1) commodities; (2) limited manufacturing; (3) advanced manufacturing and services; and (4) innovative activity. The Bank found that from 1990 to 2015, only 34 out of 146 countries upgraded, which amounts to just 23 per cent of the countries surveyed (Selwyn & Leyden 2020: 176). Fourteen countries upgraded from tier 1 to tier 2, 11 from tier 2 to 3, and nine from tier 3 to 4. It is true that two of the 11 in the second category were India and China, but focusing just on high population countries ignores important constraints faced by developing countries as a whole (see Chapter 2 for a similar argument related to poverty reduction). Indeed, China's industrialization may in part be at the expense of these same countries (China's upgrading is further discussed in Chapters 5 and 6). What is clear is that there is no general tendency towards upgrading at the level of individual countries for those who participate in these value chains.

This becomes even clearer if we return to a consideration of the Prebisch–Singer thesis. This argued that there was a tendency for the terms of trade to decline for primary producers against manufacturing exporters. Its basic contention was that primary goods exporters tended to suffer because of the low income elasticity of demand for their products, which essentially meant that as average incomes increase, so consumers spend a decreasing proportion of their income on primary products. This argument was reinforced by the fact that there was intense competition between primary producers, where barriers to entry into the marketplace were low, and by the fact that industrialized countries had relatively fuller employment and higher wages, as against low wages and "unlimited supplies of labour" (Lewis 1954) in the developing countries. With the rise of manufacturing exports from the Global South, this argument is on the face of it out of date, but in fact it can be fruitfully used to look at the terms of trade between different types of manufacturing exports (UNCTAD 2002: 118; Kaplinsky & Santos-Paulinho 2005). Based on a study of trade in manufacturing goods from 1970 to 1987, Sarkar and Singer (1991) have claimed the price of manufacturing exports from developing countries fell by an average of 1 per cent a year. This has been challenged on methodological grounds, and particularly over the use of the category of non-ferrous metals when examining price movements (Athukorala 1993), but a further study has suggested that the price of this category made no difference to the overall movement of manufacturing prices (Rowthorn 2001). Other studies have supported the claim that the price of simple manufacturing exports from the Global South have tended to fall against more complex manufacturing and services from the North (Maizels *et al.* 1998). One study of Chinese exports suggests that the net barter terms of trade fell by 10 per cent against developed countries between 1993 and 2000, but improved as against other developing countries (Zheng 2002).

The reason for these movements can be linked to the globalization of production. Essentially, the Global North still dominates in high-value sectors, based on high barriers to entry, high start-up and running costs, and significant skill levels. In the South, where there are large amounts of surplus labour, barriers to entry, skills and wages are low. While this gives such countries considerable competitive advantages, at the same time low barriers to entry mean that competition is particularly intense and largely determined by cost price, which also means low wages. Thus, the clothing industry, where the Global South has achieved considerable increases in world export shares in recent years, has a very low degree of market concentration. In contrast, sectors like machinery (such as non-electric engines and motors) and transport (cars, motor bikes, aircraft, ships, boats) have very high degrees of market concentration and are mainly located in the Global North (UNCTAD 2002: 120–23). In other words, we might argue that the old hierarchy between manufacturers and primary goods producers, identified by Prebisch and Singer, has been partially replaced by one based on different kinds of low-value manufacturing goods, and this reflects the stalled industrialization that has emerged in most of the South. Put in terms of the theory of trade outlined above, the partial shift to manufacturing in the Global South has not eliminated over-specialization.

How then does this discussion relate to older arguments about the relationship between industrialization and development? In different ways, Kuznets (1955), Furtado (1964) and Lewis (1954) envisage development as a process whereby labour is gradually transferred to and absorbed by a high-productivity modern sector associated with industrialization, from a lower-productivity so-called traditional sector. The former is characterized by high rates of productivity and output, the latter, composed largely of subsistence farming has low productivity and output (Lewis 1954). Development is ultimately the growth of the former at the expense of the latter, in part through the absorption of the latter into the former. While this approach can be far too unilinear and assume that all nation states pass through similar stages of development (see Rostow 1960), in fact much of the approach can be used to highlight the differences and inequalities inherent in this variegated process. This was central to Furtado's approach in particular (see Furtado 1965). In the case of transitions based on participation in global value chains, this has been associated with stalled and premature deindustrialization, so the income enhancing effects of industrialization have been limited (although these effects have historically varied and been associated with political pressure and public policy interventions; see Kiely 1998). Indeed, Diao and McMillan (2018) suggest that contemporary development is less associated with a dualism between a modern industrial sector and a traditional rural sector, and instead identify a further "dualism" within the modern sector: an "open non-agricultural" sector of relatively sophisticated technology and some degree of high productivity, alongside an "in between" or "closed non-agricultural" sector based on low technology, low productivity, which includes the informal sector and is dominated by the urban poor (Moser 1978; Davis 2004). The existence of this massive reserve army also helps to keep wages low, even in sectors where productivity levels are similar to those in the richer world (Selwyn 2019). In contrast to linear accounts of various political persuasions (World Bank 2020; Warren 1980), there is little evidence that this in-between sector will be absorbed by the "open non-agricultural" sector (Kiely 2008).

We might also briefly note that this has implications for the optimistic take on globalization discussed in Chapter 2. As Ferguson (2006: 14) suggests for Africa, its participation in globalization "has certainly not been a matter simply of 'joining the world economy'; perversely, it has instead been a matter of highly selective and spatially encapsulated forms of global connection combined with widespread disconnection and exclusion". In other words, rather than theorizing in terms of being sufficiently or insufficiently globalized, an approach which lies at the heart of dualist analyses, we need to better understand the forms of global integration. This then provides us with a better understanding of deindustrialization, and how we might overcome simplistic analyses that suggest either a straightforward positive-sum game, or a straightforward negative-sum game.

At the same time, the discussion in this section has made it clear that we cannot simply focus on the ways that developing countries are "included" in global value chains. This is partly because of the constraints faced by these countries and the difficulties of upgrading, which is reflected in the stalled industrializations and premature deindustrializations discussed above. This also partly reflects the shortcomings of poverty measurements that rest on too low a conception of what constitutes absolute poverty (see Chapter 2). As Selwyn (2018: 74) points out, optimistic approaches, such as Sachs' (2005: 11) claim that "sweatshops are the first rung on the ladder out of extreme poverty", rest on an arbitrary measure. But we also need to reject the dualist approach which assumes that in the long run labourers will eventually be incorporated into these value chains and upgrading and higher wages will be the inevitable result (Kiely 2008). For the story of these chains is not simply one of (unequal) inclusion through incorporation, but (uneven and unequal) exclusion through what Werner and Bair (2019) have called "disarticulation", whereby most labourers are not incorporated into such production networks. Indeed, low wages in the former are in part a product of the existence of the latter. This then suggests that we are a world away from notions of the South "stealing" the jobs of workers in the North, but also ideas which suggest that deindustrialization in the North has simply been caused by the industrialization of the South.

CONCLUSION

This chapter has discussed a much more negative account of deindustrialization than that outlined in Chapter 2. While we have at times reiterated some of the problems of the optimistic scenario discussed and critiqued in the previous chapter, our main focus has been on the ways in which deindustrialization is said to be a problem for the Global North. This has a number of forms, and includes a focus on import competition, foreign investment and relocation, the use of global value chains and subcontracting, and exchange rate undervaluations from Southern exporters. All of these add up to an argument that the rise of manufacturing on the South has had negative effects on industrialization in the North, and is the principal reason for the deindustrialization of the so-called advanced countries. But we have shown that while this might be true within specific sectors, it is not true for developed countries as a whole. The evidence from trade, trade deals, and so on, clearly shows this is the case. Our discussion of trade deficits in the US shows that while there may have been some short-term issues, and the China shock was significant, it was still not the main reason for manufacturing jobs losses in the US. This argument – that trade deficits per se did not causes manufacturing job losses at an aggregate level – has also been borne out by comparative studies of manufacturing employment in as many as 60 countries in the period from 1995 to 2011 (Lawrence 2020). Furthermore, in terms of the globalization of production, manufacturing in the South is overwhelmingly concentrated in lower-value production characterized by low barriers to entry, intense competition and diminishing returns. It is in these sectors – clothing, textiles, toys, and so on – that the South has a cost advantage, particularly in low wages. But precisely because they are characterized by low barriers to entry, they do not provide the basis for upgrading to sectors with higher barriers to entry, where rents can be accrued to the most dynamic producers (Kaplinsky 2005; Kiely 2007). Indeed, since 1990, the growth of China's exports in absolute amounts has exceeded that of the rest of the top ten leading manufacturing exporters from the developing world, and since 2000, the latter nine countries' combined export share has fallen while China's has risen (Eichengreen *et al.* 2004). This reflects the fact that competition in low-value sectors is particularly intense and not necessarily a springboard to further development, and the fact that competition with China – and not the Global North – has deleterious consequences for the rest of the South. This is not lost on the Chinese Communist Party, which essentially operates aid policies designed to extract raw materials from the South to aid its own industrialization. It also attracts foreign investment and enters into subcontracting agreements while at the same time trying to continue the promotion of industrial policy – import-substitution industrialization (ISI) – in order to upgrade into higher value activity (Nolan 2001). In recent years this has had serious economic and geopolitical consequences which take us beyond a discussion of deindustrialization, and we examine these in Chapters 5 and 6. For now however, we need to emphasize the fact that at best, competition with the Global South, is a very limited explanation for the deindustrialization of the North, perhaps above all because manufacturing output has continued to expand in the developed countries. The next chapter therefore looks at an alternative explanation which highlights this fact.

CHAPTER 4

DEINDUSTRIALIZATION AS A PRODUCT OF TECHNOLOGICAL CHANGE (AND WHY AUTOMATION'S SIGNIFICANCE IS REAL BUT EXAGGERATED)

The previous chapter questioned the extent to which deindustrialization in the Global North was and is a product of import competition from the Global South and/or the relocation of capital from North to South. While there is evidence that this might be the case in *specific sectors*, at an *aggregate level* it is problematic, and the fact is that in many cases manufactured goods are produced using less workers. It is also the case that wage stagnation and/or loss of benefits such as pension levels is an issue across the board – in manufacturing and services and indeed in the public sector – regardless of whether or not there is intense competition from imported goods or services. The issue of more output being produced with less workers is addressed further in this chapter, as it speaks to a different potential explanation for deindustrialization in the North, namely that it is a product of technological change, including automation.

The chapter examines this thesis, first by reiterating and further developing the debate between the "relocationists" versus the "technologists". It then moves on to consider in more detail the debate about technological futures, including those around robotization and automation, in both the North and South. This discussion about a second machine age is related to wider debates about a second "Great Transformation", which highlights the importance of the new post-industrial age. The third section then provides a critical assessment of this debate, and in particular introduces the powerful critique made by Benanav (2020a) of the technologists, whose wider arguments are also considered in the next chapter. The chapter concludes that while the technologists provide a useful corrective to the relocationists considered in the previous chapter, there are some serious issues not fully addressed by this perspective.

THE RELOCATION THESIS QUESTIONED: THE TECHNOLOGIST CRITIQUE

Chapter 3 considered the question of the extent to which deindustrialization in the Global North can be explained by the industrialization of the Global South. While the discussion did not reject the relocation and/or import competition arguments outright, it did suggest that there were important reasons for questioning its central claims. These included the stalled industrialization and deindustrialization of parts of the Global South in the context of the rise of global value chains, and the fact that much economic activity there continues to focus on agriculture or insecure service work, alongside low-value, low-labour productivity in the manufacturing sector. Although this latter sector might account for some degree of deindustrialization in the Global North in particular sectors, it does not provide an adequate account in terms of manufacturing at an aggregate level. This is above all because total manufacturing output has increased in much of the North, even as the share of manufacturing in total output and employment has fallen. This suggests then the need for a different explanation for deindustrialization in the North, and it was suggested that we need to look at technological change and productivity increases, whereby increasing levels of manufacturing output require less labour.

This was discussed in the previous chapter but here we need to develop this argument further. We examined changes in the US economy and the shift from one where trade surpluses were common (up to 1976) to one where deficits are the new normal. It was suggested in that discussion that the deficits per se were not the cause of deindustrialization or declining employment levels. Here we examine this issue further by looking at more recent developments in the US economy, and specifically the period after 2000, which saw a sharp decrease in manufacturing employment. Hicks and Devaraj (2017: 3) claim that there were 5,647,700 jobs lost in manufacturing in the period from 2000 to 2010. At the same time, manufacturing output grew, even with the declines that took place in the period of the global financial crisis and its immediate aftermath (2007–09). In the period 2006–13, which included those three years of declining output, manufacturing grew by an annual average of 2.2 per cent per year (*ibid.*: 2). There were some sectors that saw significant declines, including wood products (a decline of 22.5 per cent), non-metallic mineral products (a decline of 19.1 per cent), textiles (a decline of 21.3 per cent), and computer and electronic products (a decline of 11.6 per cent). On the other hand, some sectors saw significant increases in output, including primary metals (a 22.8 per cent increase), machinery (a 27.5 increase), automobiles and automobile parts (14.6 per cent) and goods/beverages/tobacco (37 per cent) (*ibid.*: 3). With these increases more than compensating for some sectoral declines, this amounted to a total increase of 17.6 per cent for all manufacturing in that period (*ibid.*: 2).

In terms of productivity, this is measured by dividing the value of all manufacturing goods by the number of workers employed in manufacturing. Hicks and Devaraj (2015: 3) suggest that in 2012, the average value of the product of labour was $149,299, which ranged from $45,930 in the apparel and leather goods sector to $733,861 for petroleum and coal products. When adjusted for inflation, productivity grew in all manufacturing sectors in the period 1998–2012 (*ibid.*: 3). In computer and electronic products, growth was as much as 829 per cent, but this is an issue of some controversy, and we return to it later in the chapter. As already stated, this coincided with a sharp fall in manufacturing employment, but Hicks and Devaraj argue that trade only accounted for a small share of these job losses. There were significantly high job losses in some sectors, including apparel, leather and allied products (44.6 per cent), and furniture and related products (40.2 per cent), but in terms of total employment losses, trade accounted for 13.4 per cent, and 87.8 per cent of total productivity increases, while increases in domestic demand accounted for small increases in employment (*ibid.*: 4). Although in many respects on opposites sides in the "China shock" debate (see Chapter 3), this account is broadly consistent with Acemoglu *et al.* (2014) which estimate a total of 2–2.4 million job losses in manufacturing in the period 1999–2013, a higher figure but one measured across different years and one that includes job losses beyond direct manufacturing.

TECHNOLOGICAL CHANGE, AUTOMATION AND THE FUTURE OF EMPLOYMENT

The critique in the previous chapter and the section above highlights the issue that at an aggregate level, it is quite possible for manufacturing output to increase, both with less workers and a declining share of manufacturing to national output. But this leads to the obvious question of whether the issue is less that of relocation and import competition in the developed countries, and actually one of technological displacement, in both developed and developing countries. But this begs a further, troubling question, namely whether or not we are living through a new post-industrial age, based on computerization, automation and the "rise of the robots" (Ford 2015), in which old jobs have been displaced but not replaced by new ones, or at least it has seen replacement largely in more insecure sectors of employment. Although the precise arguments of this automation discourse vary, all agree that we are living in a new, "second machine age" or "fourth industrial revolution" (Brynjolfsson & McAfee 2014; Schwab 2016).

This argument can be usefully understood by thinking of recent technological and socio-economic change in terms of a "second Great Transformation" (Burawoy 2010; Harriss 2021). While both transformations are not solely about technology, they involve different technological developments that are relevant for our discussion in this chapter. The idea of a first Great Transformation often involves discussion of the transition from feudalism to capitalism (Hilton 1976) and from rural agriculture to urban industrialization (Hobsbawm 1999), but it is the work of Karl Polanyi (2001), published in 1944, which is most relevant here. Polanyi talked about two stages, or "movements" in the first Great Transformation. The first movement was based on steam power, which laid the basis for mechanization and eventually globalization. It involved a shift from agriculture to industry and urbanization in what came to be called the "developed" countries. Late nineteenth-century globalization was facilitated by the extensive development of railways (which had started earlier in the century) and then steamships. In the developed world at least, industrialization and advances in transportation, and a labour force increasingly separated from direct access to land, laid the basis for an unprecedented expansion of wealth. In terms of employment, in Britain, manufacturing was dominant throughout the nineteenth century and remained central in the first half of the twentieth century. In 1800, manufacturing accounted for 48 per cent and agriculture 30 per cent of the labour force. By 1890 the figures were 44 per cent for manufacturing and 18 per cent for agriculture. By 1950, the figures were, 48 per cent for services, 42 per cent for manufacturing and 10 per cent for agriculture (Herrendorf *et al.* 2014).

At the same time, this expansion exacerbated social problems or created new ones, including urban squalor, heightened inequality, economic crises and geopolitical rivalries. Polanyi argued persuasively that the expansion of the market did not take place independently of the state, and indeed the former was a deliberate policy of the latter, especially in Britain. But this led to uneven development between countries (and regions) and much of Western Europe, the US and Japan responded through protectionist policies in order to build up their own industries, rather than simply trade surplus raw materials with the dominant industrial power, which at the time was Britain. In other words, such countries made the deliberate decision to develop and catch up through industrialization, and this policy was extended to the dominant white settler colonies in the British empire. This protectionism – part of Polanyi's second or double movement – was not necessarily progressive however, and took a variety of forms, including socialist revolution and then Stalinism in what became the Soviet Union, and fascism in Italy and Germany. It also involved heightened geopolitical conflict, including a new round of colonialism from the late nineteenth century, two world wars and the Great Depression of the 1930s, all of which were closely linked. This double movement also involved domestic pressures for social reform as an increasingly concentrated working class began to organize into trade unions and political parties and demand the vote, and it was this "fear of the masses" and the labour question which partly led to authoritarian responses by elite groups within society.

Polanyi's work is useful but there were two areas where he was not necessarily wrong, but incomplete. First, he saw the second movement as part of a re-embedding of the economy back into society. As we have seen, a complete dis-embedding had not taken place and laissez-faire was in some respects planned, but the ideology of "market fundamentalism" tended to distort this fact. Nonetheless, Polanyi was not very precise about which groups in society – and the interests they had – that led to protectionist pressures, and the diverse forms that they took. He was well aware that these were often reactionary but did not say much about why this was the case (Burawoy 2010). Second, Polanyi's focus was largely on the so-called developed world and had far less to say about the developing world, colonialism and the hierarchies of the international division of labour created in this era. He was certainly aware of these, not least as his work represented such a powerful critique of the market economy and free trade, but the hierarchies which we outlined in the previous chapter were not particularly prominent in his work. More specifically, the colonial world and Latin America were integrated into the nineteenth- and twentieth-century world economy largely as producers of raw materials, and therefore did not reap the benefits of industrialization. While this did not preclude growth, specialization in comparatively low-value, low-productivity goods left them at a disadvantage compared to industrial producers, and it failed to generate the favourable spin-offs associated with industrialization, as outlined in Chapters 2 and 3. In short, they essentially traded on the basis of high ubiquity (a lot of countries exported these products) and low diversity (not many products were exported by each country) (Hausmann *et al.* 2011).

In the period of the first Great Transformation, there was an initial period of rising inequality. For example, from the late seventeenth century to around 1867, the share of income of the top 5 per cent in England and Wales rose from around 35 to 40 per cent. This was reversed through the re-embedding process outlined by Polanyi, and in concrete terms the share of the top 5 per cent fell from around 40 per cent in the late nineteenth century to under 20 per cent by the 1970s (Roser 2014). In the United States, the share of income going to the top 10 per cent fell from 45–50 per cent in the 1910s and 1920s, to around 35 per cent from the 1950s to around 1980 (Piketty 2014: 24). This reflected significant reforms associated with the double movement, including the extension of the franchise (although this remained limited in the South of the country until 1965 and still is to some extent), the New Deal, welfare states and so on.

The second Great Transformation started in the 1970s and intensified in the 1980s and 1990s. In terms of technology, information and communications technologies (ICTs) were crucial, and in terms of jobs, this accelerated the trend away from manufacturing in the developed world towards services. Computerization and automation saw the destruction of jobs in manufacturing, an explanation which accords with that outlined in the opening section of this chapter. But from the 1990s, the use of ICTs enabled the organization of manufacturing across national boundaries whereby information was collected and production organized in global production networks, in what Castells (1996) called the rise of the "network society". This explanation is thus compatible with the relocation and/or import competition explanation outlined and critiqued in the previous chapter, but it is sufficiently nuanced to point out that these processes applied only to selected parts of the globally fragmented production process (and is thus compatible with the stalled industrialization and deindustrialization arguments previously discussed).

These developments lead us back to a consideration of the optimistic and pessimistic accounts of new technologies. The automation discourse is far from completely pessimistic and some point out that in the past new technologies and new investment led to new jobs, so this might happen in the future, an argument not dissimilar to that addressed in Chapter 2. Part of the argument here is the much older one that technology and markets will lead to growth, and progress will automatically follow, a by-product of the free exercise of self-interest in the marketplace. This is often associated with relatively sophisticated work by the likes of Hayek (2001, 2013) and Friedman (1962), as well as Adam Smith (1981), albeit with considerable caveats (Kiely 2018). More recently we have seen populist books like *The Rational Optimist* (Ridley 2010) argue along similar, if much cruder, lines. The argument here is that the state is in many respects a parasite on the wealth-creating activities of entrepreneurial individuals, and so taxation, subsidies, bail-outs and regulation should be regarded with suspicion.[1] Although somewhat more subtle,

1. It should be noted that Matt Ridley was himself chair of the British bank Northern Rock from 2004 to 2007, which was subject to a bank run, the first on a British bank for over 100 years. The bank was subsequently bailed-out and nationalized, and then taken over by the Virgin Group in 2012. Ridley resigned in 2007.

Pinker (2018) similarly suggests that progress is a result of Enlightenment values and market innovation. Historically, these arguments assume a more or less straightforward link between technological development, economic growth and improvements in living standards, but the evidence suggests that progress was a far more uneven and complex process. For instance, historians have long debated whether or not the British industrial revolution led to improvements in living standards (or what today might be called social development). Although much of this debate is couched in terms of optimists versus pessimists, all sides agree that at some point there was an improvement in living standards (Snooks 1994; Crafts 1997; Voth 2004). The disagreement is about when this happened, and the reasons why such improvement occurred (Gallardo-Albarran & de Jong 2021), although it still tends to mainly focus on the impact within Britain rather more than its empire. The evidence appears to show a decline in real wages from 1760 to 1830, and then a small increase from 1830 to 1850. Life expectancy at birth improved from 1760 to 1800, from 35 to 40, but was then static from the next 50 years. Annual working time increased over the period 1760–1850, as did inequality (*ibid.*). So, even where there were some improvements from 1760 to 1850, these were far from impressive and hardly kept pace with the benefits of technological change, and it was only in the second half of the nineteenth century that improvements became more substantial, above all in public health. Furthermore, if we include the impact of what became the colonial division of labour then any improvement – narrowly defined as increased income – in British colonies was extremely slow, involved repression, famine and, in India, the destruction of industry (Bairoch 1993: 95; Davis 2001), as even apologists for colonialism have accepted (Ferguson 2004: 195). What this suggests then is that "progress" is not guaranteed by combinations of markets and technology, and that "shared prosperity emerged because, and only when, the direction of technological advances and society's approach to dividing the gains were pushed away from arrangements that primarily served a narrow elite. We are beneficiaries of progress, mainly because our predecessors made that progress work for more people" (Acemoglu & Johnson 2023: 6). This point applies to all kinds of technological developments: as Acemoglu and Johnson (2023) show, this includes better ploughs, crop rotation and improved mills in the early modern period, which had little impact on peasant producers but which allowed privileged groups to use wealth to build luxury churches; improvements in shipping which played a role in the intensification of the Atlantic slave trade; and the cotton gin which intensified the savagery of slavery in the southern United States. One might add to this current debates over AI in which a version of technological determinism fears that the new technologies will come to dominate humanity, an argument that downplays the ways in which human interaction alters the technology (Harding 2023; Acemoglu & Johnson 2023: ch.9).

Despite all this, the conflation of technology, markets and progress has persisted into the "post-industrial" era, and these arguments are all the stronger according to proponents of the "Californian ideology", which combines the anti-statist counterculture of the 1960s, with the "anti-statism" of neoliberalism (Barbrook & Cameron 1996; Turner 2006). This in itself has a longer history, which links fears about the impact of new technology with criticisms of the welfare state and New Deal, particularly in the postwar period. While basic income proposals pre-date the twentieth century, these usually took the form of payment-in-kind relief measures, or were linked to property or tied to particular modes of behaviour (Jager & Zamora Vargas 2023: ch.1). Milton Friedman made the case for a negative income tax from the 1940s onwards, arguing that there should be a floor of unconditional income for all individuals and he rejected the view that this should be linked to certain duties or obligations. This would allow individuals to make their own choices as opposed to the paternalist (welfare) state making decisions for them, and so it was regarded as a challenge to the postwar development of the New Deal (Friedman 1962) and the alleged "creeping totalitarianism" of the welfare state (Hayek 2001: 125). This "negative income tax" (Friedman 1962: 190–95) is a form of universal basic income (UBI) and is discussed further in Chapter 8, but we should note here that advocates crossed the political divide and it was linked, not only to criticisms of the welfare state, but also to the growing fear of technological change displacing workers, which is not as recent a phenomenon as is sometimes thought. For instance, in 1948 the US mathematician Norbert Wiener warned of the possibility that technological change could displace workers through a cybernetic revolution (see Jager & Zamora Vargas 2023: 68–70). The Triple Revolution manifesto of 1964 was an open memorandum sent to President Johnson and which focused on the potential absence of jobs as a result of the cybernetic revolution (see Jager & Zamora Vargas 2023: 72). Among its signatories was James Boggs, an African American who had migrated from the South to Detroit in the 1930s. Given the growing deindustrialization in that city, he increasingly questioned his Marxist views centred on the primacy of the proletariat, as African Americans were increasingly likely to be unemployed. He came to argue against a civil rights project that focused in part on integrating Black workers into the New Deal project of full employment. Technological change had rendered this project unsustainable, not only for those African Americans displaced by technological change, but also for white workers likely to face a similar prospect in the near future (Boggs 2009). These ideas influenced the civil rights movement, which shifted gradually to a critique of "welfare colonialism" to one of Black autonomy, through the rise of Black Power (Jager & Zamora Vargas 2023: 81). Ironically, this occurred at a time when the right was intensifying its own attacks on the welfare state, in part through advocacy of Friedman's negative income tax, but also through conservative attacks on the behaviour of the (mainly African-American) poor (discussed further in Chapter 8). In Europe too, although mainly from the 1970s, the left focus on the proletariat was challenged from within the "post-workerist" left, which reflected the breakdown of the postwar social contract, technological change, and the argument that new class forces were displacing an increasingly conservative – and declining – industrial proletariat (Negri 1991; Gorz 1987; Marcuse 2002). On the other hand, this did not mean a complete rejection of the idea of work – for instance in the US calls for basic income through the National Welfare Rights Organization in the 1970s and 1980s made the point that "welfare mothers" were entitled to a basic income because they were already carrying out work in the home, an argument that overlapped with Wages for Housework campaigns in Europe. This was less a break and more a reconstruction of the idea of what constituted work, and one that upset any straightforward association of the disappearance of work with the rise of automation.

These arguments have continued and developed in new contexts in recent years. More specifically, the argument made is that the IT revolution has created non-hierarchical knowledge networks that have connected individuals in virtual communities. Furthermore, new technologies have the potential to liberate people from jobs that are tedious, environmentally unfriendly and dangerous. In many respects this is an argument that overlaps with that discussed and critiqued in Chapter 2. In fairness, this account does recognize the dangers of inequality and therefore calls for appropriate policies designed to enhance human capital, and so sees a role for the state (in alliance with the private sector) through investment in education (Schwab 2016) to deal with this challenge. But these policies have had limited impact, not only on the "left behind" (see Chapter 7) but also most of those that have benefited from an advanced level of education (see Chapters 2, 7 and 8; see also below).

More broadly, one can also point to the reality of manufacturing in the IT sector through global production networks and the low wages and poor conditions experienced by these workers (Selwyn 2018). For reasons outlined in the previous chapter, it is far from certain that these sweat-shops will see rapid upgrading in the foreseeable future. For progress to happen in these circumstances, it is likely to be the product of resistance on the part of the labourers themselves and through public policy, but this is something that is regarded as politically unacceptable for Ridley's market fundamentalism or Pinker's recourse to technocratic rationality. Similarly, all cases of industrialization have relied on state interventions, including subsidies and tariffs, not only in the cases of Ridley's misplaced examples of South Korea and Taiwan, but also the supposedly libertarian IT sector in the US (Amsden 1989; Wade 1990; Chang 2002; Weiss 2014; Kiely 1998, 2018; Mazzucato 2013). Despite the utopian dreams of the Californian ideology, the reality is less one of networked individuals, and more that of highly concentrated, oligopolistic firms exercising authority and surveillance over everyone else (Zuboff 2019). While it might be the case then, that technological development can be progressive and has the potential to liberate humanity from work, to some extent at least, it is also true that technology comes with a particular rationality that intensifies domination over individuals, an argument made by romantics at the start of the industrial revolution through to theorists of the Frankfurt School, and perhaps above all Herbert Marcuse, from the 1930s onwards (Pepper 2002; Marcuse 2002).

Furthermore, as we saw in Chapter 2, much of the new service-sector jobs are relatively low skilled and insecure, and in terms of technology, the argument is now made that technologies might displace unskilled as well as skilled work. The digital revolution, including computerization, Big Data and AI, means that technological innovation is job displacing more than it is job enhancing. This is because it is human brains that are being displaced and so there is now a substitutive rather than complementary relationship between human and non-human work (Schlogl & Sumner 2020: 43), with the result that we may now be at a "peak human" period of technological transformation (DeLong 2017b). The issue here then is that while some jobs displaced in manufacturing have been replaced by service-sector jobs, the expected upgrading has only taken place among a small proportion of the labour force and so comparatively few jobs have been created for those that work with their minds, and certainly not on the scale required to replace those who worked with their hands. In the US, service jobs accounted for around 60 per cent of total jobs in 1970, and this had increased to around 80 per cent by 2018 (Herrendorf *et al.* 2014). At the same time, inequality has returned to early first Great Transformation levels, with the share of income going to the top 1 per cent in the US increasing from 10 per cent in 1981 to 23.5 per cent in 2007 (Piketty 2014: 24). In a 2013 study of the US labour market, Frey and Osborne (2013) estimate that around 47 per cent of total jobs in the US are at risk of being replaced by computerization. This is also a potential problem in the Global South. The World Bank (2016) recently estimated that around 1.8 billion jobs, which is around two-thirds of the formal labour force in the South, are potentially at risk from automation. The McKinsey Global Institute (2017) examined employment susceptibility to automation in 52 countries and while less pessimistic than the World Bank, still suggested potentially high rates of technological unemployment. These included figures of around 50 per cent or higher in China, India, Malaysia and Thailand (see Schlogl & Sumner 2020: 65). On departing the presidency in the US, Barack Obama suggested that the issue of unemployment and underemployment is less a problem caused by overseas trade and more "the relentless pace of automation that makes a lot of good, middle-class jobs obsolete" (quoted in Benanav 2020a: 4). More recently, it has been suggested that developments in AI could impact around 80 per cent of the US workforce. While this might impact only around 10 per cent of their work, for around 19 per cent of the workforce, it is likely to impact around half of their work (Eloundou *et al.* 2023).

On the other hand, critics have suggested that the impact of automation has been exaggerated. This is discussed in detail in the next section, but a recent re-evaluation of Frey and Osborne's estimates put the impact on jobs at around 10 per cent rather than their estimate of 47 per cent (Benanav 2023a). The online datasets used to estimate job losses included some odd candidates such as central bank monetary authorities and the clergy, so some scepticism is required, especially when we combine this with the productivity statistics discussed below. What is perhaps more telling is that the deployment of new technologies has coincided with an intensification of insecure jobs in the Global North. Standing (2011: 109–10) suggests that a new precariat has developed across the globe, based on a lack of secure, work-based identity, which affects around 25 per cent of the global adult population. This of course also has implications for thinking about possible agents to lead the second phase of a new double movement, for as Castells (1996: 475) noted in the 1990s, "[l]abour is disaggregated in its performance, fragmented in its organisation, diversified in its existence, divided in its collective action". While industrial unrest in the early 2020s suggests that this scenario is something of an exaggeration, it does still point to some important social and political realities in the 2020s.

One of the most common criticisms made of the automation thesis is that it tends towards a technologically determinist explanation for social change, which is implicit if not explicit in Ridley (2010) and Pinker (2018). But the more sophisticated accounts do at least reflect on the social impact of these developments, and suggest that appropriate social arrangements need to be put in place to ensure that the benefits of technological change accrue to everyone, and not just a small minority (Acemoglu 2021). While technological change might provide the potential for a better future, some suggest that this will depend on factors beyond technology. Benanav (2020: 2) suggests that the "automation discourse" refers to four key themes: (1) workers are being displaced and this has led to technological unemployment or underemployment; (2) we are on the verge of living in a largely automated society;

(3) however, more radical accounts highlight that most people remain wage dependent; and (4) therefore we need to sever the link between wages and income, with many (from left and right) suggesting that we need to introduce something along the lines of a universal basic income (UBI).

Much of these arguments rest on the assumption that the new technologies of this new era have led to high rates of productivity and increasing output. To some extent this is true, as we have seen, because trends in aggregate manufacturing output do undermine simplistic relocation explanations for deindustrialization. However, there is a significant problem only partially addressed by the technological displacement thesis. This is perhaps best illustrated by the famous Robert Solow quote, which suggests that "[w]e see the computer age everywhere, except in the productivity statistics" (Solow 1987: 36). In the US, productivity growth rates are exaggerated by the method of measurement, where productivity in the computers/electronics sector rose by high levels but outside of that sector growth rates actually fell in the period 1987–2011 (Benanav 2020a: 18). This has led some to argue that we need to look again at the relocation/import competition arguments (Houseman 2018), but we have argued elsewhere why this might be useful in some but not most sectors of manufacturing. There is also some debate about productivity in the context of new technology, with some emphasizing time lags between technological diffusion and productivity increases, and some questioning how measuring productivity is distorted by inflation (Brynjolfsson & Hitt 2003; Feldstein 2019). Nonetheless, we can still accept the strength of the technological change thesis' critique of the relocation argument, while holding on to some scepticism about the claims made by the former. The next section examines a critique of the automation thesis, one that at the same time does not endorse the relocation/import competition alternative.

THE TECHNOLOGICAL PARADIGM: A CRITIQUE

What this suggests then is that technological change and productivity increases might be more significant in terms of job losses than relocation to parts of the Global South. However, this then leads to a number of further problems, because while we might point to productivity and output increases in *particular sectors*, there is also a considerable debate about the relative lack of productivity increases in *the economy as a whole*, particularly in Britain but also in the US and to some extent Germany as well. Not unrelated to this point, and as we saw above, why is it that technological change has not led to significant numbers of highly paid jobs during this period of deindustrialization, whereas previous periods of technological change have? (Blanchflower

2019). To understand this we need to move beyond questions of technology and deindustrialization per se.

This section examines in particular Aaron Benanav's critique of the technological change thesis. It will be suggested that this is indeed a powerful critique, although the next chapter will problematize some of the wider contentions of his thesis. For now, however, we shall just focus on this critique. Benanav (2020a: 16) accepts the basic definition of deindustrialization and demonstrates its importance by contrasting proportions of the labour force employed in manufacturing from 1970 to 2017. In the US the decline in the proportion of manufacturing employment was 22 per cent in 1970 to just 8 per cent in 2017; for France the figures were 23 per cent and 9 per cent; for Japan, 25 per cent and 15 per cent; for Germany, 29 per cent and 17 per cent; and for the UK, 30 per cent and 8 per cent. Thus, the actual numbers fell by around one third in Germany, the US and Japan, one half in France and as much as two thirds in the UK (*ibid.*). Some of this might be accounted for by the relocation of manufacturing in some sectors (see Chapter 3), but none of these countries saw a decline in total manufacturing *output* over this period. Indeed, from 1970 to 2017, manufacturing value added (MVA) more than doubled in all of the countries mentioned above, except for the UK, and even in there MVA increased by around 25 per cent over the same period (*ibid.*: 17).

Technological change may also be a factor, and indeed it has been, within certain sectors of manufacturing (see above), where output has increased but with fewer workers being employed. However, as we saw in the previous section, there is a productivity paradox in which it is widely assumed that the IT revolution has sharply increased productivity, but this belief is not borne out by the official data. Thus, in Germany, manufacturing productivity grew at an average annual rate of 6.3 per cent in the 1950s and 1960s, but only by 2.4 per cent from 2000 to 2017 (*ibid.*: 18). The high rates from the earlier period might partly have been caused by recovery from the devastation of the Second World War, but we would still expect high rates in the second period when industrial robotics were widely introduced (and there was indeed scope for high rates of productivity increases due to the impact of reunification ten years before).

Moreover, Germany is far from unique in this regard. In the period from 1950 to 1973, France saw average annual productivity growth rates of 5.2 per cent, but only 2.7 per cent in the years following 2000 (*ibid.*: 19). At this point, Benanav introduces a further measure which is central to his overall argument. Specifically, he highlights not only the 5.2 per cent average annual manufacturing growth rate from 1950 to 1973, but also the average annual output growth rate of 5.9 per cent in the same period (*ibid.*). In other words, in the period 1950 to 1973, both productivity and output grew at relatively high rates, but crucially, *the rate of growth in output was faster than the rate of growth in productivity.* As a result, while productivity increases were rapid, this did not lead to a decline in employment, and technological advance went hand in hand with the (proportionate) expansion of manufacturing employment. For the period since 1973, Benanav (*ibid*: 19) correctly identifies some important changes in this scenario. If the average annual productivity growth rate of 2.7 per cent has gone hand in hand with an annual average growth rate in manufacturing output of 0.9 per cent, this means that in the latter period, not only has productivity and output growth slowed down when compared with the former, but also that in the second period productivity growth has been faster than output growth (*ibid*.: 21).

More generally, in the 1950s and 1960s, global manufacturing production expanded at an average annual rate of 7.1 per cent in real terms, compared to 4.8 per cent in the 1970s, 3 per cent in the period 1980–2007, and just 1.6 per cent from 2008 to 2014 (*ibid*.: 23). It should be stressed that these figures include China. In the period 1991–2016, global manufacturing employment rose by an average of 0.4 per cent a year, but once population growth is factored in, this translated to a 3 percentage point proportionate fall in the share of manufacturing in total employment (*ibid*.: 22).

Benanav is essentially arguing then, that earlier periods of industrialization saw higher productivity increases alongside increasing employment in manufacturing, as output growth outstripped productivity growth, but in recent years these trends have reversed, while at the same time the growth in both productivity and output has slowed down (*ibid*.: 29). The result is that higher productivity has outstripped higher output in an era of slower growth. Thus, in contrast to the technology and automation theses discussed in this chapter, it is not technological change per se that has led to deindustrialization, but slower growth in the world economy. Indeed, the argument of the technology/automation thesis is further undermined by the fact that those with higher levels of robotization have not had the worst degrees of deindustrialization. In 2016, Germany used 31 robots per 1,000 manufacturing workers, South Korea 63 and Japan 30, compared to 19 in the US and 7 in the UK. But the first three countries had higher manufacturing employments shares (South Korea 17 per cent, Germany 17 per cent and Japan 15 per cent) than the US or UK, both of which had only shares of 8 per cent (*ibid*.: 28).

This is a powerful critique of the technology thesis, although it will be argued in the next chapter – which goes beyond a consideration of deindustrialization per se – that the wider arguments made by Benanav are more contentious. For now, however, we should just note the importance of his critique of the technological change/automation thesis.

CONCLUSION

This chapter has considered an alternative approach to understanding deindustrialization, focusing on technological change rather than industrial relocation as the prime explanation for the decline in manufacturing employment in the Global North. The first section demonstrated that this account has a powerful critique of the relocation/import competition thesis, at least when looked at in terms of aggregates rather than specific sectors. The chapter then considered further argument around the focus on technological change and higher productivity, and this was where some scepticism entered the picture. The idea that progress is caused by a combination of reason, markets and technology, and this is all the more true in the era of information technology, was challenged. The role of the state, public policy and social resistance were shown to be as relevant in the information age, which has seen an intensification of corporate power more than dispersal to individuals. But it is also the case that for all the hype about new technology, it has not led to unprecedented increases in productivity and output.

Where does this leave us in terms of the deindustrialization debate? What we have seen in our discussions so far is that deindustrialization is a significant phenomenon, but there is no single explanation that can account for it. It might be associated with manufacturing in the Global South in some sectors, but not as a whole, not least because of stalled industrialization and premature deindustrialization there. Technological change and some productivity increases might also work as an explanation in some sectors – indeed at an aggregate level it is more convincing than the relocation/import competition thesis – but some of the wider claims made about productivity miracles and jobless futures are exaggerated. Similarly, the claim that a post-industrial society in the Global North automatically represents progress flies in the face of the low-paid service work that has largely "replaced" manufacturing jobs. What this suggests then, is that while the perspectives discussed in Chapters 2, 3 and 4 have some utility, we need to widen out our discussion beyond a simple focus on deindustrialization per se. That is the task undertaken in the second half of the book.

PART II

DEINDUSTRIALIZATION AND ITS WIDER CONTEXT

CHAPTER 5

CONTEMPORARY CAPITALISM: LONG DOWNTURN OR UNEVEN AND UNEQUAL EXPANSION?

This chapter in part provides an assessment of an additional explanation for deindustrialization, namely that it has occurred through slow growth and investment in the context of manufacturing overcapacity. But it goes beyond this to examine some wider questions about contemporary global capitalism, which takes us beyond a consideration of deindustrialization in itself. This is because the claim made about deindustrialization in effect draws on some wider contentions, most notably that capitalism entered a period of a long downturn in 1973, from which it has not recovered (Brenner 1998, 2002). Therefore, in order to fully assess the specific claims made about deindustrialization, we need to consider these wider claims. A consideration of these arguments then form the basis for a further examination of the previous accounts explored in the previous three chapters, and then forward to an assessment of more overtly geopolitical questions in the next chapter.

The chapter starts by further investigating the claim that deindustrialization is a product of slow growth, relative stagnation and manufacturing overcapacity, which we discussed in the previous chapter when focusing on the work of Aaron Benanav (2020a), and it also alludes to the wider arguments that this account draws on. Part of Benanav's claim is that capitalism entered a long downturn in the 1970s from which it has not recovered and it is this contention that is the main focus of this chapter. The next section further develops and explores this contention, through an assessment of another version of the "stagnationist" thesis, which links it to global imbalances, trade surpluses and deficits, and underconsumption (Klein & Pettis 2020). Although the approaches explored in the first two sections are very different (Benanav 2020b), both characterize the current era of global capitalism as one of stagnation, of which deindustrialization is one part. The three sections that follow challenge this thesis, by focusing (in the third and fourth sections) on two manifestations of financialization, and how this has laid the basis for capitalist expansion in the neoliberal era. The first of these (third section) considers the question of debt but centrally places this in the context of what we call "assetization" (Birch 2015; Adkins *et al.* 2020) and the rise of the asset economy, while the second (fourth section) examines financialization in the context of changes in global production and the rise of global production networks. This discussion is then used to identify the very real problems that existed in the era of neoliberal capitalism, but which also suggest that identifying these as indicative of an era of ongoing crisis and stagnation, and comparing this unfavourably with the postwar boom, is too one-sided. This argument is developed further in the fifth section in the context of an alternative account of the global imbalances explored by Klein and Pettis. The conclusion then draws the argument together and provides a bridge to a consideration of more openly geopolitical questions in the next chapter.

THE BENANAV THESIS: DEINDUSTRIALIZATION AS THE RESULT OF OVERCAPACITY AND LOW INVESTMENT

Aaron Benanav's work, discussed in terms of his critique of the automation thesis in the previous chapter, requires further consideration here. His starting point (Benanav 2020a: 16) is to highlight the reality of deindustrialization in the world today, and like others, this is measured by a decline in the proportion of manufacturing work in the total employment within countries. As we saw in the last chapter, Benanav rejects both the relocation/import competition argument on the one hand, and the technological change/automation thesis on the other, and he provides a compelling critique of these – particularly the latter. In contrast to the relocation thesis (Chapter 3), it can be pointed out that manufacturing output has increased, including in countries where manufacturing employment has declined. But in contrast to the technological change/higher productivity thesis (Chapter 4), we can point out that earlier periods saw higher productivity increases alongside increasing employment in manufacturing, as output growth outstripped productivity growth, but more recently these trends have reversed, while at the same time the growth in both productivity and output has slowed down (*ibid.*: 29). The data provided in Chapter 4 shows how Benanav reaches these conclusions.

Benanav's task then, is to account for slower productivity and output growth and the fact that the latter is now outpacing the former. His argument here draws on Brenner's (1998) contention that the world economy has suffered a long downturn, in part due to manufacturing overcapacity, and this in turn reflects and reinforces heightened competition for market share, falling rates of profit, lower rates of investment and lower output growth rates. In the 1950s and 1960s, global manufacturing value added grew at an annual average of 7.17 per cent and GDP at 5 per cent, but the rates of growth of both have slowed considerably since then (Benanav 2020a: 33). In the period 2001–17, German manufacturing productivity grew by 2.2 per cent a year while the economy grew by just a 0.7 per cent annual average; in Japan, manufacturing grew by an annual average of 2.7 per cent but GDP by just a 0.7 per cent annual average (*ibid.*).

What this has led to is declining investment rates. In the US, capital stock grew at a rate of 5.3 per cent a year from 1951 to 1973; it then grew by 2.8 per cent a year from 1974 to 2000, and it grew by just 1.8 per cent from 2001 to 2017 (*ibid.*). In other words, companies have invested less in expanding their fixed capital base, and so while labour productivity has increased, its rates of increase have slowed significantly. Thus, for all the talk of the IT revolution and automation, there remains a basic, longstanding problem for the world economy, namely that: "When the growth engine of industrialization has spluttered due to the replication of technical capacities, international redundancy, and fierce competition for markets, there has been no replacement for it as a source of rapid growth" (*ibid.*: 35).

This leads to an account of deindustrialization somewhat at odds with those associated with technological change and robotization, for "What automation theorists describe as the result of technological dynamism is actually the consequence of worsening economic stagnation, following on decades of manufacturing overcapacity and underinvestment. These theorists assume that an accelerating pace of productivity growth is the main driver of the declining demand for labor, when in reality, the main driver is a decelerating pace of output growth" (*ibid.*: 39). In order to provide an assessment of these arguments, we need to further examine a number of contentious issues, but equally we should also acknowledge the great merits in Benanav's work. As regards the latter, we should recognize that, in focusing on aggregate levels, he does a very good job in challenging the relocation and automation theses discussed in the previous two chapters. In particular, he is correct to identify certain tendencies in the world economy, including slower growth rates in investment, output and productivity from around the 1980s, when compared to the postwar boom. He also usefully provides global examples, rather than just providing data from the so-called developed countries, even if the data from developing countries is still comparatively thin. Nonetheless, some of his data is sufficient to partially undermine the relocation arguments discussed in Chapter 3. So Benanav's account is in some respects a compelling one as it highlights the global problem of relatively insecure jobs and (as we have seen) underemployment.

On the other hand, we need to explore further his arguments that attempt to explain what he calls relative stagnation. This means that we need to further examine the overcapacity thesis, issues around wage stagnation, a more detailed consideration of manufacturing in China and the South (and global value chains in this process), a more detailed consideration of history (and whether or not the period 1950–80 is an appropriate point of comparison), and the role of finance in the recent history of capitalism. We shall examine these issues in more detail later. First, we examine a second version of the stagnationist thesis.

GLOBAL IMBALANCES, UNDERCONSUMPTION AND STAGNATION

Klein and Pettis's (2020) excellent work on the relationship between trade wars and inequality within countries, and how this affects relations *between* countries, is a very different approach to that of Benanav, but equally it is one that still partially fits within a stagnationist perspective. In particular, their focus is on the relations between trade-surplus and trade-deficit countries. In doing so, they draw on and develop the work of John Hobson (2018), first published in 1902, and perhaps best known for influencing Lenin's 1916 pamphlet, *Imperialism: The Highest Stage of Capitalism* (Lenin 1977). In that work, Hobson argued that the export of capital from Britain to the rest of the world was linked to the weakness of labour organization, reflected in the suppression of labour income and the consequent rise in surplus capital looking for a profitable outlet, which resulted in the massive growth of finance and the export of surplus capital.

Klein and Pettis (2020: 7) draw a parallel between early-twentieth-century Britain and Germany and China in the current era. They argue that both are characterized by an under-numerated working class and the export of capital, which in turn has encouraged the creation of credit bubbles. In effect then, underconsumption at home is linked to the export of capital abroad. Klein and Pettis (2020: 7) thus argue that "[i]n the late nineteenth century, the 1920s, and today, the harm caused by extremely unequal income distributions was spread to other countries through the global trade and financial systems", and today it is the United States that acts "as a sink for foreign gluts".

In the case of Germany, it has exported surplus goods while not raising domestic consumption and specifically the consumption of imported goods. Instead, German surpluses have been recycled into capital exports, including financial flows that have facilitated credit bubbles, especially within the European Union (Germann 2021). The 2008 global financial crisis could have led to a rebalancing by Germany raising wages and importing more goods, but instead it was an era which saw the burden placed on deficit countries through the imposition of austerity (Blyth 2013: 86). This led to rising inequality and the undermining of purchasing power in the EU, thus generating even larger imbalances and thus even more capital searching for higher yields (*ibid*.: 79–80).

In the case of the other trade-surplus country explored, China, Klein and Pettis (2020: 198–201) link this to the aftereffect of the 1997–98 financial crisis which hit parts of Asia. In order to avoid vulnerability to external shocks, attacks on local currencies and intervention by international bodies like the International Monetary Fund, China accumulated trillions of dollars, much of which was then invested in the United States and the European Union, largely in the form of financial assets such as US Treasury bonds. These flows further encouraged debt in the rest of the world, and together with innovation such as the securitization of financial products, was a major cause of the 2007–08 global financial crisis (Kiely 2015: ch.5). With the slowdown in the growth of export markets after 2008, China inaugurated a massive fiscal stimulus, amounting to 13 per cent of GDP for 2009 (*ibid*.: 116–18), with investment focused on infrastructure development. This led to substantial recovery after 2009, but with limited advances in wages, this expansion was far from fully utilized, thus exacerbating the longstanding problem of overcapacity, and by 2018 the growth of fixed asset investment was just 6 per cent compared to an annual average increase of 26 per cent from 2005 to 2011 (Klein & Pettis 2020: 119). The local limits of investment and consumption meant that China had to further deal with the problem of searching for an outlet for its capital. In contrast to those accounts of the Belt and Road Initiative that regard it as indicative of China's global hegemonic ambitions, Klein and Pettis (*ibid*.: 124–5) see it as a mechanism to deal with longstanding problems of national imbalances, an argument considered further in the next chapter (see also Jones & Zeng 2019). Thus, China after 2008 has faced the problem of weakening global demand or at least slower export growth, and a strengthening of its currency, but no substantial rebalancing as import growth has also grown more slowly than in the pre-2008 period (*ibid*.: 120–21).

The US also has slow to no wage growth, but in this case, it runs annual trade deficits. Klein and Pettis (2020: ch.6) argue that this is due to the role of the dollar in the international system. On one level, this gives the US a certain exorbitant privilege (*ibid*.: 189–95), as it allows the US to run budget and trade deficits without the usual consequences faced by other countries, because the dollar is the main international currency. But they argue that this is a double-edged sword, as it means that the US is an attractive location for financial flows, but cheap credit and in particular a strong dollar has undermined US manufacturing and in turn contributed to wage stagnation and job losses, as we have seen in previous chapters. In this way the US's financial hegemony has undermined its manufacturing base, and this is their explanation for US deindustrialization (*ibid.*: 212–13).

Chinese and German exporters have benefited from this process, and in this respect US manufacturing is a victim of cheap imports and some degree of relocation, or at least drawing on global supply chains. But, in an argument that has echoes among some sections of both the US left and the Trumpian conservative right, US elites are said to have benefited from this through the attraction of US-led financial assets which has in effect accommodated much of the world's savings. In effect there is an alliance of Chinese and German industrialists with US financial elites, against US workers and US manufacturing (*ibid.*: 221–32).

This new era of a globalized capitalism has existed side by side with a global glut of goods, relative stagnation and global imbalances. It is characterized by declining opportunities for productive investment, cheap manufacturing goods, and weak worker bargaining power due to low demand for labour. In contrast to Benanav (2020b: 144), Klein and Pettis (2020: ch.1) put the internationalization of production and the shipping container revolution at the centre of their explanation, and suggest that the threat of relocation has disciplined labour and thus helped to keep wages low. They also – quite correctly – point out that more than half of world trade involves the movement of unfinished goods within global production networks, centred largely on the US, Germany and China (*ibid.*: 27), an important point considered further in a later section (and see Chapter 3). Their solution to this problem draws on a combination of Keynes and Hobson, and essentially calls for surpluses to be redistributed. In China, this involves an expanded social safety net, or what might even involve the *partial* return of the "iron rice bowl", involving greater job security and social benefits for those in work, and higher wages. Within the eurozone, this would involve greater federalization of economic policy, allowing the EU to issue more debt, levy taxes and invest in green policies and allow for higher budget deficits. In the US it would involve greater investment in infrastructure, more generous welfare provision, support to manufacturing and, in the absence of international cooperation, a partial process of "deglobalization" in which the US would gradually protect its capital and consumer markets (*ibid*: 221–4).

The issue of political solutions will be considered in the next three chapters, but here we should reiterate that Klein and Pettis (2020: 221ff.) in effect explain what they call the "global glut", and global imbalances, by reference to inequalities within countries, and competitive pressures between countries in the context of globalization, including the rise of the container revolution in the 1980s (*ibid.*: 23–7). Some of this argument draws on the relocation thesis discussed in Chapter 3, but it also appears to imply that the threat of relocation, or what we might call the discourse of globalization, is a major factor in keeping wages down. In contrast, Benanav (2020b: 144) argues that "the global glut is real and causally primary: the pressures it has induced to cut wage costs and depreciate currencies, to gain competitive advantages, are stark". He goes on that these competitive pressures are less the result of the container revolution and the globalization of production of the 1980s, and more the competition with Japan and Germany that emerged in the 1970s (see also Brenner 1998), an argument considered further below.

Some of the political implications are discussed more fully in the next chapter, but some further discussion is essential at this point because it does point to some of the problems with Klein and Pettis's analysis. For Benanav (2020b: 144), the focus on trade imbalances addresses the symptoms but not the causes of the global glut and reducing trade surpluses "would not resolve the tendency towards global overcapacity, which has ushered in under-investment and worsening economic stagnation worldwide. It would merely redistribute its consequences differently across nations – which is precisely what has happened in the past, with the US as the primary agent shaping its redistribution".

We shall shortly return to the question of stagnation, but Benanav is correct that the US is hardly a victim in these processes. While the US did indeed face (among other things) heightened competition in the 1970s, this was followed by a period of dollar devaluation in which US manufacturing was very competitive, even as jobs were lost in the sector (see Chapters 3 and 4). With the breakdown of Bretton Woods in 1971, and the shift of the dollar away from being tied to gold, and then the re-emergence of floating exchange rates, Japan and West Germany faced appreciating currencies and so tried to hold down wages in order to maintain competitiveness. One of the aftereffects of this breakdown of Bretton Woods, and the oil price rises of 1973–74, was a growth in lending to the Global South, and Latin America in particular. When interest rates rose from the late 1970s, this led to unsustainable debt repayment burdens for much of the South, which was managed by IMF-led programmes to secure repayments through conditions attached to any new, and increasingly scarce, loans. In the short term this meant that overexposed Western banks largely received ongoing interest payments, but this was mainly at the expense of significant cuts in living standards (apart from in East Asia) during the lost decade of development (Singer 1989). But in the longer term, this laid the basis for a shift in the Global South away from developmentalist ISI policies and towards policies that prioritized export promotion. While some parts of the developing world, especially in Asia and above all China, successfully industrialized, other parts underwent a process of what we described in Chapters 2 and 3, following Rodrik (2016) as "premature deindustrialization". But crucially – and while both Benanav (2020b: 145) and Klein and Pettis (2020: 27–34) recognize this, they downplay its significance – the industrialization that did occur was in many respects a product of the rise of global production networks (discussed further below).

At the same time, US manufacturing recovery in the face of German and Japanese competition was formalized through the 1985 Plaza Accord, which managed a further devaluation of the US dollar. Japan attempted to manage currency appreciation through the ongoing purchase of US dollars, but a massive credit bubble burst in 1991. When this threatened to intensify in 1995, a further round of currency management led to a partial revaluation of the dollar, which the US agreed to in part because a crash in Japan, which held so many dollar-denominated assets, would impact the US economy. This had the side effect of adversely affecting economies where local currencies were pegged to the dollar and was a significant factor in the Asian financial crisis of 1997–98, which in turn led to the Chinese response of accumulating dollars as a safeguard against a repeat of the crash and the foreign intervention that followed. It also undermined US manufacturing and facilitated the promotion of a new asset bubble in the form of the dot-com boom, which crashed in 2001. This in turn was followed by the growth of Chinese exports and credit to the US, ongoing trade imbalances between the two, and then a housing boom and bust in the US. This was caused by low interest rates and the expansion of home ownership including in the subprime sector, aided and abetted by cheap credit, including from China, but also a growth in interest rates to deal with growing inflation, which was in part caused by high commodity prices, which in turn were a product of demand from China to fuel its own industrialization process. This paved the way for the financial crisis of 2008, which spread from the housing market to the rest of the financial sector, as mortgage loans were in effect securitized and sold on as part of massive bundle of loans, which in turn spread beyond the financial sector and led to extended bail-outs to private firms from 2008 onwards (Kiely 2015: 92–105).

The key question for Klein and Pettis's analysis is, as we have seen, whether the imbalances are a cause or symptom of what they call the global glut. We have also seen that Benanav is quite explicit that they are a symptom. We shall consider this further in the next chapter, but we might initially note that the uneven development and global imbalances that have arose since the 1970s have in some respects changed form but have not actually ended. However, their claim that "Chinese government policies before 2008 destroyed millions of US jobs" (Klein & Pettis 2020: 2) has been questioned, to some extent at least, in Chapter 3. But more relevant at this point is that in contrast to Klein and Pettis, Benanav argues that the focus on imbalance is a focus on symptoms and not causes, but he is in agreement with them that this is indeed an era of relatively slow growth and stagnation. We need to consider this claim further, and we do so in the following sections.

FINANCIAL EXPANSION CONTRA CAPITALIST STAGNATION 1: THE ASSET ECONOMY

It should be clear from the previous section that Benanav's thesis has some wider implications which take us from a narrow focus on deindustrialization to a much wider consideration of global capitalist development in recent years. In particular, what is central to Benanav, following Brenner (1998), is the argument that capitalism entered a period of stagnation from the 1970s, from which it has never fully recovered. This is highly contentious and much of the argument that follows is in essence a critique of this contention. But in order to unpack this case we need some building blocks, which consider the arguments in a focused way.

We start this by examining the question of finance. For Benanav (2020: 35) and others (Brenner 2002; Arrighi 1994), the increased prominence of finance reflects the weakness of capitalism in recent years. The shift to what is often called neoliberalism, based on privatization, economic liberalization and the marketization of the state and indeed of individuals has not resolved the problems that emerged in the 1970s, and capitalism remains stuck in a long downturn of which deindustrialization is one manifestation. In contrast to this argument, we now consider a very different account of the role of finance and debt in capitalist development, one which suggests that it is indicative of a new wave of capitalist expansion (Adkins *et al.* 2020; also Panitch & Gindin 2012) rather than stagnation. It is one, however, that accepts much of the argument about wage stagnation and the undermining of labour, but sees this as the basis for a new wave of capitalist expansion in the neoliberal era. Like Benanav, this account focuses on the changes that have taken place since the 1970s but does so by focusing less on (de)industrialization per se, and more on wider structural changes and in particular the role of finance. In the Global North, the 1970s saw a combination of rising inflation and increasing unemployment. This eventually gave rise to a shift in which high interest rates led to a recession in the early 1980s, which saw the defeat of organized labour through lower unemployment and the end of wage increases linked to productivity gains, and eventually the control of consumer price inflation. Previous chapters have highlighted the erosion of benefits such as defined pensions, wage stagnation, and unemployment and underemployment. This account is well documented, including by those who believe that capitalism entered a long downturn in the 1970s from which it has not recovered (Brenner 2002). Where there is disagreement is over the extent to which these changes constituted a significant restructuring of a new dynamic capitalism and specifically – for now at least – the ways in which the increasing importance of finance represented a significant break from the so-called Golden Age, and indeed earlier periods of capitalism as well.

In particular, the 1970s saw a distributional struggle between labour and capital, and wages and profits, in the context of slower growth. Alongside this slower growth and increased US military state spending, this gave rise to inflationary pressures, which impacted on consumer prices, which in turn further fuelled the demand for higher wages. One effect of this was to undermine asset wealth such as stocks, bonds and US Treasury bills. In effect then, wage and consumer price inflation coexisted with asset price deflation. However, in Britain and the US in particular, a number of reforms were implemented in the 1970s and 1980s, so that by the 1990s this scenario was reversed, and there was a shift to wage stagnation and low consumer price inflation, alongside soaring asset price inflation. This included the Revenue Act of 1978 in the US, which cut taxes for richer households and won support among homeowning middle-income earners fighting tax on their housing wealth, and the 1981 Reagan tax cuts on capital gains, and which raised the threshold on estate tax. While this was partly reversed in 1986, George W. Bush slashed the top rate of capital gains to 15 per cent and introduced lower tax rates on dividend payments, and Donald Trump further cut taxes for the rich in 2017. In Britain, the 1988 budget cut the top rate of income tax to just 40 per cent, while the 2008 Labour government budget introduced a new capital gains tax rate of 18 per cent. The result of these changes was that "capital gains and investment income are currently taxed at a much lower rate than income from labour, with predictable effects on the overall distribution of wealth and income" (Adkins *et al.* 2020: 37).

This is central to Piketty's (2014) argument that growing inequality in capitalist society has its basis in capital income growing at a faster rate than labour income. But this tendency in some respects depends in part on public policy, and the tax cuts for the rich were promoted alongside policies in the 1990s which included attempts to control public spending, continued regressive taxation, and inflation targets that focused on consumer prices. Central bank independence was seen as an important component of this "depoliticization" (Burnham 2001), designed to ensure that financial technocrats were insulated from the political pressures of trade unions demanding wage increases and other social benefits. However, this was far from a neutral political process, for: "If central banks had once sacrificed the value of assets to permit wage growth, they now strove to repress wages and consumer prices in the service of asset price appreciation ... What was once seen as a major source of moral hazard – the creation of expectations of financial assistance – was increasingly treated as a policy instrument" (Adkins *et al.* 2020: 42; see also Hay 2013).

On the face of it this might be interpreted as a sign of desperate attempts by governments to promote continued expansion in the face of deindustrialization, wage stagnation and so on – and some have argued this as we saw above. We might further add that rising inequality compounds this problem and "post-industrial" capitalism therefore faces an ongoing legitimation crisis. This is not necessarily completely incorrect, but it is too one-sided, because we need to examine further the ways in which the growth of finance, and specifically "assetization" (Birch 2015) was extended. In essence, by the 1990s, Third Way governments attempted to make as many people as possible into asset holders (Kiely 2018: ch.7). This took a number of forms such as pension fund capitalism, which attempted to compensate for declining defined-benefit pensions by promising increased values through pension fund investment in stock markets.

The Third Way also promised gains to be made, either through increased wages or access to assets such as stocks and bonds, or through education. As we saw in Chapter 2, the argument here was that entrepreneurial individuals could invest in themselves, in their human capital, in the post-industrial new economy. The state would play a role in expanding this human capital through investment in skills, education and research and development, and workfare policies, thus in effect exhorting individuals to behave in "entrepreneurial", market-expanding ways (Finlayson 2003). The asset here was one's own labour, which could somehow be converted into capital and reap significant rewards. But as we have also seen, there was actually a limited number of high-paid jobs in the so-called new economy, and indeed many job losses from the industrial sector in effect gave way to low-paid service work (see Chapters 2 and 6). This was reinforced by the fact that in the US, where Clinton successfully committed to cutting government deficits, there was limited public money for human capital investment. Payment through stock options was available, but only to high-income earners who already held considerable assets (see further below).

But the biggest problem with this policy of "supply-side liberalism" (Cebul 2019) was that the strategy involved a contradiction between the promotion of higher wages on the one hand, and higher asset prices on the other. In effect, it "is impossible to create a new middle class of highly paid knowledge workers while at the same time enacting the rule of generalized wage suppression and public spending austerity" (Adkins 2020: 50).

But there is one asset held by a significant proportion of the adult population, and that is housing. What is perhaps most significant in Britain and the

US is the link between wealth, potential and actual income streams, and home ownership. This was extended in Britain under Margaret Thatcher through the sale of publicly-owned council housing to private individuals and families from the 1980s onwards, and in the US through subsidies for potential homeowners. While it is mistaken to see such subsidies as the cause of the global financial crisis of 2007–08, as subprime mortgages were initiated by private companies, and the only "market distortions" that existed were ones that attempted to expand the market and not restrict it (see Payne 2012; Mirowski 2013; Kiely 2018: ch.8), public policy undoubtedly helped to fuel the housing booms. This led to an initial increase in homeownership in both countries, but increased house prices alongside stagnant wages have inevitably led to declining proportions of homeowners. In a 2020 report (ONS 2020), the Office for National Statistics found that a third of 35–44-year-olds in England were renting from a private landlord in 2017, compared to less than one in 10 in 1997. Almost three-quarters of adults in the generation that includes baby-boomers born after the Second World War own their own homes outright, up from just over half in 1993 (Partington 2020). Since the launch of the "right to buy" scheme, the proportion of council properties in Britain fell from 33.2 per cent to only 17.6 per cent in 2017. The current generation of adults under the age of 65 are poised to enter retirement in worse financial health than their parents, as ONS figures suggesting that 15.8 per cent of 45–54-year-olds rent from private landlords, compared to only 5.6 per cent in 1997. Around a third of millennials (those born between the mid-1980s and mid-1990s) are unlikely to ever own a home (ONS 2020). An earlier ONS report (ONS 2019) suggested that in 2018, the average full-time worker could expect to pay about 7.8 times their annual earnings on purchasing a home, compared with about 3.5 in the early 1990s. Indeed, in the Covid-19-related slowdown in 2020, annual average house prices in Britain rose (by an average of 8.5 per cent) even as GDP contracted (ONS 2021). Thus, people in every age group under 65 were considerably more likely to rent rather than own their home compared to 10 or 20 years ago (ONS 2019). This problem is exacerbated by the erosion of final-salary pensions and in many cases a lack of automatic pension savings. If neoliberal capitalism is indeed, in the words of Wolfgang Streeck (2014), "buying time", it is less, contra Streeck, because of the rise of debt in itself, and more because of rising inequality in terms of access to the asset economy.

It should be clear then that this has led to the growth of a generation, many of whom are unable to access homeownership (Milburn 2019). However, it is too simplistic to suggest that inequality is now rooted in generation, rather than say, class, gender or race. Instead, inequalities are reproduced in part through inheritance, as has always been the case, but also through inter-generational transfers based on asset ownership in the here and now. Transfers might include remortgaging, down payments on homes for adult children and even allowing adult children to live rent free in the parental home, as the age of first-time buyers has increased (Adkins *et al.* 2020: 70). These inter-generational transfers sustain inequality *within* as well as between generations and affect for example access to education and home ownership for younger people.

Most work on social class focuses on employment. Even Marxists largely theorize class based on the social relations of production, which can actually form the basis for a wider definition of class than simply narrow employment relations (Sayer 1987), but which still tends to see work as the main basis for inequality. The late Erik Olin Wright (1985), for example, developed a theory of "contradictory class locations", but these locations were largely focused on different aspects of the employment relationship, such as wage labour alongside managerial positions. While obviously employment remains an important source of class location, in terms of securing an income and wider life chances, the significance of assets also needs to be highlighted, for what in effect has happened in parts of the developed capitalist world is that workers have effectively settled for wage stagnation while trying to secure growing income from rising asset prices (Soederberg 2010). This of course has meant rising debt levels, as we have seen, and for many workers with low-value or no assets, this may be unsustainable, as it was for low-income homeowners who took out subprime mortgages in the run up to 2007. But it is also the case that many workers who have lost labour rights made in the so-called Golden Age have been (unevenly and unequally) integrated into what Birch (2015) has called "assetization".

The relationship to the asset economy is one that is highly stratified and indeed disproportionately benefits the global 1 per cent (Piketty 2014). But an exclusive focus on this group underestimates the wider significance of this phenomenon. Adkins *et al.* (2020: 63) identify five groups: investors with diversified portfolios, outright homeowners, homeowners with mortgages, renters and the homeless. It is also one that is by its nature narrowing for younger people, particularly in the last two categories, but also to some extent in the third. This is because inflated asset prices co-exist, and in many respects rest on, wage stagnation, which makes it difficult for newcomers to enter the housing market without access to inter-generational transfers. In Britain, data suggests the richest 5 per cent and the poorest 5–10 per cent spent a similar proportion of their income – around 15 per cent – on housing in 1961. Over the next 20 years there was some divergence with the richest spending smaller proportions and the poorest larger proportions of their final income on housing. There was then a sharp divergence after 1981 and again after 1997, so that by 2015–16, the richest 5 per cent spent just 9 per cent of their income on housing and the poorest 5–10 per cent of households spent 31 per cent, while the poorest 5 per cent spent as much as 44 per cent of their final income on housing (Hindmoor 2018: 151–2).

This section has suggested an account of capitalism in the neoliberal era that, in contrast to the deindustrialization as relative stagnation thesis, instead identifies important sources of expansion. Benanav and Brenner (2002), and a number of other writers from different Marxist and neo-Marxist traditions (Arrighi 1994), suggest that financial expansion is only a short-term fix for capital, one that hides longer-term issues rooted in the real economy of capitalist production. Financialized capital reflects the weakness of capitalism, the stagnation of production and the build up of capital "chasing returns to the ownership of relatively liquid assets rather than investing long term in new fixed capital" (Benanav 2020: 35). Moreover, the post-Bretton Woods period, where global deindustrialization has really set in, has also been one of periodic financial crises, stretching back to the Latin American debt crisis of 1982, through (among many others) the East Asian financial crisis of 1997–98 and the dot-com bubble of 2001, and ultimately the 2007–08 global financial crisis and the great recession that followed. In effect then, this is a period of what Polanyi called the dis-embedding of the market economy from society, and more specifically the irrational commodification of money from the real world of production (Germain 2009). What is therefore needed is a re-embedding in which finance and the asset-holding class are subordinate to production.

However, it is one thing to point to weaknesses and tensions within neoliberal capitalism, but quite another to then make the leap that capitalism has effectively stagnated since 1973. There have indeed been regular financial crises, and these do reflect some of the tensions within neoliberal capitalism, but it is also the case that capitalist dynamism and crisis tendencies are "necessarily two sides of the same coin" (Clarke 1999: 70) rather than symptoms of stagnation. Moreover, the financial crises of recent years, including the one in 2007–08, have been managed on a far more effective scale than the three years following the Wall Street Crash of 1929. Furthermore, while many have suffered as a result of the fallout from such crises, asset prices have largely recovered, not just in stock markets but also in housing, and policies such as quantitative easing have disproportionately benefited asset holders. While many criticisms can be made against the return of the rentier class (Christophers 2020), it is too one-sided to regard finance as simply a parasitic hindrance to productive investment. Indeed, the Bretton Woods era also saw compromise and limits, as social programmes, defensively powerful trade unions and developmentalist ISI policies of import-substitution industrialization all slowed the processes of open-door trade and investment, and wider commodification. Gindin (2000: 357) usefully contrasts Bretton Woods with the neoliberal era: "Where the state had turned to fiscal policy and public debt to support growth and the realization of surplus, finance offered the alternative of stimulus through the expansion of *private* credit – supporting individual rather than collective consumption and reinforcing rather than moderating existing inequalities".

This then is an era that reflects what Crouch (2009) has called a privatized Keynesianism, in which living standards are expanded or sustained, not through higher wages, but through debt. This debt however, or at least much of it, is linked to the extension of the asset economy, which in turn has helped to facilitate capitalist expansion (Birch 2015: 129). This might be an expansion that is uneven, unequal, prone to financial crisis, and it is also one where "financialized individuals" (Lazzarato 2012) face the stresses of running their lives as an ongoing and ever-changing balance sheet, and many do not even have this "privilege", but *stagnation* is too simplistic a characterization of this scenario. Following slowdowns in the US and UK economies – for instance after the dot-com bubble burst and the 9/11 terrorist attacks of 2001 – central banks lowered interest rates, which helped to encourage remortgaging and the accumulation of unsecured personal debt and thus ensured that aggregate demand was maintained. The US Bureau of Economic Analysis has suggested that "home equity extractions led to an additional GDP growth rate of 1.5 per cent per year between 2002 and 2007. Excluding that, the US would not have grown faster than the supposedly sclerotic eurozone" (Marazzi 2010: 35). Financial expansion and the asset economy persisted in the context of post-2008 quantitative easing and low interest rates, although as we shall see the period from 2022 onwards saw the return of higher interest rates, which had all kinds of implications for the asset economy.

This section then has suggested that financial expansion has become a significant feature of capitalist economies in the Global North, especially in the Anglo-liberal economies of the US and Britain (and Australia). On the other hand, in identifying assets and debt as an alternative to wages as a source of expansion, this alternative account only provides an important corrective to Benanav's stagnation thesis and does not engage directly with his account of deindustrialization. The next section turns to an account of capitalist *production* in the age of deindustrialization.

FINANCIAL EXPANSION CONTRA CAPITALIST STAGNATION 2: SUNK COSTS, CAPITAL MOBILITY AND GLOBAL PRODUCTION NETWORKS

The previous section showed how in at least some countries, particularly those associated with the Anglo-liberal growth model, the increased importance of assets, and of housing in particular, has been central to the expansion of capitalism in the neoliberal era. One possible objection to this argument is that it does not undermine the wider context of deindustrialization and a long downturn in capitalist development. Seen in this way, financialization and assetization are limited ways of dealing with the ongoing crisis in the real economy of production (Brenner 2002; Benanav 2020a). This section challenges this perspective by suggesting that in fact the processes of financialization and assetization are not something to be considered outside of production, but in fact have become central parts of it.

As we saw in the previous section financialization and assetization refers to the rising dominance of finance and of asset holders in the economy, and their domination over workers, renters and customers, and as we shall see suppliers. How then do these processes of financialization and assetization influence the process of production? The idea and strategy of shareholder value maximization (SVM) is a useful starting point for understanding these changes. Lazonick and O'Sullivan (2000) have described SVM as a new mode of corporate governance in which greater emphasis is placed on maximizing shareholder value, even if this is at the cost of long-term growth. Crucially for our purposes, this transformation from what was essentially "retain and reinvest" to "downsize and distribute" (see Milberg & Winkler 2013: ch.6) has meant less investment from retained earnings and the financialization of the non-finance corporate sector, driven by an expansion in financial services and the massive purchase of a company's own shares aimed at rising stock prices. A share buyback is where a company repurchases its own shares, which may involve liquidation of existing shares and therefore an increase in profitability per share, thus increasing shareholder value. A further practice is the use of stock options for senior employees such as chief executive offices of companies, who generally receive annual stock option rewards that are larger on average than their salaries and bonuses combined, a practice that has soared since the 1980s (NBER 1998). The rationale for executive stock options was to better align manager and shareholder interests, and to therefore improve company performance, but it has done so only in the sense that it has led to "greater incentives for managers to focus on short-term movements in share prices" (Milberg & Winkler 2013: 216).

In the US, the proportion of share dividends and share buybacks increased from around 20 per cent in the 1980s to 100 per cent of internal funds in the early 2000s (Milberg & Winkler 2013: 220). While these collapsed following the 2008 crisis, they recovered after that. The tax cuts handed out to US corporations in the US in 2017 was followed by a massive bonanza in share buybacks, which totalled a record $806 billion in 2018 (Troise 2019). What is crucial then, and puts the slower rates of investment discussed by Benanav in a new light (see above), is that increases in profitability do not necessarily translate into higher rates of investment, and instead is linked to greater demand for financial assets including within the firm itself in the form of share buybacks.

Corporate practices have been reinforced by changes in accounting practices, and it is here that the emphasis on the knowledge economy (discussed in Chapter 2) is relevant. Significant here is the question of intangible assets, which can be contrasted with tangible assets such as buildings, machinery, tools and equipment. Intangibles are essentially assets with no physical substance, and include software data, intellectual property rights (IPR), brand value and goodwill (Palma 2009). The importance of intangible assets has increased significantly since the 1970s, and Birch (2015: 137) suggests that they constituted as much as 80 per cent of the assets of the largest corporations in 2010, compared to just 20 per cent in 1975.

Among the most significant corporate assets are patents and intellectual property rights, which in effect gives legal backing to companies to monopolize knowledge for a given period of time. This has been reinforced by the WTO TRIPS (Trade Related Intellectual Property Rights) agreement, first negotiated in 1994 but since subject to considerable debate and controversy. Since the 1970s, the life span of copyrights and patents has been extended in US law, and the WTO TRIPS agreement requires developing countries to adopt increasingly Americanized laws on these issues, and these have been extended by other international agreements (see Baker 2016: 80). Over 90 per cent of all patents and most copyrights and patents are held by rich countries,[1] which means that the cost of acquiring new knowledge for developing countries is increasingly expensive. The cost of the increase in technology licence payments alone for developing countries was $45 billion a year in 2004–05 (Chang 2007: 141). The extension of IPR is thus a classic example of the assetization of production.

But perhaps of most relevant to our discussion of deindustrialization is the point that the rise of global production networks must also been seen in the context of the reorganization and financialization of production. Offshoring is intrinsically linked to SVM as it involves cost reduction such as cheaper labour (and low transport) costs, and indeed in the case of subcontracting it means that there is no need for direct investment. In focusing too much on the excess capacity of what is assumed to be national capitals, Brenner and Benanav both underestimate the significance of the rise of global production networks or global value chains. Of course, they do not deny their existence (Benanav 2020b: 145), but they do not significantly analyse the full implications of their development. In Chapter 3 we saw that different versions of the

1. See more detailed data in Kiely (2015: ch.8) and Kiely (2016: ch.3) which shows the limits of the rise of the BRICs.

hyper-globalization thesis exaggerate the mobility of productive capital, and wrongly assume that productive capital can simply bear the sunk costs of moving from one location to another. But at the other extreme, both Brenner (2000) and Benanav (2020a: 24–5) appear to imply that manufacturing capital is so immobile and sticky, that it can barely shift investment from one sector to another. Gindin (2000: 348) thus suggests that "Brenner's case rests on the combination of new entrants (generally via trade) and limited exit (because of high fixed costs) leading to excess capacity and therefore a lowering of average profits. But if a defining element of this period is the overall *mobility* of capital ... then ... an already weak argument about inadequate exit is further invalidated".

Moreover, the rise of global value chains should be seen less as a desperate response to industrial overcapacity, and more a dynamic restructuring that has taken place since the 1970s. Again, the use of subcontracting by major firms does not translate to a sharp increase in investment but instead can mean both higher profits and lower rates of investment. In the period from 1996 to 2000, US import prices fell by an annual average of 1.4 per cent, and from 2000 to 2006 by 0.7 per cent (Milberg & Winkler 2013: 212). It has been suggested that in the 2000s, up to 2013, in the US offshoring accounts for up to 27 per cent of goods input purchases in a significant number of industries, 50 per cent or more of US imports, and provides cost savings of 40–60 per cent (Milberg & Winkler 2013: 213), and this is a tendency that can be found across all of the developed capitalist countries (*ibid.*: ch.4). Alongside government legislation in many countries, the growth of intra-firm trade has facilitated tax avoidance, whereby companies can declare profits in lower tax locations, even if they have been made in territories with higher rates of taxation, and this includes the common practice of parking funds in tax havens (see Palan *et al.* 2010). Estimates vary, but possibly as much as $21 trillion was held offshore in 2010, the equivalent of the combined GDPs of the US and Japan (Urry 2014: 47).

Nonetheless, the rise of global value chains at least suggests that the industrialization of parts of the Global South is an important phenomenon, and even if much of the South has experienced *deindustrialization* in recent years (see Chapter 3), this is indeed the case. On the other hand, as we saw in Chapter 3, this has not led to a straightforward convergence between Global North and South, nor is it a major cause of deindustrialization in the former at an aggregate level. While some have suggested that global value chains have promoted the rise of the South (World Bank 2020: 3), the picture is more complicated than this. As we saw in Chapter 3, the World Bank's own data show limited evidence of upgrading, as Selwyn and Leyden (2021: 3) point out, its report "provides evidence to suggest that GVCs concentrate wealth, repress incomes, create many bad jobs ... and reproduce new forms of in work poverty". This then is hardly a story of straightforward global convergence and reflects an international division of labour in which higher value activity with high barriers to entry is relatively concentrated in the richer world and lower value activity with lower barriers to entry tends to concentrate in the Global South. On the other hand, this does not support the idea that this reflects capitalist stagnation, but rather shows how these value chains or production networks should be regarded as a case not of an ongoing stagnant capitalism, but rather as a case of capital overcoming barriers to the postwar order and the so-called Golden Age of capitalism.

Furthermore, the rise of global production networks in part means that one cannot assume that the diversification of manufacturing within different nation states always means an intensification of competition, because at least some of this manufacturing will be complementary, as it will represent different stages of an increasingly globalized production process. We have already come across this argument in terms of China, Apple and trade and value added (in Chapter 3), but it also applies in distinct but related ways, if we measure the share of manufacturing in national trade data, which can similarly be misleading. As we saw in Chapter 3, the share of global value chains in world trade rose from around 37 per cent in 1970 to 52 per cent in 2008 and, following a fall after the financial crisis and great recession, stood at around 48 per cent in 2015 (World Bank 2020: 3). According to UNCTAD (2013: 122), in 2012, about 60 per cent of global trade was trade in intermediate goods and services that are incorporated at various stages in the production process of goods and services for final consumption. Given the significant rise of cross-border trade, it is not surprising that this means that there is "a significant amount of double counting in global trade" (*ibid.*: 122), something that is not factored in to Benanav's claims concerning intensified competition within the manufacturing sphere.

This point is also relevant to the discussion of profitability, which it is (problematically) claimed has fallen because of intensified competition between manufacturing producers. But, as well as being empirically questionable (Mohun 2012), this argument is theoretically problematic because Brenner,

> focuses on competition for export markets without acknowledging that somebody's exports are somebody else's identical imports. Within a sector, new investment can be recipe for excess capacity and falling profitability for all producers. However, if occurring, it necessarily has its counterpart in falling prices for 'consumers'. If those consumers are other producers, the falling profitability of their suppliers necessarily raises their own profitability in the form of lower input prices. (Fine *et al.* 1999: 55)

This is a particularly important point in the context of the growing importance of the rise in trade within global production networks, and again reflects the fact that both Benanav and Brenner do not sufficiently integrate this into their analysis and focus too much on the idea of capitalist stagnation. This is considered further in the next section.

GEOPOLITICAL ECONOMY, STAGNATION AND CRISIS

This chapter has moved us some distance from a narrow focus on deindustrialization to a consideration of an understanding of global capitalism in the twenty-first century. In many respects, this is a debate about the relationship between financial and productive capitalism, and the extent to which the former has become dominant because of a crisis in the latter, of which deindustrialization is one manifestation. This final section further examines this debate, and in doing so further considers important factors discussed above such as the rise (or resurgence) of the rentier, or what Christophers (2020) calls "rentier capitalism", and the importance of knowledge and information, or what Wark (2019) calls the vectoral mode of production. In keeping with the arguments made above, it will be suggested that while these are important phenomena in the current era of capitalism, they do not point to an era of a long downturn of stagnant capitalism or even less its transcendence.

Christophers argues that Britain is based on a form of rentier capitalism in which, following Anderson (1964), commercial and landed interests have dominated industrial, productive capitalism. While it is true that this dominance saw some temporary displacement in the early to mid-twentieth century, it was revived via the Thatcherite neoliberal revolution (Christophers 2020: 22–3). Rentier capitalism is based on the extraction of rent, which is defined as "income derived from the ownership, possession or control of scarce assets under conditions of limited or no competition" (*ibid.*: xxiv). The system of rentier capitalism "is an economic system not just dominated by rents and rentiers but, in a much more profound sense, substantially scaffolded by and organized around the assets that generate those rents and sustain those rentiers" (*ibid.*: xviii). The clear argument here is that dynamic, productive capitalism has increasingly been displaced by a parasitic capitalism based on proprietorship rather than innovation. For Christophers this is not the same as nineteenth-century British capitalism, where rent was derived from landlords and financial capitalism. While these practices continue, there are new sources of income for the rentier class, including digital platforms, natural resources reserves, intellectual property, subcontracting service agreements and infrastructure. The Thatcher and Blair revolutions encouraged at least some of these with the privatization of state-owned enterprises, buildings and land (see also Christophers 2018), as well as the housing booms discussed earlier in the chapter. The high monopoly profits in these sectors led to the redirection of economic activity to low-productivity sectors, which led to slow growth alongside increasing rates of inequality (Christophers 2020).

Wark (2019) makes some related arguments but suggests that reference to ideas like rentier capitalism fails to capture the significance of the changes that have taken place in recent years. She argues that capitalism is increasingly being displaced by the vectoralist mode of production, in which control of vectors of information is central to power in this new socio-economic order. Those that control these vectors have the power to organize the means of production through patents, copyrights, brands and other forms of rent. In this new order, companies are characterized less and less by what they make and more by intangibles like data about customers, intellectual property rights, marketing, and so on. For Wark, these changes reflect relative stagnation since the 1970s in which capital makes profits through the privatization and enclosure of information, even as this undermines individual liberties associated with privacy.

Wark and Christophers undoubtedly point to important changes in the international order, much of which have been highlighted in this chapter. But there are some problems with their tendency to exaggerate changes and particularly to separate these entirely from manufacturing production and industrial capitalism. Christophers (2020: 1–3, 412) for example highlights the importance of Anderson's (1964) account of the backwardness of British capitalism from the outset, but if rentier interests were so dominant, why did Britain ever emerge as the industrial workshop of the world in the first place? It is true that Britain then did enter a period of relative decline in the face of the rise of manufacturing competitors, but to some extent this was inevitable (Edgerton 2018) and reflected not the incompleteness of Britain's industrial capitalist transition, and rather more the fact that its early victory was followed by an institutional failure to deal with this competition (Thompson 1965; Wood 1991). Furthermore, the idea of British decline was central to the Thatcherite revolution, which included a kind of "right-wing" version of the Anderson thesis (Bacon & Eltis 1978). The irony is that it was in many respects decline exacerbated by Thatcherism, both in terms of the closest case we have to an example of "negative deindustrialization", as outlined in earlier chapters, and the excessive reliance on finance and housing as leaders in the British economy (Albertson & Stepney 2020).

This in turn leads to two more points. First, it is not clear how much one can generalize from the British example and second, to what extent can we actually separate the rentier economy and finance from productive, innovative capitalism? In terms of the first point, one of the most important recent debates in political economy, implicit in the discussion above, is the extent to which parts of the world economy have shifted from a capitalism based on accumulation through technological innovation, to one where profits are based on the extraction of rent, without innovation. This can actually be traced back to an important debate over the origins of capitalism and the transition from the feudal to the capitalist mode of production (Hilton 1976). In feudal society, surplus was appropriated in various forms (money rent, labour, goods) but was rarely reinvested. International trade did of course take place, but this alone did not reflect any ongoing and substantive development through innovation, or what Marx called the development of the productive forces. While some argued that the expansion of trade was central to the development of capitalism (Sweezy 1976), others argued that the primary factor in its development was the separation of the producers from the means of production, which in those days basically meant land (Marx 1976: 874; Dobb 1976). This had significant long-term implications, because this separation has the effect of undermining production for immediate use, and therefore generalizing commodity production, whereby people have to buy their goods to survive rather than (in the first instance) producing directly for their own use. Thus, "[o]nly under conditions of free wage labour will the individual producing units (combing labour power and the means of production) be forced to sell in order to buy, to buy in order to sell and reproduce, and ultimately to expand and innovate in order to maintain this position in relation to other competing productive units" (Brenner 1977: 32). This is the basis for a wide debate over the transition from feudalism to capitalism, between those that emphasize a trade-based explanation such as Sweezy (1976) and Wallerstein (1974), against Dobb (1976) and Brenner (1977), who emphasized the way in which the historically specific relations of production paved the way for the competitive accumulation of capital. Crucial here is the argument, too rigidly demarcated, that capitalism relies on "economic" exploitation, where workers are paid a wage less than the value of the commodities they produce, as opposed to the extra-economic or political compulsion associated with non-capitalist exploitation such as forcing the exploited to work for a landlord which then extracts a rent. Similarly, the debate was in effect abut global capitalism, based on a contrast between a process of surplus transfer from one region to another, that did not in itself define the specifics of capitalism, despite the claims of underdevelopment theory (see Frank 1969), and which effectively reduced metropole–satellite or core–periphery relations to a kind of zero-sum process of rentier surplus extraction, thus leaving aside the dynamics and specifics of capital accumulation (Brenner

1977). In many ways however this debate was one in which both sides talked past each other. The Brenner position on the specifics of capitalism was in many ways convincing, but at the same time it tended to downplay the ways in which the uneven development of capitalism, the hierarchies of the world market and the use of state/colonial exclusionary practices served to create and perpetuate core–periphery relations, even within the context of a dynamic, but uneven and unequal, global capitalism (Kiely 1995: chs.2–3; 2010: ch.2; Campling & Colas 2021: ch.1).

But what is most relevant to the discussion here is Brenner's insistence on the dynamism of capitalism in the original Brenner debate (Aston & Philpin 1987), which focused on its transition from feudalism, and how this contrasts with his characterization of late twentieth/early twenty-first-century capitalism in what we might call a second Brenner debate (Brenner 1998; Fine *et al.* 1999; Gindin 2000). We have already outlined his broad argument above, and while he does not necessarily go as far as others, what he appears to outline is a relatively stagnant capitalism in which profit is increasingly extracted through unproductive rent, rather than the productive and dynamic competitive accumulation of capital. Brenner (2006) is aware of the irony that this sounds more like his characterization of feudalism in the first Brenner debate, even if he does not go so far as calling it that. Others on both right (Kotkin 2020) and left (Durand 2017), identify a system of techno-feudalism, which in many respects complements the arguments of Christophers and Wark discussed above.

This argument is made, not only to describe finance, but also the "post-manufacturing" IT sector. For instance, in her account of surveillance capitalism, Zuboff (2019) argues that companies and brands like Facebook and Google derive their profits from the "colonization" of people's personal data, which is then monetized through advertising. This is not incorrect, but it is incomplete. As Morozov (2022: 111) shows, Google's parent company Alphabet made a profit of $41 billion in 2020, and much of this was a result of advertising. But at the same time, "Google does sell a commodity, namely access to its users' screens and attention – to advertisers". Rents are extracted in this and other processes, including patents, copyrights, trademarks, but also through innovation which is the exclusive property of companies. This then is a combination of rent and innovation, and as Morozov (2022: 118) suggests, "if the tech giants are lazy rentiers who are ripping everyone off by exploiting intellectual property rights and network effects, why do they invest so much money in what can be described as production of some kind?" Moreover, while selling advertisements is not new, this has been taken to unprecedented levels and exists alongside all kinds of novel developments in communication that spin off to the rest of the economy, including YouTube, email, Google Maps, Google Earth, which are central to the gig economy, real estate and indeed the fusion of financial power and techno science, which relies on big data for managing financial portfolios (Strom 2022). Indeed, in this respect we might argue that Morozov does not go far enough in emphasizing the innovation of tech companies, for as Strom (2022: 39) argues: "Biotech, robotics, artificial intelligence, logistics and urban infrastructure: the sprawling diversification of Alphabet – in common with that of other tech giants – shows that the conglomerate is much more than a narrow indexer of web pages or selling of advertisements".

Thus, just as the original transition debate too easily demarcated productive capitalism from rentier extraction, so too does the debate about the so-called post-industrial society.[2] More specifically, it is far from clear that the rentier economy and financialization can be separated from industrial capitalism as easily as these accounts suggest. We have already seen how production itself has become increasingly financialized and the rise of global production networks is part of a new era of dynamic productive capitalism, based in part on SVM which is an intrinsic part of the financialization of production (see above). Moreover, while financial institutions have led to over-leveraging and excessive risk taking, it is also the case that the "internationalization of finance allowed for the hedging and spreading of the risks associated with the global integration of investment, production and trade with the dollar at its centre" (Panitch & Gindin 2010: 10). Furthermore, China's rise would indeed have been unthinkable without its role within global production networks, and the growth of the world's most populous country in the world is hardly a reflection of capitalist stagnation. Crucially, as we have discussed above, globalization and digitalization "allowed top firms in the Global North – think Walmart – to leverage their positions at the apex of global commodity chains in order to extract lower prices for final or intermediate goods from the actors lower down the chain" (Morozov 2022: 114).

It is of course true that the world has seen regular financial booms and busts in recent years, but as already suggested, this itself is part of the expansion of capitalism in recent years. Seen in this way, periodic "crises" are not so much a reflection of long-term stagnation, but rather should be seen as intrinsic to the expansion and dominant forms of capital accumulation that have taken place. The expansionary logic associated with financialization,

2. Much the same point can be made about attempts to set up a rigid dichotomy between state and market, as for example is apparent in the case of the libertarian ideology that pervades much of Silicon Valley, which as Chapter 4 showed, celebrates the rise of digital platforms at the expense of the "archaic nation state"; see Barbrook & Cameron (1996). However, in contrast to this belief, there are close links between the state and the new technology sectors; see Chapter 4; and Weiss (2014).

including of the "non-financial" corporate sector itself, is one that mirrors that of expansion in the housing market, namely that these assumptions are not based on individual market assumptions about share (or housing) prices. Similarly, corporate accounting systems are not based on the value of tangible assets, but instead, "accountants looked simply at the stock market values of these assets, a value formed by traders' beliefs about others traders beliefs', etc" (Crouch 2012: 100). What this means is that corporations,

> have been turned into assets whose value needs to keep rising forever; this is because their share value represents the aspects of institutional investors who are dependent on these rising assets values to ensure returns for their constituents (e.g. pensioners, savers, insurers, etc). All this, however, has been underpinned by assumptions about rational self-interest on the part of *individual* human actors, rather than the consequences of the emergent properties of *inter-subjective* expectations. (Birch 2015: 141)

This logic is both expansionary and crisis prone, and it is one that permeates all aspects of contemporary global capitalism.

This has meant that the neoliberal era has seen regular financial crises, but (leaving aside 2008 for a moment) these have been managed by states and above all the US state, and the period since the 1980s has also seen periods of significant growth. As we have seen, some have argued that the resurgence of finance since the 1970s is indicative of capitalist stagnation, and some add that this in turn is linked to the question of US hegemonic decline (Arrighi 1994, 2007). In fact, the rate of growth of the US economy was faster than all other G7 countries at the time, and the real GDP of the US was 20 per cent higher than the total of the top 12 Western European countries by 1999, compared to relative parity in 1982, and a gap of only 13 per cent in 1950 (Panitch & Gindin 2005: 151). Furthermore, while it is the case that global growth rates from the mid-1970s to the early 2000s were lower than the so-called Golden Age period from the late 1940s to the early 1970s, the average was still higher than any other period since the 1820s (Maddison 2001: 265). This puts the claim of a long downturn since 1973 into historical perspective.

On the other hand, this kind of evidence leaves two significant factors out of the equation, namely the period since 2008, and the rise of China. These two factors are of course important, and we can partly tackle them alongside each other (although the latter will also be considered in the next chapter as well). First, the period from the early 1990s and especially the early 2000s, was in many respects the era of a new globalization, which saw the expansion of finance, global production networks, and indeed deindustrialization and

China's rise. The immediate causes of the global financial crisis were related to financial expansion, and the build-up of loans that were usually repackaged and securitized to agents that were not party to the original loans, and which were increasingly incapable of being repaid. But this in part reflected closer ties between China and the US, and the ways in which a virtuous cycle of interdependence became increasingly "vicious". The long 1990s boom from 1992 to 2007 (Schwartz 2009) relied on cheap exports from China to the US, which increased US trade deficits and thus debt, but obligations were met by cheap credit, a product of securitized loans and money from China. In effect China exported cheap (finished) goods to the US, and cheap credit which helped to pay for these cheap goods, including in the housing market (Thompson 2011). At the same time, China used this export success to promote a development strategy of industrialization, including upgrading from low-value, labour-intensive exports. This stimulated demand for primary commodities, which in turn led to inflationary pressures due to higher commodity prices. This was nothing like the inflationary pressures of the 1970s, but it did represent a threat to asset values, and so the US responded in the two years prior to 2007–08 by increasing interest rates. The problem with this is that it also meant increased mortgage repayment prices, and this was the beginning of the financial crisis, which spread from mortgage defaults to the wider economy due to securitization (Kiely 2015).

This in effect brought the long 1990s boom to an end, but it did not lead to anything like a clear replacement in terms of a new dominant mode of capital accumulation. The 2008 crisis, the eurozone crisis of 2010 and the emerging markets crisis of 2014–15, were in effect managed "by government spending and central bank interventions that drove a coach and horses through firmly held precepts about 'small government', and 'independent central banks'" (Tooze 2021a: 3). In particular, there was the practice of quantitative easing, whereby new money is released into circulation through the purchase of assets and specifically government bonds. Purchasers might include private investors, but the main buyer after 2008 were central banks. Combined with low interest rates, quantitative easing had the effect of avoiding a 1930s-style depression, but recovery was slow and the main beneficiaries were those asset holders discussed above, who benefited from an era of cheap money. In China there was a much more substantial fiscal stimulus (see above), but by 2015 this had run into difficulties as the infrastructure boom led to significant overcapacity (see Chapter 6). The response to the Covid-19 pandemic in many respects repeated and extended these interventions, this time not to save individual banks but rather entire markets deemed too big to fail (Tooze 2021a: 14–15). As well as the shutdown of a great deal of economic activity, this included tax relief and deferrals, massive income-support measures, capital injections to businesses, employment protection, and moratoriums on debt payments, including mortgages, although of course this varied across countries (Danielli *et al.* 2021). This era of quantitative easing and low interest rates did save the world from a depression of 1930s' levels, but growth was sluggish and asset owners were the main beneficiaries (see above). In 2004–07, annual world growth rates were always above 4 per cent. Between 2012 and 2019, four years saw growth rates of around 3 per cent, including four years actually below 3 per cent (World Bank 2023b).

While the interventions of 2008 and 2020 can be seen as ways to try to maintain, or return to, the long 1990s of 1992–2007, it was clear that this era of globalization had stalled. This did not necessarily mean a reversal of the condition of globalization (see next chapter), but it certainly did mean a slowdown in processes and indeed that it was in crisis (Green 2019). Important here – and again this takes us back to the original transition debate discussed above – was the ways in which before and indeed in some respects after the financial crisis of 2008, global capitalism rested on a combination of both "economic" and "political" exploitation. As Morozov (2022: 124–5) states: "That the political was also instrumental in securing cheap supplies of energy and food, of unfree labour and minerals, of knowledge and, perhaps eventually of data – the very conditions of possibility that make the (expanded) conception of the 'economic' possible – was left unsaid".

Indeed, one can argue that it is the unravelling of these conditions since 2008, alongside and related to the global financial crisis in 2008, eurozone crisis in 2010, emerging markets crisis in 2015, the rise and impact of right-wing populist "anti-globalization" politics, trade tensions, Covid, the interruption to global supply chains, and the war in Ukraine, which led to a period of huge instability by the early 2020s. In 2023, a number of bank failures occurred (including Credit Suisse and Silicon Valley Bank) due to the shift from low to higher interest rates. These developments left banks exposed due to price falls on bonds paying low fixed rates, tensions in housing markets as mortgage rates increased, companies paying higher rates on their debts, exposure to bad investments that were in effect hidden in an era of low interest rates, and a new wave of government bailouts. In addition, this meant the prospect of lower growth, the reality of government debt servicing costs sharply increasing, and a new developing country debt crisis. In March 2023, the IMF suggested that 60 per cent of low-income countries and 30 per cent of middle-income countries were at high risk of debt distress (New Economy Brief 2023). All of this was happening at the same time as a serious cost of living crisis across the world. Rather than arguing that capitalism has been in crisis since the early 1970s then, we can instead argue that the crisis of 2008 has been managed but far from resolved and developments in 2023 look like "a further mutation of capitalist economies, hit by multiple crises, away from the free market model of the recent past and into this ... new state-supported variant – in which billions are pumped by governments into industries considered strategically important, like semiconductor manufacturing, whilst zombified financial institutions limber about, kept alive only by the promise of unlimited government support" (Meadway 2023a). The political implications of these issues are addressed further in the next chapter.

CONCLUSION

This chapter has suggested that debates over deindustrialization need to be put into a wider context. The approaches to deindustrialization discussed in previous chapters do capture some of the issues around the phenomenon – the shift to services, global value chains, relocation, import competition, technological change – but we need to broaden our account to an understanding of changes in global capitalism to get a more complete picture. This chapter considered approaches which emphasize the idea that capitalism has in many respects stagnated as part of a long period of crisis, characterized by intense competition and overproduction, which has paved the way for financialization, which is a symptom of, but also something that exacerbates, this crisis. There is some use to this approach and the chapter demonstrated examples of where "rentier" practices – in housing, intellectual property – have increased and intensified. But it has also cast doubt on the idea that this simply represents a long- term period of stagnation, and showed how capitalism has continued to expand, above all through the rise of both global value chains and China, which are closely related. This paved the way for the rise of "Chimerica" (Ferguson & Schularik 2007), whereby China provided cheap exports and cheap credit to the US, while US capital benefited from cheap Chinese labour and consumers benefited from cheap goods and cheap credit (and where one part of the deindustrialization debate can be – one-sidedly – located, as outlined in Chapter 3). The global financial crisis in effect broke this link and if we can identify an economic crisis, then 2008 is the appropriate year, rather than the Brenner/Benanav 50-year downturn. Furthermore, the unfolding of the crisis after 2008 was protracted, partially managed, but not resolved, and the political fallout from this (alongside longer-term issues) has persisted. This is the subject of the next chapter.

CHAPTER 6

THE QUESTION OF GEOPOLITICS

In Chapters 2–4, we considered three approaches to understanding deindustrialization. The first of these was that the phenomenon did not necessarily matter because jobs lost in manufacturing would be replaced by jobs in the service economy. We noted two problems with this approach, namely that the new (and existing non-manufacturing) jobs often had worse conditions than what had previous existed and wage growth was often lower than in the past, and that deindustrialization was also taking place in much of the Global South. The second approach argued that deindustrialization in the North was caused – at least partly – by competition from the rise of manufacturing in the South, through cheap goods, low labour costs, relocation of production (through foreign investment or subcontracting within value chains) and undervalued currencies. We suggested that while this might be the case in some sectors, it could not explain longer term trends of deindustrialization and again it failed to properly take account of deindustrialization in much of the South. The third position suggested that most deindustrialization in the Global North (and beyond) was caused by productivity increases and technological innovation, including automation. While this approach had its merits, it did not sufficiently explain why this also meant worse "replacement jobs" (as in the first perspective), nor the falls in growth rates in productivity and output in recent years. This led to a consideration of trends beyond deindustrialization per se, as discussed in Chapter 5, and specifically the idea that global capitalism has in effect stagnated for a long period of time. While the data on productivity and output were significant, the argument about stagnation over the past 50 years was rejected as it failed to account for the continued dynamism of capitalism, even with lower growth rates. The argument made was that rentiership has indeed increased in the neoliberal era, but this was less a reflection of capitalist stagnation, and more one of new and intensified sources of expansion, including in finance and global value chains. It was also noted how this led to the boom of the long 1990s, which took place from around 1992 to 2007. However, the chapter also suggested that the global financial crisis of 2007–08 had been managed but not satisfactorily overcome, and it was here that we could identify a crisis, of which recent deindustrialization in the US for example (the China shock) was but one manifestation.

The chapters that follow further develop this argument by looking at the various interlinked crises, or what many have called the polycrisis, in which a number of crises (climate, food and energy, geopolitics, inflation and slow growth, populism) interact (Tooze 2023a). In attempting to cover most of these in at least some detail, this chapter focuses specifically on the issue of geopolitics, and the growing tensions that have undermined the optimistic scenarios associated with liberal peace and a flat earth globalization. This is done with particular attention paid to China and the US. The first section examines globalization and interdependence between China and the US, which is sometimes known as "Chimerica". While there were tensions in this period, from around 1992 to 2008, these were successfully contained. The second section then shows how these tensions intensified in the context of the financial crisis and growing economic nationalism from 2008 onwards. Finally, the third – concluding – section briefly addresses wider theoretical questions around geopolitics. It will become clear that while deindustrialization was not the cause of these tensions, it was an important contributing factor, and the selective treatment of geopolitics that follows is intended to show how this was significant in understanding these growing tensions.

CHIMERICA AND GLOBALIZATION

The 1990s was in many respects a period of optimism in the Western world. The Cold War ended and the lost decade of development of the 1980s was replaced by a foreign investment boom, and the rise of subcontracting and expansion of global value chains. This gave rise to the idea that globalization represented a new level playing field or "flat earth" (Friedman 2005), which would end the global North/South divide and geopolitical conflict, especially between major powers. While the latter claims were in some respects challenged in the early 2000s, the liberal wars of intervention that took place in Afghanistan and Iraq (and later Libya) were rationalized as necessary in order to overcome (failed and rogue) states that were not embracing the opportunities of globalization (Barnett 2005). Much of the rhetoric around manufacturing and poverty reduction was part of this optimistic globalization discourse (see Chapter 2).

On the other hand, it was also clear that since at least the late 1970s China had been rising, and its industrialization was a central part of this process. From the early 1990s in particular, China focused increasingly on its Special Economic Zones which concentrated on manufacturing exports, and in January 1994 devalued its currency, the renminbi (RMB) by 30 per cent. Following the crackdown on protest and especially the Tiananmen Square massacre of 1989, there was increasing suspicion of China in the US. China had been granted Most Favoured Nation status under the GATT (General Agreement on Tariffs and Trade) agreement in 1979, which essentially meant similar treatment for China as all GATT members. This had been renewed by Reagan and George H. W. Bush but in the presidential election of 1992, there was some question that this would be renewed by the Democrat candidate, Bill Clinton. At the same time, that campaign also saw a third candidate, Ross Perot, who was particularly concerned with trade agreements like the imminent NAFTA agreement and whose running mate James Stockdale held paleoconservative views that were broadly hostile to "globalization". At the time, most of the focus was on NAFTA as trade levels with China were relatively low and so much of the Most Favoured Nation (MFN) debate was more about geopolitics rather than economics (Hung 2022).

Nonetheless, Clinton's victory led to business uncertainty and a slowdown in the rate of growth of trade. This led to lobbying by some firms, which were also offered incentives by the Chinese state, and included companies like AT&T, Boeing and IBM, many of which looked at China in terms of market access more than investment location (*ibid.*: 17–24). Indeed, future major investors like Walmart and Apple were not involved in the initial lobbying efforts to maintain MFN status. It was only after Clinton retreated, and continued to grant MFN status to China, that investment by these companies began to increase – in the case of Apple, investment really took off from 1997–98 (*ibid.*: 22). Clinton continued to grant MFN status and then when in 2000 Permanent Normal Trade Relation status was granted (the new name for MFN), this essentially paved the way for China's accession into the World Trade Organization. As we saw in Chapter 3 this was opposed by organized labour in the US, but it was granted and led to the so-called China shock, which saw a large increase in the loss of manufacturing jobs in the US, although as we also saw this was in many respects a continuation of long-term trends, albeit in a short space of time. But in many respects the issue here was more fear of China's rise and the way in which economic growth might have geopolitical implications, and the 1990s also saw some considerable distrust between China and the US, which included disputes over the South China Sea from the mid-1990s, the Taiwan Strait Crisis in 1996, the US bombing of the Chinese embassy in Belgrade in 1999, and the US spy plane clash with a Chinese war plane in 2001.

Nonetheless, in terms of political economy a new era had emerged in which China exported goods (often finished in China but designed and made in a number of countries) to the US (and the EU), as outlined in the previous chapter. At the same time, and following the 1997–98 Asian financial crisis, China invested its foreign reserves in US Treasury bonds and by the time of the 2008 crisis had emerged as the largest foreign holder of US bonds. Since 2014, China's purchase of US Treasury bonds has flattened, and by the end of 2022, China's holdings, with a total of $862 billion, were the lowest since 2010 (McGeever 2023). A sharp decline in 2022 was more to do with the devaluation of Treasury bonds, plus some reaching maturity, rather than sell-offs per se, and at the same time China actually increased its holdings of US agency bonds (McGeever 2023). So, although the financial crisis of 2008 has had some negative impact, it has not led to the complete abandonment of US–China interdependence. This was the virtuous circle outlined in the previous chapter, in which: "The US consumer market and Washington's policy of integrating China into the global free trade system enabled the latter's export driven economic ascendancy. China's low cost exports fuelled a consumption boom in the United States, while China's recycling of its USD earnings in government bonds helped finance America's expanding fiscal deficit" (Hung 2022: 24).

Although there were some tensions in this era then, there was also some degree of cooperation and interdependence based on a virtuous circle between China and the US, or what Ferguson and Schularik (2007) called "Chimerica". The implicit tensions in this scenario were however increasingly exposed by the financial crisis of 2008, and its aftermath.

FROM GLOBAL FINANCIAL CRISIS TO RISING GEOPOLITICAL TENSIONS

As we saw in the previous chapter, this circle of interdependence was broken by the financial crisis, which itself was in part a reflection of the interdependence that preceded it (Kiely 2015: chs.4–5; Tooze 2018). In 2002, export growth accounted for 29.4 per cent of GDP; in 2003, 26.8 per cent; and in 2004, 28.4 per cent. However, by 2008 the figure was down to 8.6 per cent and in 2009 the figure stood at minus 10.4 per cent (Akyuz 2012: 27). By 2010 the figure was back up to 27.6 per cent but this in part reflected the previous year's contraction, and by 2011 the figure was 12.4 per cent (*ibid.*: 27). By 2019, the figure was around 18 per cent (Klein & Pettis 2020: 124). US imports of Chinese goods grew most sharply in the period prior to the 2008 crisis, from $125 billion in 2002 to $337 billion in 2008. After falling back and then recovering in 2009 and 2010, the figure for 2011 was $399 billion which had increased to $538 billion by 2018. Trade wars and the Covid pandemic led to some falls but by 2021 the figure was $536 billion (Statista 2023). What we see then is continued but slower (and interrupted) growth in US imports from China after the global financial crisis. This suggests less favourable international conditions for Chinese exporters and alongside this, some attempt to reduce export dependence, but quite a limited one. From the late 1980s to 2010, the share of Chinese GDP consumed by Chinese households fell by 15 percentage points, as China curtailed wages to maintain and increase export competitiveness. Even by 2018, the household consumption was as low as 40 per cent, a ratio far lower than any other major economy in the world (Klein & Pettis 2020: 111).

As we saw in the previous chapter, the 2008 crisis and immediate sharp fall in export markets, was followed by a massive fiscal stimulus by China, which led to a strong recovery driven by debt-financed infrastructure, fixed assets, and real estate. However, in the context of weakening export growth and thus less foreign exchange to be used for investment, debt increased sharply from 148 per cent of GDP in 2008, to over 250 per cent in late 2017, and then 330 per cent during the Covid pandemic (Hung 2022: 27). The Chinese economy thus faced serious pressure in the context of overcapacity and debt without a substantial expansion of foreign exchange reserves, which in turn led to fears of capital flight (despite considerable capital controls), a stock market fall and a sharp devaluation of the renminbi in 2015–16, which was only stabilized by a strengthening of already strong capital controls in 2016 (*ibid.*: 27).

At the same time, despite these growing economic problems throughout the 2010s, Chinese companies were becoming much more visible, and Chinese companies in the Fortune 500 grew from just ten in 2000 to 124 in 2020 (*ibid.*: 25). Most of these were state owned (91 of the 124) and private companies like Huawei and Alibaba, still had close ties to the state. This reflected the fact that while China had emerged as a major exporter to the West, at the same time the party-state apparatus adopted protectionist policies in some sectors, in order to promote national champions. Under this system, in 2015 around 26 sectors prohibited foreign capital investment and a further 38 insisted on joint ventures with foreign capital (Starrs 2015). This was in effect a policy of combining export promotion with import substitution, designed to promote upgrading of Chinese companies so that they could "climb up the value chain ladder" (Kiely 2016). This intensified with the 2025 Made in China initiative, which made these plans quite explicit. In particular the plan attempts to develop an advanced services sector and upgrade manufacturing in ten core industries: information technology, robotics, aerospace, renewable energy vehicles, raw material extraction, pharmaceuticals, medical equipment, ship building, agriculture and mobile phones (Starrs & Germann 2021: 1126–7). While its success in upgrading is mixed (see below), China has become less dependent on the import of manufactured goods, which includes supplies of intermediate goods, which suggests that China has had some success in displacing foreign with local suppliers (Klein & Pettis 2020: 121).

The Chinese political system became if anything, more concentrated in this period, with a shift away from collective leadership and a concentration of power in the presidency of Xi Jinping, and a crackdown of dissent and the effective abandonment of the one country two systems policy in Hong Kong in 2020–21 (Tooze 2021a: ch.10). This led to growing geopolitical tensions, as did the spread of the Covid virus which originated in Wuhan, China in 2019. But in contrast to the 1990s, this happened alongside growing economic tensions as well.

The old concerns about China as a currency manipulator were revived, alongside an intensification of concerns that China continued to be protectionist and favour Chinese firms and was stealing intellectual property. The American Chamber of Commerce in China reported a growing sense of unfair treatment against US companies operating in China in the 2010s (Amcham China 2018, 2019), and some firms resorted to legal action. In 2010, Motorola sued Huawei for stealing its wireless technology, although the suit was dropped after pressure from the Chinese Ministry of Commerce and in 2011, the company sold its wireless business to Lenovo (Davis & Wei 2020). American Superconductor (AMSC) successfully sued Sinovel in 2018 in a US court over non-payment by the latter to the former. However, while the number of US lawsuits increased in the 2010s, US companies faced the threat of counter-suits in China. The California based company Micron Technology, which is a memory chip manufacturer, successfully sued a Chinese competitor Jinhua in a US-based court over intellectual property theft. However, Jinhua counter-sued in a Chinese court, backed by the party-state apparatus, and won. The US Department of Commerce then blacklisted Jinhua and so barred it from obtaining US technology and components, on the grounds of national security, which effectively meant the end of Jinhua as a viable operation (Davis & Wei 2020: 265). Something similar occurred in the more well-known case of Huawei, which relied on high-end computer chips from the US and its allies in Taiwan and South Korea. From 2013 pressure grew to exclude Huawei, and while the Trump presidency increased the rhetoric, there was actually a short-lived attempt to ease the ban in early 2019 in the context of a cooling of trade tensions. However, this led to a bipartisan Congressional backlash, and so Huawei continued to be excluded from access to US technology.

The issue of currency manipulation intensified in the period from August 2019 to January 2020, when China was designated a currency manipulator, which thus renewed the trade war with a greater intensity. In the period since the late 1990s, accusations of currency manipulation persisted, but companies that benefited from outsourcing were happy with cheap labour and exports from its Chinese operations, and also made the case that the renminbi had actually appreciated in value since 2005. Among the main beneficiaries were Walmart, Kodak, Apple, Footwear Distributors and Retailers of America, the US-China Business Council, some Wall Street banks, and Caterpillar (Hung 2022: 40). The shift away from a largely favourable view of China was however best illustrated by Caterpillar. This was one of the main companies that led the lobbying for China to maintain MFN status in the 1990s, and by the early 2000s it was the main player in China's construction machinery market. However, with the 2009–10 fiscal stimulus, Chinese companies began to expand in the market, thus threatening Caterpillar in the Chinese market and potentially the export market. Fearing Chinese exports to the US, the company began to lobby for the idea of China as a currency manipulator. But it was actually over the questions of market access and intellectual property that saw a noticeable shift in US corporate policy, with companies like Oracle, IMB, Google, GM, Eli Lilly, Morgan Stanley and United States Steelworkers all lobbying Congress in the year 2019 (*ibid.*: 42–3).

This growing corporate hostility to China also took place at the same time as fears intensified in terms of geopolitics. There were fears that Chinese initiatives such as the Asian Infrastructure Investment Bank, created in 2015, and the Belt and Road Initiative, which began in 2013, represented a new, aggressive challenge to US hegemony. China also played a growing role in the South through investment and aid policies, and its demand for raw materials led to a commodity price boom in the period 2002–07, and from 2010 onwards following the fiscal stimulus and investment in infrastructure. Under Obama, there was the 2011 "pivot to Asia" which reflected a growing unease with China's rise, and in 2017, the National Security Strategy for the first time designated the Indo-Pacific as the decisive area of Great Power competition (Tooze 2021a: 18). It is also true that Putin hoped that Russia's invasion of Ukraine would be followed by an extension of the BRICS (Brazil, Russia, India, China, South Africa) alliance, first formed in 2009, into something like a firm diplomatic alliance that could challenge Western hegemony, although this was far from having been achieved by late 2022 (SAIIA 2022). Ukraine was also important because it exposed energy dependence of a number of the US's allies in Europe, and victory for Russia might encourage a more belligerent Chinese approach towards Taiwan and the region more generally. So while Putin's hopes for a full-scale alliance may not have been realized, the war in Ukraine has brought Russia and China closer together (Callinicos 2023: 107–108).

At the same time, we need to keep the rise of China in perspective and recognize its very real limits (and of course remind ourselves of the other reasons for US deindustrialization that were considered in earlier chapters). In terms of the rise of the South, Chinese demand for raw materials was important and useful for some countries, but we should also remember why industrialization is important, and indeed that commodity price falls from 2014 onwards left some countries vulnerable. Commodity prices fell sharply in 2009, by as much as 16.9 per cent (excluding petroleum), and while they recovered in 2010 and rose in 2011 following demand from China due to its investment in infrastructure, prices fell back again in 2012 and fell back sharply – by 13.1 per cent in 2015 (UNCTAD 2015: 12). After that, commodity prices more or less stagnated until a surprisingly sharp increase in the latter half of 2020–21, largely explained by China's initial recovery from Covid, but fell back once China faced difficulties again in 2022 (IMF 2023). This has differential impacts on developing countries as some suffer from commodity price increases. But even those that might benefit from price increases face vulnerability when prices fall back down again, not least because they are so dependent on one or two exports in contrast to the diversified economies associated with industrialized countries (see Chapters 2 and 3) At this point then, it needs reiterating that China essentially wants raw materials from the South, in order to promote its own industrialization process and does not want manufacturing competitors. On the eve of the BRICS summit in Durban, South Africa in 2013, the then-governor of the central Bank of Nigeria stated that Africa is "opening itself up to a new form of imperialism … China takes from us primary goods and sells us manufactured goods. This was also the essence of colonialism" (cited in Hung 2022: 55–6). Since then, there have been accusations of colonialism, perhaps most infamously in the cases of high levels of debt that Pakistan owes to China, and the leasing of the Sri Lanka port of Hambantota as collateral for default on loans. While it is questionable to describe this as a deliberate debt trap that aims at acquiring territory, it still has a negative impact in terms of perception and it does involve the exercise of Chinese power, albeit in unintended – and incompetent – ways, as the Belt and Road Initiative, discussed below, shows (Jones & Hameiri 2020).

The new initiatives led by China also have serious limitations, and the initial pledge to commit $50 billion to the Asian Infrastructure Investment Bank fell short, with $8.4 billion pledged by 2019 and in fact only $2.9 billion disbursed by that year (Hung 2022: 59). It should also be noted that these loans were denominated in US dollars and attempts to internationalize the renminbi (largely in response to the 2008 crisis) have not led to any significant results. The currency is not freely convertible and so there is bound to be limited demand, and if China did change this it could lead to significant capital flight. Indeed, the slowdown in growth and the debt bubble that peaked in 2015 (see above) led to a tightening of foreign exchange controls, thus further undermining the internationalization of the renminbi. It is therefore not surprising that most of Chinese trade, loans and outward investment is denominated in US dollars.

Even the Belt and Road Initiative, often portrayed in the West as an example of Chinese expansionism, "can best be understood as a way to manage the trade-offs associated with its internal rebalancing, rather than as part of some strategic plan to gain territory or military bases" (Klein & Pettis 2020: 124). In effect China avoided domestic debts by exporting goods to the rest of the world and accumulating financial assets in the process. This was undermined (although not fully reversed) by 2008, and so the government then invested in domestic infrastructure and real estate, but this again reached limits by 2015. The purpose of the Belt and Road Initiative is thus to stimulate further demand for Chinese exports and construction overseas. This has led to some borrowers taking on bad debts (see above) and there is still the problem of far more limited markets in territories affected by the Initiative (and why its pre-2008 export markets remain so important). This then, is less expansionist policy and more the search for new "spatial fixes" for China's accumulation strategy (Jones & Zeng 2019; Jones & Hameiri 2021).

The discussion above also made clear that for all China's protectionism and nationalist economic policies, which intensified after 2008, the US can and has responded in ways harmful to Chinese companies, above all in the case of Huawei. The Made in China 2025 initiative has seen some important developments in terms of upgrading, but at the same time there have also been significant limitations. While there has been an increase in patent registration in China, over 90 per cent of these are not renewed after five years, which suggests limited innovation (see Appelbaum *et al.* 2018). While the US ran high and increasing balance-of-payments surpluses on intellectual property from 2001 to 2019, China's *deficits* actually increased over the same period. The US's surplus increased from around $24 billion in 2001 to close to $70 billion in 2019, and Germany and Japan had surpluses that had grown to about $18 billion each by 2019, while China's deficit increased from below $5 billion for each year in the early 2000s, to over $20 billion in 2019 (Hung 2022: 35). In other words, China "pays a lot more for foreign patents and copyrights than foreign entities pay for Chinese ones" (*ibid.*: 35).

More broadly, we should also observe that while some Chinese firms have become significant players (although most are still only "big in China"), US companies remain at the top. Starrs' (2013) comparison of the national sectoral profit share of the top 2000 corporations in the years prior to (2006), and after (2012), the financial crisis shows the extent of US dominance. In aerospace and defence (from 66 per cent in 2006 to 67 per cent in 2012), casinos/hotels and restaurants (46 to 64 per cent), computer hardware and software (70 to 74 per cent), financial services (45 to 53 per cent), media (59 to 67 per cent) and transport (27 to 31 per cent) US leadership increased in this period. The share of Chinese companies in all these sectors was minimal, and never as much as 5 per cent except in the case of transport (Starrs 2013: 822). Even in electronics, a sector in which China is the world's largest exporter, its share in 2012 was just 4 per cent, reflecting China's role as an assembler of final goods produced as part of a global production network dominated by multinational companies. In 18 of the 25 sectors outlined by Starrs, US companies were still the global leaders in 2012, and in 12 of them had a share of 40 per cent or more – and in two others they had a share close to 40 per cent (*ibid.*: 823). China did increase shares in the banking, construction and real estate related sectors, which reflected outcomes that emerged out of the fiscal stimulus after 2010 (Kiely 2016: 52–3). Since 2012, there has been increased concentration by US companies in sectors like aerospace and defence, and media, and while China has seen advances in some sectors like auto, electronics and finance, their companies profit shares remain considerably lower than those of the US (Wagner & Starrs 2022).

Despite these limitations, it is still true that tensions have increased since the global financial crisis. China's share of global manufacturing value added has increased from about 9 per cent in 2004 to 30 per cent in 2021, while the US's had declined from 22 per cent to 16 per cent (McGee 2023). There has been pressure, geopolitical and economic, for US companies to begin to roll back their links with China, and President Biden has intensified cutting off Chinese company access to US technology (*ibid.*). The Korean company Samsung closed much of its Chinese operations by 2019 after a significant loss of market share to Chinese companies, and there is some expectation that Apple might follow suit. However, the expectation that this might mean a substantial growth of operations in India is somewhat hindered by the fact that the government there expects the whole supply chain to be located in India, while currently India's role for Apple is limited to the final assembly of some products in Taiwanese-owned factories. Vietnam is a possible alternative, but Apple could then face similar problems to Nokia after it relocated out of China to Vietnam in 2013, in terms of organized crime networks and infrastructure facilities far worse than China's (McGee 2023; Beattie 2023). The fact is that China has a better infrastructure and a ready supply of labour guaranteed by the party-state apparatus (Chan *et al.* 2020), and indeed Apple has increased its operations with Chinese contractors in recent years, at the expense of foreign companies operating in China like Foxconn and Pegatron (McGee 2023). At the same time, while Foxconn has diversified some of its operations out of China, to Vietnam and India, it is still the case that 70 per cent of its operations are in China (Weber 2020). China's share of manufacturing value added to GDP has declined since 2007 (from around 32 per cent in 2007 to 27 per cent in 2021), and while some of this may be due to rises in MVA in Vietnam and even Turkey (Beattie 2023), it is also as likely to be a product of the shift to construction after 2009. Similarly, while the trade war saw significant falls in some of China's supply lines, there is a massive way to go before we can talk of decoupling. For example, the computer and tablet sector saw a 4 percentage point fall in the trade war in 2019, but China still accounted for 45 per cent of exports in that sector (Weber 2020). At the same time, China would have much to lose from anything like a full decoupling process, in terms of exports, technology and its reliance on the dollar system. The early 1990s saw a collapse in communist "red supply lines" and with it the shock therapy that saw catastrophic falls in living standards and mortality in Russia and Eastern Europe. China avoided that scenario but now finds itself locked into a system from which it wants some, but far from total, exit (Weber 2021).

CONCLUSION: GLOBALIZATION AND THEORIES OF GEOPOLITICS

This argument also has wider implications for understanding the links between globalization and how we understand geopolitics in the current era. Specifically, while globalization has stalled since the financial crises of 2008, 2010 and 2015, it is premature to talk about "deglobalization" (although the implementation of Green New Deals would change this; see Chapter 8 for more details). Green (2019: 3) defines the *process* of globalization as "the widening, deepening, acceleration, and intensification of cross border flows of goods, capital, people and ideas". This has slowed down since the 2008 crisis, and with the pandemic in 2020, but talk of deglobalization conflates "the slowing and partial reversal of globalization processes with a wider unravelling of the globalized condition" (*ibid*.: 11). Global trade as a proportion of global GDP did indeed fall from 61 per cent in 2008 to 52 per cent in 2009, and only increased to 56 per cent in 2016 (*ibid*.: 5). During 2011–14, annual average trade growth was 3.4 per cent, compared to around 7 per cent in the years immediately prior to 2008. Foreign direct investment (FDI) inflows stood at 5 per cent of GDP in 2008, but 3 per cent in 2016 (*ibid*.: 5). On the other hand, the world trade share of global GDP was 24 per cent in 1960, and so we are a long way from returning to a comparable figure. The 3 per cent measure of net FDI inflows is still six times larger than it was in 1970 (*ibid.*: 5–6).

Not unrelated to these points is the idea that recent tensions add up to a kind of cyclical recurrence of geopolitical competition, as argued by some realist theorists of international relations (Mearsheimer 2006), or inter-imperialist rivalries, as argued by some Marxist theorists of imperialism (Lenin 1977, 2003; Bellamy Foster 2003). For the former, it is the anarchy of the international system, and the absence of a world state, which makes rivalry between states inevitable (Mearsheimer 2001). For the latter, it is the uneven development of international capitalism that leads to conflict, although some have tried to combine the two approaches (Hung 2022), while another has linked deindustrialization and China's rise to the uneven and combined development of the world economy (Rosenberg & Boyle 2019). Our focus in this book has been on political economy and so the Marxist view is perhaps more relevant for our purposes, and here the focus is very much on the interwar 20-year crisis period from 1919–39, analyzed from a kind of Marxist-influenced realist position by E. H. Carr (2001) in 1939. The question then is to what extent are we seeing a deglobalization in which rival exclusive blocs of protected trade and controlled finance will emerge? We have already identified some tendencies in this direction, but equally have suggested that these need to be put into context, and stalled globalization is far from deglobalization. Indeed, Green (2019: 56) is surely correct when he states that "[t]he context of rival imperialism within the West, a hallmark of the period between the 1870s and 1940s, has been surpassed". In particular, the world is now composed of sovereign states and not empires and colonies (although realism was notable for ignoring this in the past), much greater levels of interdependence in terms of trade, investment, finance and global value chains, a consequent ambiguity in terms of the shared interests between nation states and national capitals, a fragmented left that in some respects has lost many battles since the 1980s, more cooperation through regional and multilateral agreements and institutions, and a right in much of the world that is prepared to be critical of its "national capitals", which it accuses of being globalist. We might of course qualify this; for instance, organized labour has shown considerable signs of resistance in the early 2020s. While it undoubtedly exists (see Chapter 7), much of the anti-globalist rhetoric of the right is exaggerated to appeal to a protectionist base: for instance, Trump talked about and implemented tariffs, but much of this was a bargaining tool led by his US Trade Representative Robert Lighthizer (Slobodian 2018). Nonetheless, this is still very different from Lenin's (2003) contention that there was a clear overlap between economic competition of national capitals, and geopolitical competition between respective national states.

What this chapter has suggested is that there were always some US–Chinese tensions from the outset, but these were effectively managed in part because of the actions of US companies with vested interests in China. After 2008, these tensions increased and the geopolitical hawks in the US eventually over-rode US corporate interests, especially as the latter faced increased difficulties in their operations in China. This is in contrast to Germany, which has responded to China's growing techno-nationalism in a far more muted way, in part because German labour has not fared so badly compared to its US counterparts, with the result that there is no alliance between national security actors and organized labour in the latter (Starrs & Germann 2021). Nonetheless, there is still a great deal of interdependence or globalization in place and therefore for both the US, and perhaps even more China, an increase in tensions, "made sense from every vantage point except 'the economy stupid'" (Tooze 2021a: 19). All this suggests then, that we are seeing intensified geopolitical tensions, but in terms of national capital and nation state, these are different from those in the run up to 1914 or 1939. Furthermore, we need to stress the contingent nature of these tensions and should not see them as some kind of inevitable product of international anarchy or international uneven and combined development. We might accept that both of these things exist (although uneven and combined development originated as a theory that focused on development *within* states, albeit one that highlighted the international as a key influencing factor), but we must also recognize the ways in which states deal with these factors, which the previous two sections attempted to do.

However, there is one more sense in which older debates may tell us something about the present. As we saw in the previous chapter, Klein and Pettis (2020) argue that global imbalances, and the trade wars that have eventually emerged out of these, reflect the fact that labour in both Germany and China is now adequately renumerated, and so an increase in wages would help overcome trade surpluses. In this respect, as was pointed out, their work draws heavily on John Hobson's 1902, account of imperialism. Lenin was influenced by Hobson's account but rejected his solution that imperialism could be overcome through increasing demand in the home countries, which would then stimulate domestic investment rather than capital export. Lenin (1977: 212) argued that such a redistribution would not happen because capital would not accept such a threat to its profits, and so the choice faced by the world was war or world revolution. War did take place but as it turned out, in the end there was an important class compromise after 1945 in the developed world, and a postwar boom which coincided with a significant redistribution of income. While this was still substantially racialized and gendered, it was still real, until the reversals that took place from the 1970s and especially

1980s onwards. There is a question, following Klein and Pettis, that needs to be asked, namely, is a new era of compromise possible in the 2020s, in a world where labour is far less organized, capital more globalized, and there are new concerns about the environment? To address this, we move partly from an exclusive focus on the geopolitical and the international, the main focus of this chapter, to one that combines an analysis of domestic politics. This is done in the chapters that follow, which focus on populism (Chapter 7), and levelling up, universal basic income and a Green New Deal (Chapter 8).

CHAPTER 7

THE QUESTION OF POPULISM

This chapter examines the question of populism. Although there is some wider discussion, especially around definitions, it is not an exhaustive treatment of the concept. Instead, the focus is mainly on how deindustrialization and the current period of global capitalism can help us to understand contemporary populism. This is done by first defining populism in the opening section and providing some brief account of its rise or resurgence in recent times, as well as some of its general and country specific features (one of which is hostility to China and to some extent globalization). The chapter then moves on to examine populism with a more specific focus on deindustrialization and contemporary capitalism. Populism has specific manifestations in particular parts of the world, and the chapter cannot begin to examine the similarities and differences between populism in Brazil, India, Hungary, and so on. Instead, it provides some details from the British (or English) case study, and especially the debate over the so-called "left behind", which is identified as a group of workers (and retirees) who live in regions affected by deindustrialization. The issues discussed here also have some parallels with the US case and the Trump presidency, and this is discussed in some depth.

WHAT IS POPULISM?

Much has been made of the rise of populism in recent years, and while political parties of the populist right have grown since the 1990s, it is the period after the global financial crisis which saw a particularly significant rise. In very different, nationally specific ways, populism has been associated with Modi in India (elected 2014), Trump in the US (president 2017–2021), Bolsonaro in Brazil (president 2019–22) as well as the vote to leave the EU in Britain in 2016. In addition, there are a wide range of parties – particularly across

Europe – that have had some degree of success (Lewis *et al.* 2018), and in some respects Putin in Russia is also seen as a central international influence and part of this right-wing populist surge (Feffer 2021: ch.2).

Populism essentially argues in favour of "the people" against a corrupt elite. At one level this is banal, because all political movements and ideology claim to represent a "people". However, populism attempts to *construct* a people, and does so in opposition to what are deemed to be non-persons (Muller 2016). This is in contrast to the implicit agreement of liberal democracy, which rests on the notion of disagreement over policy, ideas, and so on, but also the belief that losers in an election agree to concede to the winners, on the understanding that they have their chance to again represent the people in an election in the future. Populists accept this at best half-heartedly, and at worst reject it outright. This is because populist leaders suggest that only they represent the true, authentic people, and therefore electoral defeat is a product of elections rigged by the "non-people". This of course is how things played out after Trump was defeated in the 2020 presidential election, which was followed by various attempts to overturn the results, and there was some effort to do something similar in Brazil in 2022.

Who then are the "real" people as opposed to the inauthentic others? This varies from country to country, but essentially the "inauthentic" refers to liberal elites, migrants, universities, minorities, and so on. These groups are accused of "rigging" the system against the real people, the latter of whom are said to have been left behind in recent decades. In the Global North at least, but also in some parts of the South, this might be linked to deindustrialization, as we shall see below. But the main culprit identified (and sometimes blamed for deindustrialization, as we saw in Chapter 3) is globalization. The argument here is that elites within particular countries have betrayed their nation and done so through encouraging migration and/or multiculturalism, liberal wars of intervention, welfare states for the undeserving poor and foreign investment overseas at the expense of domestic investment. One of the central ideas is the notion that a corrupt elite has betrayed the real nation. This elite is not intrinsically rich capitalists, although there is some objection to their globalist outlook, but a cultural elite that patronizingly claims to speak for everyone, in areas as diverse as health, education, history, and ultimately all forms of knowledge. This is why the culture wars and conspiracy theories are so central to populism (Buchanan 1992). This was very much the rhetoric of Trump, although as we saw in the previous chapter, the extent to which he really challenged globalization as a condition was open to question. In the case of Brexit, it is true that much of the vote was motivated by some of these issues, although the leaders of the movement actually saw it as the basis for a new global project with Britain and imagined like-minded countries leading the process (Kiely 2020: chs.4, 5 and 7).

How then does the rise of populism relate to deindustrialization? As was suggested above, part of this is due to the idea that big companies have betrayed their "roots" and invested overseas. Although the tensions between China and the US go beyond the rise of populism, the latter is a factor and what is interesting here is how the "anti-globalization" of populists goes hand in hand with growing tensions with China. For example, prominent Republican Josh Hawley has stated that "When the communists in Beijing tell Apple to jump, it asks, 'How high?'" (cited in McGee 2023). Some of the intellectuals that have had some influence over populist leaders are interesting in this regard. In particular there are the examples of the late Olavo de Carvalho, who had considerable influence in Brazilian right-wing circles, including with Bolsonaro, and Steve Bannon, who advised Trump in the early period of his presidency and retained close ties, even after a very public fallout. Both suggested that authentic peoples, with a broadly conservative cultural outlook, had been undermined by globalization, and this had been led by US liberal elites and corporations in alliance with China. In contrast to many right-wing thinkers who no hope for the US at all (Dugin 2012; Benoist 2017; O'Meara 2013), the argument here was that "rural" America was a natural home for authentic traditional values, which have been lost with the rise of globalization, of which China is a central part (Teitelbaum 2020). It was in this way that right-wing populists in the US (and beyond) have come to celebrate the largely white, "Middle American Radicals" (Francis 1994). These people are said to have been by-passed by both globalization and deindustrialization. The next section considers the idea of the left behind in more detail, focusing on the US to some extent, but Britain – and England – in particular.

This is also important for understanding the foreign policy of right-wing populists. There are national differences, but the Trump-US case is a significant one, not least as some have suggested that Trump's isolationist rhetoric potentially or actively overlaps with left-wing anti-imperialism, and indeed could form the basis for some kind of alliance between left and right; see, e.g., Parenti (2023); Greenwald (2023). This represents a complete misunderstanding of what America First entails. It does promote an isolationist position, but a highly selective one. It is largely disinterested in wars that involve few if any Americans, and rejects multilateral institutions and alliances associated with liberal internationalism and (more selectively) neoconservatism. While this might point the way to a critique of disastrous wars of intervention such as in Afghanistan, Iraq and Libya, it does not mean a wholesale rejection of involvement in international affairs. Rather, the US populist right sees the international sphere as one based on civilizational conflict and power struggles between different cultures, but this differentialism still rests on ahistorical and essentialized understandings of "ethno-cultures", an account which suggests that Western culture is still the most progressive (as even French new right thinker Alain De Benoist argues). While this might include an argument for peaceful coexistence, it also accepts that conflict between cultures is likely, if not inevitable – and which therefore intensifies hostility to migrants and asylum seekers; see Spektorowski (2003); Kiely (2020: 165–6). Within this civilizational conflict America is First. This is clear if we look at the main example in the last chapter, namely US–China relations. But it is also clear if we look at the foreign policy record of the Trump administration, which combined criticism of NATO with close alliances with right-wing governments in Saudi Arabia and Israel, withdrawal from the nuclear deal with Iran, the initial escalation of war in Afghanistan (followed by ill thought-out withdrawal plans), threats to use nuclear weapons in North Korea and to lead wars against Venezuela and Mexico, airstrikes against Syria, Iraq and Somalia, military assistance to Ukraine, withdrawal from the Intermediate Range Nuclear Forces Agreement, and from the Open Skies Treaty. The administration also proposed the largest inflation-adjusted defence budget since 1945. Perhaps most in keeping with the theoretical account of the international, the administration relaxed rules of engagement designed to reduce civilian deaths, resulting in a sharp increase in civilian casualties in Afghanistan, and Trump proposed that engagement in conflict in the Middle East should be paid for by the US "taking the oil" from the region (Heer 2023; Beauchamp 2023). Not all of these policies are intrinsically bad, although most are, but what it does show is that commentary on imperialism/anti-imperialism and intervention/isolation rests on far too simplistic dichotomies, not unlike the domestic one of state intervention versus non-intervention, one also taken up by Greenwald (see Chait 2021) and what some have called the "Tucker Carlson left" (Motopu 2021). Although in many ways distinctive and in some respects "globalist", the right-wing Brexit project envisaged a liberal trading order, led by the "English-speaking peoples" of the Anglosphere (Britain, US, Canada, Australia and New Zealand), one which has broken from the shackles of the liberal European Union. More generally, we should accept that it is one thing to highlight the hypocrisies, power relations and double standards of a liberal international order (and the mainstreaming of some populist ideas among advocates of this order), but quite another to endorse the distinctive, populist right alternative, which is one that often closely parallels that of the Axis powers in the 1930s, albeit with less overt militarism and pro-colonial rhetoric.

POPULISM, THE "LEFT BEHIND" AND DEINDUSTRIALIZATION: AN ENGLISH CASE STUDY AND SOME US PARALLELS

This account portrays a loss, and, although most if not all are sceptical about a full-blown retreat to a prior Golden Age, the idea of a better and more desirable past is central to right-wing populism. It is at this point that it overlaps, not only with debates about globalization (and the assumption that this has caused deindustrialization), but also with deindustrialization itself. Although it does not explicitly engage with debates around deindustrialization, it is clear that in many respects Sobolewska and Ford's (2020) work on Brexit is the most significant political sociology of Britain in recent years. Their essential argument is that the Brexit vote is a product of long-term demographic and socio-cultural changes, and more specifically a response to mass immigration and the expansion of higher education in Britain (Sobolewska & Ford 2020: 24–54). In particular, they identify three groups: first, "identity liberals" who hold cosmopolitan values and are generally supportive of immigration and multiculturalism (*ibid.*: 66–9); second, "identity conservatives" who are essentially "ethnocentric communitarians" who have lost their status in society (*ibid.*: 59–65); and third, "necessity liberals" who are migrants and their descendants, who have a direct interest in opposing identity conservatives (*ibid.*: 70–72). It should be clear how this links to some of the issues discussed around deindustrialization in earlier chapters. Identity liberals are the product of the expansion of higher education, which in turn was partly motivated by a desire to expand higher paid, skilled service jobs in the face of deindustrialization, while identity conservatives are partly those who have been left behind through the erosion of relatively well paid and secure jobs associated with manufacturing industry.

We shall see in a moment that this account needs some qualification (and the third group requires further consideration) but it does undoubtedly have considerable merit. What we should immediately note, following Gilbert and Williams (2022: 152) is that if the identity conservatives are hostile to liberal cosmopolitanism, then this suggests that, to some extent at least, the values associated with this perspective "have acquired a degree of social authority that they did not have before. But if this is the case, then why should we not assume that "identity liberal" graduates learn to align themselves with such values at university *because* those values enjoy such authority, such that aligning themselves with them is in their social and economic interests". This does not amount to some kind of "woke indoctrination" (although there may be some individual attempts to carry this out). There is evidence that students that go to university tend to have liberal outlooks before they enter university (and indeed is a reason for them choosing higher education) (Simon 2022), and students tend to pick and choose what information they receive – and ignore – in terms of teaching and wider advice. This reflects an instrumental approach on the part of students, encouraged less by "liberal indoctrination" and more by the marketization of higher education. Having said that, the educational experience does expose students to a wider array of informational sources, as does wider access to social media, when compared to identity conservatives. This at least encourages a liberal outlook, which – contrary to many accounts by and about identity conservatives – was also true of organized labour, where institutions and workers' education encouraged internationalist approaches, alongside a sense of pride in local places (Featherstone 2012).

Sobolewska and Ford's account then, does an impressive job in showing the wider context for socio-political change and how this influenced the Brexit vote. But it also tends to separate culture/values and economy/interests slightly too rigidly. Gilbert and Williams (2022: 158) show how this is important in assessing a significant number of voters – probably close to 1 million – who voted leave in the 2016 referendum, for Labour in the 2017 election, and for Conservative in the 2019 election. These cannot simply be described as identity conservatives because it was clear in 2017 that Corbyn's Labour Party was "identity liberal" among other things. What appears to have happened is that the Labour Party's own position on Brexit after 2016 was highly uncertain, certainly compared to the Conservative Party. Some in the labour movement, such as Len McCluskey (general secretary of the trade union, UNITE at the time) argued against free movement of labour, arguing that it was a question of class interest. This was on the grounds discussed – and rejected – in Chapter 3, namely that free movement would erode wages for workers, an argument that neglects the ways in which an expanded workforce can stimulate demand and hence growth in an economy. But what is important here was the *perception* that free movement undermined labour, and again here we see that it is not simply disinterested values that need to be considered, but how such values interact with interests, both real and perceived. We might also add that populist rhetoric around migration and multiculturalism is hardly the exclusive preserve of the populist right, and indeed has been deployed by supposedly cosmopolitan elites like Clinton (on welfare and incarceration in the 1990s) and New Labour, with its talk of British jobs for British workers, schools being swamped with the children of asylum seekers and Muslim women removing their Niqabs during MP's surgeries (see Edin & Schaefer 2019; White & Travis 2002; Younge 2009).

To return to the question of Brexit, we should also point out that it was not simply a vote led by the left behind. As many have pointed out, much of the vote came from richer voters in the South-East of England, but even in left-behind locations, it tended to be those who at least had some assets, namely they owned their own homes, and thus had some degree of economic security (and are more likely to be white; Edgar 2021). This accords with some of the discussion about the asset economy in the previous chapter. But what is most important here then is that there are interests that need further consideration when looking at the Brexit vote, and it is not just migrant "necessity liberals" who vote this way (and this is important as we shall see in a moment).

Sobolewska and Ford (2020: 54–6) are fully aware of this and do not consider this basic realignment to be fixed and note that it can change as political actors respond to these changes and the rise and fall of perceived threats. In other words, they do not conflate their largely convincing political sociology with a particular political project that inevitably "captures" these different groups. This point is all the more true if we consider how interests are central to this process, and note that these can change, not least as political parties establish new positions to deal with these challenges. In marked contrast, Goodwin (2023a) appears to believe that identity-conservative political positions are not only real but will not – and should not – change. In this respect, his earlier calls to take populism seriously (Eatwell & Goodwin 2018) – a laudable aspiration but one that simply repeated the claims made by populists rather than subject them to critical scrutiny – has been replaced by what is in effect an endorsement of populist politics, one which has not gone unnoticed in approving alt-right circles (see Johnson 2019). In particular, Goodwin (2023a) claims that recent decades have seen the rise of a new elite in Britain, that represents a minority of the population, but through institutional capture has had an enormous effect beyond its sheer numbers. This new elite is far more liberal than the rest of the population, and has used its control of institutions (education, health, the media, and so on) to impose its will on those left behind, and looked down on, by the new ruling class. Goodwin cites a number of influences, including Goodhart (2017), Christopher Lasch (1996), Daniel Bell (1976) and Michael Lind (1996; see also Rutherford 2023). We might also add to this list the postwar writings of James Burnham (1972) and Joseph Schumpeter (1954), and in the 1960s and 1970s, Irving Kristol (1970) and Paul Johnson (1980). What these writers argued was that a liberal elite had emerged as a product of the New Deal and or welfare state capitalism, and had extended their power to promote liberal ideals of multiculturalism, immigration and welfare, and thus undermined individual responsibility and virtue. These kinds of arguments were deployed, alongside public choice theory's contention that state elites did not promote the public interest but were in fact self-interested (Buchanan & Tullock 1962), by the Anglo-American new right in the 1970s, to promote neoliberal economic policy alongside cultural conservatism (see Kiely 2020). In this way, critical writing on the "new class" located its origins in the New Deal in the US and the postwar era of managerial capitalism in Britain (and elsewhere). However, in the 1980s and 1990s, American conservative intellectuals divided into neoconservative and paleoconservative wings, and the latter suggested that the new class persisted even after the Reagan revolution, as was clear in the socially liberal Clinton and Obama administrations, and the Blair governments in Britain (Gottfried 2001; Francis 2016; Mount 2012). In other words, the liberal elite has intensified its dominance through the promotion of cosmopolitanism, multiculturalism and liberal identity politics (Gottfried 2005), and its support for globalization has led to deindustrialization, which has meant that many are left behind (Francis 1994, 2014). This argument overlaps with the criticism of China alluded to above in the case of Steve Bannon (see also Goodwin 2023c). But it should also be clear that Goodwin is in many respects repeating this argument in his account of the rise of a new elite in Britain, and he too is propagating the idea of an out-of-touch liberal elite, who are the "people who really run Britain" (Goodwin 2023a: 3), against "ordinary Britain" (although he says little about Scotland, Wales or Northern Ireland), the latter of which parallels Francis's "Middle American Radicals" (see above).

There is also some overlap with leftist arguments in this account.[1] Barbara and John Ehrenreich (1977) attempted to theorize the class location of the professional managerial class in the US in the 1970s, which they identified as a class of college-educated professionals which was distinct from the old middle class. Although they suggested that this class could be won over to progressive causes, this was far from certain and they also suggested that this class could become anti-working class radicals. Liu (2021) has explicitly argued that this is indeed the case and that there is a group of "virtue hoarders" that in effect look down on older working class decimated by deindustrialization, and instead champion identity politics and virtue signalling. This argument in some respects overlaps with that of Lasch on both the new elite (1996) and the culture of narcissism (Lasch 1979).

There is then some close parallels between these approaches and that of Goodwin. We look at the claims about "ordinary Britain" in a moment but first we should make some brief observations about this new elite. The notion that there is a version of identity politics that is in many respects performative is not without foundation, and it does exist, to some extent (for example), at universities (Williams 2014) – although it is also exaggerated by the right. Ozkirimli (2023: 17–25) provides many examples of left fragmentation and virtue signalling for example, including some torturous debates in the run up to the Women's March on Washington following Trump's election. We might also add that much of the diversity training established in corporations and

1. Paul Gottfried, the US's main living paleoconservative intellectual, was supervised for his PhD by Herbert Marcuse. This itself leads to a certain irony given that much of the alt-right in the US and elsewhere have deployed the idea of "cultural Marxist" influence on society, and done so in an antisemitic way.

the public sector takes place in the context of growing inequality in much of the Western world, and indeed much of this appears to be designed to change the composition of those at the top of the ladder, rather than change the nature of an increasingly unequal society (Michaels 2016). This is not an argument against diversity per se, nor does it deny the reality of corporate financing of conservative "anti-woke" initiatives, but it is one that suggests that the dominant diversity narrative is perfectly compatible with high levels of inequality, which itself is likely to leave working-class minorities even more marginalized (Jager & Zamora 2022). At the same time, we should also note that there is something of a cultural divide between those that have gone through higher education and those who have not, but this is something recognized across the board and is hardly unique to Goodwin's account (see for instance the discussion of Sobolewska & Ford 2020 above).

This is where we come closer to identifying the problems with Goodwin's account, for he makes a far greater claim about this new elite, namely that it is the new ruling class, which somehow runs Britain and the US. There are a number of arguments to be made here. First, much of the blame for the left behind is placed at the door of globalization, but it is far from clear how this supposed new elite is responsible. Indeed, he argues (Goodwin 2023b) that the roots of globalization lie in the Thatcher and Blair governments, but the former can hardly be considered socially liberal. We have already seen above that even the latter was not averse to language like "swamping" and the Clinton administrations were highly authoritarian on welfare and incarceration. But even if we leave that aside, Goodwin is not clear how this new elite is a ruling class, and indeed he talks about high-net-worth individuals, oligarchs and stateless elites in London, which have little to do with universities or the media (*ibid.*), but have a lot to do with the increasing inequality that Goodwin supposedly derides. Furthermore, he suggests a strong link between deindustrialization and foreign trade (*ibid.*) and cites a number of authors discussed in Chapter 3 to illustrate this. The problem with this argument is, as we have seen, at an aggregate level even the highest estimate of the impact of Chinese imports cannot account for most of the jobs lost in manufacturing. Furthermore, where it can, it tended to be in sectors where women are as likely to be employed, whereas Goodwin's focus is mainly on white working-class men. We might add to those sectors discussed in Chapter 3, the case of steel in Britain, where job losses soared in the early 1980s, largely because of Thatcherite economic policy and not cheap imports, which arrived 20 years later (Tomlinson 2017). There is also an irony that Goodwin (2023b) relies on Rodrik as his main source for discussing globalization but does not discuss "premature deindustrialization" (Rodrik 2016) in the Global South at all. As we have also noted, wages have stagnated in sectors with little competition from imports, including in the public sector (where the supposed liberal elite reside). Indeed, if there is a liberal elite that rules Britain, then one needs to ask why wages in sectors dominated by this "ruling class" have stagnated in recent years, and why so much of these sectors (health, education, social care) are seriously underfunded. There was increased funding in the New Labour years, but this followed cuts or increases that did not keep pace with demand (health and social care), and in addition workers in these sectors were subject to all kinds of audits via new public management schemes, which served to undermine morale and recruitment. When austerity reversed spending increases, these problems intensified, not least with the rise of precarious work in those same sectors. This is also clear when we analyse the populist construction of a professional, service worker elite against a traditional, white working class, which is too simplistic. Goodhart's (2017) distinction between culturally conservative "somewheres" and liberal cosmopolitan "anywheres" effectively collapses all of the latter into a professional class that is actually composed far more of low-grade and administrative staff as well as around 3 per cent highly salaried and wealthy elites (Bloomfield 2020). This of course is an even bigger problem for Goodwin, who believes that the liberal elite is a ruling class, and appears to think that the Third Way failed only because of the failure to supply new high-wage jobs to older workers, when in fact this is true also of most jobs taken by those with university qualifications (who also have failed to get on the housing ladder unless they have wealthy parents).

Goodwin then places a great deal of explanatory power on the impact of migration, but again he assumes that this is negative. As we have seen in earlier chapters, in terms of economic impact, migration is positive in terms of its impact on government revenue and in terms of increasing demand in the economy as a whole, and so it is growth enhancing. What all this suggests then is that we need to look beyond imports and migration to explain wage stagnation and inequality, and Goodwin is essentially assuming a right-wing anti-globalization position is the most convincing one, despite all the evidence to the contrary.

This is also clear when we come to interrogating possible alternatives. While he wants to restore the centrality of state and nation over markets and globalization, it is not clear how this could be achieved, without undermining growth in the case of migration. The authors he cites on negative trade impact are also clear that protectionism is not the way forward (see Dorn & Levell 2021), and his comments about trade unions in the 1970s, and lack of comments on strikes in the context of the cost-of-living crisis in the 2020s, suggest that trade unionism is not seen as part of any solution, and neither is redistribution (Goodwin 2023c). Instead, his doubling down on culture wars leads one to suggest that he endorses a politics that in many respects is a mirror image of the left-wing virtue signalling he derides, but one with far more dangerous implications, as these wars provide no solution to the inequality and marginalization that he criticizes.

As well as a lack of clarity about the so-called new elite, Goodwin's claims about ordinary Britons is also somewhat lacking. As we have seen, the great realignment that has followed deindustrialization has meant that more workers vote Conservative than in the past. But in fact – as has been suggested already – the picture is more complicated than this. The 2019 UK general election was supposedly proof of this great realignment but in fact the picture was far muddier than initial observations suggest. The Conservatives did best among all income groups except those above £100,000 a year and especially £150,000 a year, and those on less than £10,000 a year. However, if we exclude from the analysis retired voters, Labour continued to have a majority among all those groups earning up to £40,000 a year, which includes the location of the median-income voter. In contrast, around 75 per cent of those over 65 own their home outright, and so are in effect income poor but (relatively) asset rich, and this was because they were the beneficiaries of an era when housing was comparatively cheap, including in the 1980s when council houses were sold off. Since the 1970s and 1980s, the housing affordability ratio has – outside of market slumps – soared to increasingly unaffordable levels. In 2017, about half of Conservative voters were homeowners over 55, while in 2019, the so-called Red Wall collapse of left-behind constituencies was far greater in areas with high rates of home ownership (Flip Chart Rick 2021). Given all these tendencies, and given the low voter turnout among low-earning, high-debt, high-rent-paying liberal graduates, we might conclude that it is not the "liberal elite" that is out of step with Britain, but Goodwin and right-wing populists.

Now of course political parties may continue to launch culture wars in an attempt to win elections, but we should not conflate what is a political project with reality, and it should be clear that much of this is targeted at an ageing, homeowning population rather than all of the electorate. In the so-called Red Wall left-behind areas of England, which voted for Conservative MPs in 2019, disillusionment quickly set in. The idea that these are innately culturally conservative places, somehow cut off from wider socio-cultural change (see, e.g., Goodhart 2017: 193), is not borne out by evidence that points to similar rates of cohabitation in towns as well as "liberal cosmopolitan cities" and have ambiguous and not innately conservative views on immigration – and in many other respects have become more socially liberal compared to the population as a whole 30 years ago (Bloomfield 2020; Malik 2021). Again, this is an example where the so-called "national conversation" is dominated by ageing, largely retired, culturally conservative voters, but these do not represent the "silent majority". Indeed, the stereotype of an innately socially conservative white working class is one shared by some liberal elitists and right-wing populists (Meek 2019). What is crucial here is that common interests between workers across ethnicities is downplayed and the idea is propagated that a section of the working class has lost their status, not because of industrial decline and the "lousy jobs" that have emerged (Goos & Manning 2007), but because of their "whiteness" (Makin-Waite 2021).

Similarly in the US, Joan Williams's (2017) book on white working class resentment towards an educated cosmopolitan elite is based on an income level that would actually include much of the latter (Roediger 2017). There are some parallels here with the focus after the 2016 presidential election on the white working class in the US. While there was undoubtedly some shift towards Trump, and some of this in the Rust Belt 5 (Iowa, Michigan, Wisconsin, Ohio and Pennsylvania) was decisive in Trump's victory, a finer-grained analysis shows that the shift was very much at the margins. While there was a 10.6 per cent shift to Trump in those states, this was considerably less than a 21.7 per cent swing away from the Democrats in those states (Kilibarda & Roithmayr 2016). Above all, in 2020, Trump lost all of these states to Biden. The usual proxy for "white working class" is white, non-college educated without a degree. This is problematic, not only because it ignores all these people in working-class jobs with a college degree, but also because it also includes white middle class people like shop-owners, but even leaving that aside, it appears that Biden reversed the trend of this group trending towards the Republicans, after 2016 saw the share increase of Democrats decrease from 40 per cent in 2012 to 36 per cent in 2016. Biden saw a small but important percentage increase to 37 per cent. This is significant as in 2020 this group, although in decline, still made up 44 per cent of the electorate, and an even larger share in those key swing states. Indeed, this group comprised slightly less than one third of Biden's total vote (Ghitza & Robinson 2021). There is also evidence to suggest that in some of the key battleground states (including Arizona, Georgia, Michigan, Nevada, North Carolina, Pennsylvania and Wisconsin), turnout for Biden among low-income voters was a significant factor in securing victory (Barnes 2021).

But perhaps most relevant to our purposes, is that much of this debate betrays a "methodological whiteness" (Bhambra 2017) in which it is assumed that the working class is white and that electoral politics is largely about how these people react to migrants and their descendants. We might note in passing that in the 2016 Brexit referendum, about a third of Asian and just over a quarter of Black voters supported leave (Harris 2020). But more relevant for our purposes is the fact that minorities and migrants have been central to processes of deindustrialization and changing class composition. In the

US, the initial victims of deindustrialization were often African American, and it was also a central feature in places like Lancashire and Scotland in the UK (Wilson 1997; Lawson 2020). The impact of the China shock, discussed in Chapter 3, was largely not in the Rust Belt, but in fact in southern states following earlier rounds of deindustrialization where northern industries moved south within the US, and employed cheaper, African-American labour (Hammond & Jain 2020). Alongside civil rights gains in the 1950s and 1960s, this helped to reduce the earnings gap in the US between white and Black workers, but with deindustrialization and the suppression of Black rights, this has now reversed (Bayer & Charles 2016; Johnson 2020).The effects of these social and economic changes has been an "advanced marginality" in the US where poor urban areas are in effect marginalized from the formal labour market, and areas suffer from welfare retrenchment, and federal cutbacks (Wacquant 2009), and healthcare has expanded to deal with the fallout from deindustrialization in terms of jobs, the opioid crisis and so on (Winant 2021). Methodological whiteness is also often accompanied by gender blindness, not least in sectors where deindustrialization is more likely to be a product of relocation and import competition, as outlined in Chapter 3, such as clothing and textiles, where women were more likely to be employed, but where there has been little discussion (Lamp 2018; Tomlinson 2019).

CONCLUSION

This chapter has highlighted the links between deindustrialization and populism. Following on from the discussion in Chapter 3, it has questioned the right-wing populist argument that deindustrialization is mainly a product of the rise of manufacturing in the South. It has also discussed the ways in which there have been significant social changes alongside deindustrialization, which in turn has fostered some degree of realignment in society and electoral politics in Britain (and elsewhere), but it has also argued that this is contingent and not set in stone, and it certainly does not follow that the left behind will support culture wars against supposed liberal elites. That politicians and political parties may continue to foster culture wars does point to the need to critically examine these political projects, but serious social and political analysis should not simply replicate or apologize for these projects. The next chapter examines other attempts to engage with the politics of inequality that has in part come about because of this so-called political realignment, namely that of levelling up, and then moves on to an analysis of other alternatives around universal basic income and a Green New Deal.

CHAPTER 8

FURTHER POLITICAL ALTERNATIVES

The previous chapter argued that populism has emerged in part in response to changes in global capitalism in recent years, of which deindustrialization is one important manifestation. It also argued that – in its right-wing manifestation at least – populism provides no solutions to the problems that have arisen, and instead relies on the launching of culture wars and scapegoats, which are likely to intensify in the face of a failure to address important socio-economic issues such as growing inequality. This chapter examines three possible political alternatives, which are at least more serious than those associated with right-wing populism, even if – as we shall see – the first of these is in many respects compatible with it. The first of these is the levelling up agenda launched by the Conservative government in Britain after 2019, which is associated – if only largely implicitly – with deindustrialization, due to its supposed challenge to uneven regional development. The section takes a sceptical view about the politics behind levelling up, and indeed suggests that it is compatible with the performative politics of spectacle associated with right-wing populism. The second section considers the arguments around universal basic income (UBI) and shows how this is linked to deindustrialization through arguments around "technological unemployment", as was considered in Chapter 4. Again, there are reasons for some scepticism around UBI, although it is still far more serious than the levelling up agenda. The third section examines debates around the idea of a Green New Deal, which includes some consideration of progress in the deployment of new technologies (albeit in the context of the rising geopolitical tensions discussed in Chapter 6). It also returns to the discussion of global overcapacity in Chapter 6, and how some use the Brenner thesis discussed in that chapter to argue that any such New Deal is not feasible. This argument is rejected and while strategic political dilemmas around any such Green New Deal are discussed, it is argued that this presents the most fruitful political alternative, at least in the short to medium term.

LEVELLING UP: A BRITISH CASE STUDY

Although as we shall see, the idea is implicit in various government initiatives (in Britain and elsewhere), the term levelling up was explicitly used in the Conservative Party election manifesto of 2019 (Conservative Party 2019: 26, 36, 42, 57). Although somewhat side-tracked at the height of the Covid-19 pandemic and various lockdowns, it was deployed by the Johnson government and beyond, with Michael Gove appointed Levelling Up Minister in 2021. The idea of levelling up means "creating opportunities for everyone across the UK by: improving jobs, pay and living standards; making streets safer; protecting health and wellbeing; investing in high streets and town centres; improving local transport" (Levelling Up Campaign 2023). This involves the periodic dispersal of funds that will eventually add to £4.8 billion.

The term suffers from a lack of clarity, and indeed to some extent purpose (see below). Nevertheless, much like debates over the Rust Belt in the US, and the so-called left behind under globalization, the idea of levelling up is partly a response to the displacement of relatively well-paid, previously secure jobs, often carried out by working-class men with limited educational qualifications. It thus overlaps with the great realignment in electoral politics discussed in the previous chapter. In the case of Britain, the deindustrialization processes, outlined in previous chapters, is particularly acute, for while all developed countries have experienced this, Britain's was particularly severe, especially in the 1980s. While deindustrialization in Britain started in the 1950s, and declining proportions of employment in manufacturing started in the 1960s, an overvalued exchange rate and high interest rates saw a sharp decline in both manufacturing employment and output in the period from 1979 to 1982 (Tomlinson 2017: 87). While oil revenues certainly benefited the Thatcher government, and indeed helped to facilitate the policies carried out in the period, it is also true that the tax burden for oil companies was relatively low compared to, say Norway, and higher tax revenues could have been used to deal with infrastructure issues and other policies related to a real levelling up process, but this was squandered by the Thatcher governments in particular (Garavini 2022). What is also clear is that the decline in manufacturing jobs has not been compensated by high-paid service jobs, even with the expansion of education from the 1990s onwards (see also Chapter 2). The period from 1979 to 1999 saw the growth of relatively low-paid service work, including care assistants and attendants (up from around 103,000 to 539,000), bar staff (119,000 to 188,000), shelf-fillers (50,000 to 97,000), sales assistants (954,000 to 1.3 million) and retail checkout work (113,000 to 218,000) (Goos & Manning 2007: 124–5). This was reinforced by benefit cuts for individuals and a decline in trade union membership. The Labour government made some attempt to deal with the issue of low-paid work, but the longer-term trend from 1970 to 2009 was such that the ratio between the ninth and tenth percentiles of wage earners rose by as much as 50 per cent in this period. Most of these low-paid service jobs are done by women who may have entered the labour market in the period of deindustrialization, but it was also women who were in the lower paid jobs of the industrial era, such as in the clothing and textiles sectors. Labour introduced tax credits in 1999, which was an attempt to make low-paid service jobs more attractive, as in many cases, taking part-time jobs was not sufficiently attractive given other costs and benefits. This was seen as a shorter-term solution, alongside longer-term investment in skills and education for work in the post-industrial knowledge economy (see Chapter 2). The introduction of the minimum wage in 1999, and alongside recovery from the economic downturn in 2001, there was some shift to work as the tax credits intended. However, wage growth was slow at best, in the period up to 2008, and stagnant afterwards, and so the proposed temporary solution of tax credits became increasingly permanent. Although there is some debate on the official figures, it appears that there was a sharp increase in tax credit payments, from around £1.1 billion in the first half year of introduction, to close to £30 billion by 2015. At this point George Osborne as Chancellor of the Exchequer in the Coalition government made plans to reduce tax credits, but he retreated (Butler 2015). It is also clear – despite Goodwin's assumptions discussed in Chapter 7 – that university expansion has not translated into graduates automatically getting high-paid jobs, and indeed five years after graduating, more than one third of graduates are in jobs also available to non-graduates (Pabst 2023). What had become clear was that a central part of Labour's welfare to work programme had become one of welfare *in* work, which worsened as the boom years gave way to austerity (Guinan & O'Neill 2021). In the postwar era most of those who were officially poor were either not in work (disabled, pensioners, single mothers) or those in work with large families of at least four children. While in much of the 1970s, around 3–4 per cent of working households were in poverty, by 2000–01 the figure was 14 per cent (Tomlinson 2017: 93). Today, the majority of the poor are members of households with at least one member in work, and for all the talk of record numbers of people in work and full employment, the reality is that the British economy (among others, especially the US) is characterized by underemployment, a tendency that has intensified in the years following 2008 (Blanchflower 2019).

It is also clear that levelling up refers to regional inequalities, and again we have seen an intensification of uneven development. In 1919, the South-East and London accounted for around 35 per cent of national output and the North of England around 30 per cent. By 1999, the former accounted for 40 per cent and the latter just 21 per cent (Geary & Stark 2018: table 1). In the next 20 years, London increased its share by a further 5 percentage points and by 2016, output per head in inner West London was eight times higher than that of West Wales and the South Wales valleys (Hazeldine 2020: 1, 2). The contribution of manufacturing to national output has stagnated at a particularly low 10 per cent from 2007 to 2020, around a third of the figure for Germany. While some of this data reflect long-term trends, since the 1980s it has been particularly strong. In early 1982, when unemployment reached over 3 million, regional unemployment trends ranged from 9 per cent in the South-East to almost twice than in the North-East of England (Hazeldine 2020: 165). Employment in iron and steel fell by as much as 50 per cent in the years 1979–81 (Tomlinson 2017). The Labour government elected in 1997 attempted to address these regional inequalities and between 1999 and 2006, public spending grew at an annual average rate of 6 per cent a year. Erturk *et al.* (2012: table 3) suggest that public bodies and state-funded jobs accounted for 73 per cent of employment growth in the North-East over the pre-recession decade, 67 per cent in Yorkshire and the Humber, and 62 per cent in the North-West.

The levelling up agenda has been criticized on the basis of political bias and allegations of pork-barrel politics, and the fact that the funds were not protected against inflation. Areas deemed to be of the highest priority included 14 areas with higher than average wealth levels, all with Conservative MPs. Indeed, Conservative areas tended to be favoured, leading to accusations of electoral considerations trumping areas most in need (Bounds 2021; Bounds & Smith 2021; Walker *et al.* 2021). Furthermore, even after levelling up funds had been awarded, this still left 143 out of 151 local authority areas facing the reality of real-term cuts since 2018 (Crerar 2023). In short, the levelling up agenda neither adequately deals with the impact of austerity since 2010, or the longer-term decline of certain areas since the 1980s. Indeed, given the limitations of New Labour's own, in effect, levelling up agenda through tax credits in the boom years of the 1990s and early 2000s, the short-term prospects for levelling up in the context of slow growth, inflation, and yet more austerity, are not good. This is in sharp contrast to Germany. Immediately after reunification, productivity in the former East Germany (including Berlin) was about 60 per cent that of the former West Germany, but by 2020 it was up to around 85 per cent. The East now has a GDP per capita higher than many parts of Northern England and Wales. In total, around €2 trillion was spent on the reunification project between 1990 and 2014, the equivalent of around £71 billion every year, compared to the UK's *total* fund of £4.8 billion (Enenkel 2021). In this context, the Conservative practice of governing through spectacle – tokenistic projects whose significance is exaggerated combined with culture war populist rhetoric – is likely to intensify (Jennings *et al.* 2021).

UNIVERSAL BASIC INCOME

As we saw in Chapter 4, the idea of a universal basic income (UBI) has become increasingly prominent in recent years, and includes famous advocates like Elon Musk, US politicians like Andrew Yang, Silicon Valley true believers, and a range of intellectuals from both right and left. While basic income has a long history of advocacy stretching back to the likes of Thomas More and Thomas Paine, most of this was linked to private property or was conditional on certain behavioural requirements (Jager & Zamora Vargas 2023: ch.1). In its current form it usually involves unconditional cash transfers without conditions. One of the main reasons for its growing visibility is the fear that technological change will lead to jobless futures for many, and most of the automation theorists discussed in Chapter 4 discuss the idea in some depth (see, e.g., Brynjolfsson & McAfee 2014: 232–41; Ford 2015: 257–9). In one sense the idea of UBI is an appealing one as it appears to have a quick, technocratic fix for the problems of underemployment and unemployment, and so deals with some of the fears about an automated future.

On the other hand, once we explore the details of what would constitute an effective UBI, the issue of politics quickly returns. Interestingly, a number of neoliberals have advocated something like UBI, and have done so for many years before there were debates over "the rise of the robots". As we saw in Chapter 4, Milton Friedman (1962: 191–5) argued for a negative income tax which could replace public welfare and would involve tax credits to low-income groups who would be given money so that they could participate in the market economy. Hayek argued for a basic income as long ago as 1944 in *The Road to Serfdom* (Hayek 2001) and later in 1973 in *Law, Legislation and Liberty* (Hayek 2013). More recently, Charles Murray (2012) has emerged as a prominent advocate, who has argued that UBI will both end poverty in the Western world and restore the moral foundation of Western civilization as it will lead to stable family units and a restoration of Christianity. Arguing that US welfare state programmes costs $1,000 per capita per month, he argues that this should be distributed to individuals/families directly and so the welfare state can in effect be broken up (Murray 2016: 11–15). On the other hand, Murray (2016: 7) insists that there also needs to be a constitutionally backed agreement that inequality should not be challenged. What unites these approaches is the belief that the welfare state is bureaucratic and paternalist, and in effect tells individuals what their needs should be. Cash transfers – in the form envisaged by Friedman, Hayek and Murray at least – leave it up to the individual to decide what is good for them, and in most respects this version of UBI is seen as an alternative to the welfare state, rather than a supplement. It was therefore part of a package of reforms that included the rollback of public provision in other areas such as housing and education, one which amounted to what Arthur Kemp in 1966 called "welfare without the welfare state" (cited in Jager & Zamora Vargas 2023: 55).

At the same time as these challenges from the right, the left increasingly questioned the effectiveness of the welfare state. In the 1960s, this included the charge of paternalism, alongside arguments in the US calling for independence from the racist state and the call for Black autonomy (*ibid.*: 75). Writing from the socialist left, in 1966 Cloward and Fox Piven (1966) called for the extension of welfare through a guaranteed national income, an argument that became increasingly vocalized in Europe from the 1970s (Gorz 1987; Negri 1991), and one that – particularly in the case of André Gorz – had a strong influence on UBI's main left proponent in Europe, Philippe van Parijs (Jager & Zamora Vargas 2023: 119). At the same time, liberal economists otherwise critical of Friedman and others increasingly turned from New Deal emphases on public provision to a "new Keynesianism" which argued that demand could be stimulated through private individual consumption, through tax cuts that would stimulate purchasing power, thus reflecting a "transition period between post-war Keynesianism and contemporary neoliberalism" (Major 2014: 131). As we saw in Chapter 4, while much of these debates reflected disagreements about the New Deal and welfare state after 1945, concerns over technological change, automation and deindustrialization were also present and became increasingly central.

More recent left-wing accounts are also concerned about automation, and at the same time have suggested much larger amounts than that proposed by Murray for example. The most prominent case has argued for something like $40,000 per household per year, and that this is a supplement to, rather than substitute for the wider welfare state (van Parijs & Vanderborght 2017). The case is also made for a gradual, targeted – and conditional – approach at the start before moving to a more universalist approach. This is seen as the starting point for a wider transformation, in which communities and trade unions are revived, precarity is displaced and the bargaining position of labour in the market is enhanced (Srnicek & Williams 2015: 120–23). Much is made of the potential of new technologies and the necessity of the left to hasten the shift to a fully automated society that would accelerate the transition from capitalism to communism (Bastani 2020), based on a largely workless society and a universal basic income.

As we saw in Chapter 4, while it would be foolish to dismiss the significance and potential of technological change, it would equally be misguided to assume that technology per se can provide the potential for liberation. As Sutcliffe (1984) long ago pointed out, technologies are introduced in capitalist societies to make profits, and are the product of private research and development (R&D) for precisely this purpose, or rent is extracted by private companies following long processes of publicly funded R&D. In the case of the former, the motivation for introducing technologies is bound to influence their character, such that a simple socialization would not be sufficient, not least for environmental reasons (one thinks of cars for example). But while publicly funded R&D might have more potential, even here there are difficulties, and indeed a great deal of successful R&D can be located in the military sector. Furthermore, the notion that technology per se can empower workers is problematic. This can be seen in cases such as the internet and social media, which in many – although not all – respects, intensified individualization. But perhaps above all, the idea of a workless society – or more likely a radical reduction in necessary work time – through technological change appears at best to be something that might exist, but in a long distant future. We have already seen that in the era of supposedly advanced technological change, there has been relatively slow growth in productivity and growth rates are not unprecedentedly high. This does not mean that global capitalism has seen a long 50-year downturn, but equally it does not mean that we have seen an era of high growth. There are issues around developments like AI and so on, and how this might impact on skilled work (and indeed, education), and there are of course issues of unemployment and underemployment. But this is very different from attributing these problems to technological change per se, and still less does it point to a jobless future.

Given this low growth, any introduction of UBI is likely to intensify a distributional struggle between capital and labour (Kalecki 1943; Benanav 2020a: 70). Benanav (2020a: 78) makes the point clearly:

> While UBI has the laudable goal of separating the income people earn from the amount of work they do, it would do nothing to alter the relation between income and assets, keeping us tethered to a system in which a sizeable fraction of total income derives from interest (from extending credit), rent (from leasing land or homes), and profit (from running businesses). In other words, UBI would empower workers without disempowering capital, providing people more autonomy in the fulfilment of their "animal functions", but no greater role in shaping the wider social conditions under which they do so.

In the Global South, the issues are even more problematic. Chapters 2 and especially 3 discussed the dominant development strategy following postwar decolonization, namely import substitution industrialization (ISI). This involved a commitment to social transformation through a transition to a technologically advanced society, and which included a central role for the state through "market unfriendly" policies such as subsidies, targeted credit, tariffs and so on. This "big push" strategy (Rosenstein-Rodan 1943) united left and right in the view that industrialization was necessary for development. Although the "developmental era" from the 1950s did see substantial growth, by the 1970s it was increasingly compromised by lower growth rates and from 1979 onwards by higher interest repayments on debt, culminating in the debt crisis of 1982. While the left generally argued that this reflected the constraints of a hierarchical international economic order (see Chapter 3), the right, and especially neoliberals (of right and left) argued that the problem was bad policies which involved protectionism and therefore economic inefficiency. While this paved the way for economic liberalization in the 1980s, the results were disappointing. However, from the 1990s there was some recovery, poverty reduction and indeed manufacturing in parts of the developing world, giving rise to the optimistic position that globalization was good for development (and the pessimistic right-wing populist position that globalization led to deindustrialization in the developed world). But we also saw in Chapters 2 and 3 that in fact, outside of East Asia, much of the Global South experienced stalled industrialization or even premature deindustrialization, and the record on poverty reduction was far from impressive, and indeed rested on the use of questionable poverty measurements (Oks & Williams 2022).

Nonetheless, the critique of developmentalism echoed that made against the welfare state, namely that they are both paternalist and do not speak to the demands or needs of individuals. This paved the way for an approach that combined market-friendly reforms with cash transfers. Poverty was increasingly defined as a lack of income and so "development" was redefined, with a switch in emphasis from structural transformation to one that focused on giving money to the poor (Hanlon *et al.* 2010). This in effect celebrated the local knowledge of individuals in contrast to the "knowledge imperialism" of development planners, saw micro-credit as a way of converting the income of some individuals into a proto-capitalist entrepreneurialism, and saw cash transfers as a quick-fix solution to the problem of poverty. This was one that in effect saw an alliance between neoliberalism on the one hand, and small-scale populist "post-development" on the other (Easterly 2014; Ferguson 2015). Much of its origins could be traced back to advocates of basic income policies in the US in the 1960s, on both left (Michael Harrington) and right (Daniel Patrick Moynihan), and is more recently linked to philanthropy which by-passes development planning and – potentially – the welfare state (see Jager & Zamora Vargas 2022: ch.5). In practice, the cash transfers that did occur were not ones that could be considered examples of UBI and were instead based on certain behavioural conditions. By 2016 there were more than 60 countries that had state-led transfer programmes (*ibid.*: 159), and these did have some immediate impact on poverty, perhaps most successfully in the case of the Bolsa Familia programme in Brazil from 2003. On the other hand, it also represented a break from the aspirations of socio-economic transformation and while ISI did have its limitations, these in part reflected structural constraints that an emphasis on individuals and potential entrepreneurship simply ignore. On the other hand, pro-modernization approaches associated with pro-US approaches in the Cold War (Rostow 1960), or with a dogmatically unilinear Marxism (Warren 1980; Sender & Smith 1986) are hardly useful in a world of insecure work. In contrast to previous – and at the time, accurate – critiques of the "development debate" (Seers 1979), growth-oriented approaches are no longer converging between neoliberalism and Marxist unilinear approaches, but rather between basic needs and neoliberal cash transfer perspectives. One reason for this paradigm shift is that the issue today focuses less on *poverty* within countries, rather less than on *inequality* between (as well as within) them (and how this impacts on poverty). Moreover, it once again shows that industrialization is sectorally significant when it comes to issues around productivity, linkages and spin-offs into the rest of the economy (see Chapter 2).

For all these reasons then, a UBI more like that envisaged by Murray and/or Silicon Valley ideologues than van Parijs and Vanderborght, let alone more radical views such as those of Srnicek and Williams (2015), has proven to be closer to the realities of cash transfers (and one where – in the US and UK – welfare benefits have expanded at aggregate level but declined at the level of individual payments). Put another way, and referring to a question asked at the end of this chapter's first section, it would appear that without further reforms, this would be an area in which Lenin's account – on the limits of reform – is more convincing than Hobson's. This does not of course mean that Lenin's alternative is convincing, and indeed the idea of socialist revolution in the classical Marxist sense is entirely implausible, and UBI should not be rejected out of hand (see Chapter 4). Nonetheless, the critique of UBI in terms of its wider potential is a powerful one. Indeed, one of the most problematic issues associated with UBI has been that "adequate basic incomes were unaffordable, while affordable basic incomes remained inadequate" (Jager & Zamora Vargas 2023: 88). One result has been that even the proposals associated with Friedman have in effect been watered down, and governments across the Global North have drawn on rhetoric about "hard working" versus idle families and the deserving and undeserving poor in the neoliberal era, while in the South it has been a propping up mechanism at best, despite some rhetoric about the informal sector providing the raw material for a new entrepreneurship. In the US, President Nixon's attempt to introduce a guaranteed minimum income was rejected by Senate. Instead, the Earned Income Tax Credit was introduced post-Nixon, and was essentially tax relief for low-income earners in work, a policy extended by Reagan and Clinton in particular, and it remains one of the major – inadequate – tools for dealing with poverty to this day. It is, however, a long way from the foundational ideas of UBI, and the danger of such tax credits is that they incentivize employers to continue to pay low wages, a major issue in both the US and Britain, as we have seen in earlier chapters and above. This is not to say that UBI will automatically be watered down, and some of the more radical approaches to UBI essentially envisage a challenge to the commodification of labour power and the consequent dependence on employment for a sustainable income, something that – alongside other reforms – takes us a long way from Friedman's proposals, let alone tax credits, conditional transfers and the linking of welfare to work. Nonetheless, as things stand, actually existing welfare reforms have increasingly taken place as a propping up mechanism alongside limited public provision in housing and education, and the expansion of healthcare in a crisis-hit US (Winant 2021), and this is certainly compatible with Friedman's initial vision.

A GREEN NEW DEAL

The idea of a Green New deal is essentially one that tries to reconcile environmental protection with what we have identified in this book as the global crisis of labour. Although there are various different kinds of Green New Deals, what unites them is the belief that there needs to be government investment to compensate for the failure of capitalism as a whole to invest in decarbonization. Seen in this way, it is argued that government will take a lead in delivering green investment in the future, and above all deal with the threat of climate change.

The idea was suggested in rather vague terms by the US journalist Thomas Friedman in 2007, in response to the global financial crisis, but it has really gained traction since 2019, with the development of a proposed legislation package in the US, led by Alexandria Ocasio-Cortez and Edward Markey in the Democrat Party. It essentially envisages a package of environmental targets on pollution, biodiversity, waste and above all climate change; fiscal policy to invest in sustainable projects including green energy, but also tackling issues around social inequality; and industrial policy focusing on production and consumption systems of provision, transport, housing and food (Bloomfield & Steward 2020). This may include major public infrastructure investment to convert the energy grid and generate green jobs, the extension of public transport projects, and financial incentives (above all subsidies) to promote sustainability. In terms of the environment, this is seen as necessary so meet the Intergovernmental Panel on Climate Change (IPCC) targets that global temperatures should not rise by more than 1.5°C (or possibly 2°C), and to achieve this, global CO_2 emissions have to fall by 45 per cent from 2010 levels by 2030, and by 2050, global coal use will have to decline by 97 per cent, oil by 87 per cent and natural gas by 74 per cent (Seymour 2021). This then, presupposes a major challenge to the fossil fuels industry, which is worth over $4 trillion globally (Seymour 2019), and which continues to enjoy massive loans from financial institutions (Callinicos 2023: 37). Indeed, the rise of industrial capitalism was closely linked to the use of fossil fuels, and the use of steam as opposed to say, water power, gave capitalists a great deal of flexibility in locating factories (Malm 2016). This was rooted in the industrial revolution, but at a global level this has continued into the twenty-first century, and between 1870 and 2014, a quarter of all CO_2 emissions occurred in the last 15 years of that period (*ibid.*: 265), largely because of the rise of China. The years 2015–22 have been the warmest on record according to datasets consolidated by the World Meteorological Organization (WMO 2023). Such is the nature of the climate crisis, that the IPCC (2021) has recently suggested that people born in 2020 will experience a two- to seven-fold increase in extreme weather events during their lifetimes, compared to people born in 1960, and that 3.3–3.6 billion people live in contexts highly vulnerable to climate change.

The Green New Deal has been limited so far, but at the same time, the Chinese government has adopted green investment transition strategies, aiming for carbon neutrality before 2060 (Tooze 2020). In the US, the Biden administration introduced the Inflation Reduction Act in 2022, which planned around $375 billion in subsidies for green industries, and subsidies to consumers for environmentally friendly products (Meadway 2023b). The European Union has in effect relaxed state aid rules and focused more on an EU-wide (green) industrial policy, while China's investment in a green transition in 2022 was 70 per cent greater than that of the US and EU combined (Tooze 2023b). We saw in Chapter 6 that the slowing of processes of globalization did not necessarily mean a retreat from the global condition, but progress on the promotion of Green New Deals in the future would significantly impact on the latter. Indeed, to some degree, there is a race for leadership in the development of green technologies, which in part is a geopolitical question. Nonetheless, it is still one that is necessary given the climate crisis, in which ongoing, supposedly one-off events like extreme weather or pandemics like Covid-19 are impacting on the global economy through health crises, lockdowns, food supply shortages and interruptions to global value chains, all of which were important factors in the inflation spikes in 2022–23 (PEF 2022). President Biden's National Security Adviser Jake Sullivan outlined 4 key issues for what has been called the "new Washington Consensus" in April 2023, based on: a new industrial policy to reinvigorate US industry; new geopolitical and energy competition in the context of the rise of China and the Russian invasion of Ukraine; the climate crisis; growing inequality, which had an adverse impact on democracy (WhiteHouse 2023).

Indeed, there is a parallel here with the Roosevelt New Deal in the 1930s, when policies such as social security, rural electrification, subsidies for farmers, and public works for roads, bridges, dams, hospitals, housing and schools were introduced, alongside significant regulations on finance. As we saw above in our discussion of UBI, the danger is a struggle over distribution, in which capital resists as government spending increases, claiming that it is bad for investment. This was Kalecki's (1943) warning in 1943 about the original New Deal and while it did not happen then, and a "Hobson like compromise" did occur after the Second World War, his warnings proved prophetic for understanding the shift to neoliberalism in the 1970s and 1980s (Gerstle 2022: chs.4–5). Adam Tooze (2021b) has argued that this is a danger in the context of calls for a Green New Deal, and specifically the fossil fuel industry will use the crises of the early 2020s to blame investment shortfalls on green regulations, ultimately leading to a watering down of zero-emissions targets.

This suggests then that like UBI, the introduction of a Green New Deal is not simply a technocratic question but a political one, as it involves challenges to powerful actors in the global economy, as well as significant disruptions to everyday life. Of course, disruptions will happen without such a deal and in the long run these will be worse, for some at least, but this does beg the question of how to win popular support for such policies. As already noted, ideas around the Green New Deal attempt to move beyond stark opposition between environmental sustainability on the one hand, and decent work and livelihoods on the other (Calhoun & Fong 2022). This book has noted that for all the promise of a "positive deindustrialization", the reality has been low-paid, precarious service work in both the Global North and South, alongside continued subordination in global value chains for much of the South. The question then is how would the Green New Deal reverse this trend? There is no denying that these involve considerable strategic dilemmas. Deploying what is essentially a "Leninist" interpretation of Hobson's underconsumptionist approach, Riley (2023; see also Benanav 2023b) contends that there is no possibility of a Green New Deal because it would intensify the problem of overcapacity, which was discussed in the context of Brenner and Benanav in Chapter 5. For Riley and even more for Benanav (2023b), the rise of one country is increasingly at the expense of another, but this argument replicates the fallacies of the import competition thesis discussed in Chapter 3 and downplays the rise of global value chains and their centrality to China's rise, and the fact that this led to a boom in the long 1990s (see Chapter 3). This boom did eventually give rise to the global financial crisis and the slowdown that followed 2008, but this is a long way from the longer-term secular stagnation thesis outlined by Brenner, Benanav and Riley. In terms of the Green New Deal, these writers contend that the US's plan to increase onshore production of chip manufacturing (through the US CHIPS and Science Act 2022) and green technology (through the Inflation Reduction Act 2022) would intensify overcapacity because of the context of competition across the globe.[1] This will simply exacerbate the problem of rent extraction in the context of stagnation, and state subsidies for a Green New Deal are simply the latest in a long round of "de-risking" subsidies that involve the appropriation of the public "commons" by the private sector (Brenner 2020; Riley & Brenner 2022). It is certainly the case that, for all the talk of marketization and private risk, the public sector has become increasingly involved in research and development and the production of new technologies in recent years, while much of the gains has gone to the private sector (Keller & Block 2023). But this is not an inevitability and the apparent belief that it is, leaves us once again with the kind of maximalist Marxist revolutionary "politics" as the only solution, but this is simply not likely or feasible. More specifically however, the introduction of new green technologies should not be regarded simply as adding to a generic overcapacity problem, as a new wave of green technology would lead to the depreciation of old capital. In other words, the Brenner–Benanav issue of "too much entry, too little exit" would not be the insurmountable issue that they think, because depreciation would in effect hasten "exit" (Mason 2023). There would still be significant political questions to address, such as the relationship between public and private sector, and the problem of private appropriation of public resources is a real one (Gabor 2021), but this is a question of politics and the appropriate role for the public sector in any Green New Deal, rather than one of outright rejection. This involves the setting of certain conditions on subsidies and investment, including around wages, profit share, linkages and so on, in order that profits and not just losses are socialized (Mazzucato 2020), so that corporate dependence on the state should be regarded as a two way process, and not an inevitable plunder of the public sector by private interests (Keller & Block 2023). Durand (2023) is therefore

1. The argument appears to be contradictory, namely that there is both too much and too little investment. There is low investment because of overcapacity, and at the same time that overcapacity has been caused by too much investment.

close to the mark when he outlines the limitations of the shifts represented by a new Washington Consensus, but without dismissing them outright. In particular, there are questions around: (1) limited sums of money committed to the climate crisis; (2) where subsidies will be targeted, some of which need to displace existing commodities (EV cars are prioritized rather than EV public transport); (3) growing military spending and the ways in which green industrial policy has been too closely aligned with growing geopolitical competition; (4) the ways in which finance and the problem of "rentiership" *may* continue, for example as asset managers take advantage of new state-backed infrastructure investment (see Christophers 2023: 136–47), but this should not be regarded as an inevitability.

These are not the only political questions that need to be considered. A central argument of this book is that the partial industrialization of parts of the South has not eroded the global North/South divide, and this is important when considering questions around a Green New Deal. For example, battery-powered "cleaner transportation" would rely on the mining of rare earth minerals, and there are tensions and trade-offs to be made between decarbonization, increasing transportation and mobility, and decreasing mining, and how these might operate both against each other, but also in terms of the global North/South divide (Battistoni 2023). Mining in the Global South is associated with long hours, low wages and dangerous work, and is dominated by large multinational companies that are often major carbon emitters, sometimes involved in the displacement of indigenous communities, and have been associated with land grabs (Paul 2020). On the other hand, but equally problematic in a different way, is the expectation that the South makes sacrifices for years of environmental degradation, that historically has largely been associated with the Global North. For workers in the developed world, there is the question of how to overcome low-paid service work, the erosion of benefits and relatively slow or stagnant wages increases.

These are difficult strategic dilemmas that any genuinely global New Deal would have to tackle. It is likely that they would involve challenges to corporate power, a heightened role for labour rights implementation through for example the International Labour Organization, and some forms of global redistribution of wealth that factors in the environment as well as wider social inequalities. While a wholesale "degrowth" strategy would actually exacerbate these problems, it may well be the case that there would have to be some selective degrowth strategies in particular sectors. So again, we see that the debates around the Green New Deal come up against questions of agency and power, and what we crudely identified in Chapter 6 as the "Lenin–Hobson" debate. This is of course a problem for all politics, and the ultimate weakness of the Lenin side of the argument is the implicit assumption that its maximalist politics will give way to minimalist politics, where difficult political questions somehow disappear through some kind of "revolution". Specifically on the question of the Green New Deal, why it perhaps has more potential – in terms of jobs and the environment – is that, unlike UBI, it lends itself much more easily to a collectivist politics, not only in terms of state power, but also local organization through the promotion of trade unions, and a more collectively self-confident working class. UBI does not necessarily prevent this, but it does lend itself to an individualized version in which payments are made to simply generate participation in the marketplace, as indeed some neoliberals advocate. In some – although not all – respects, UBI has emerged as a neoliberal challenge to the gains made during the original New Deal. Indeed, for all its flaws and limitations (Katznelson 2014), which intensified in the 1960s for reasons already outlined, the New Deal saw significant, if limited and still racialized, inroads in terms of broader organization and wage increases, even if these were contested and sometimes defeated in that period (Schickler 2016).

CONCLUSION

This book has argued that deindustrialization has occurred in recent years in both the Global North and much of the South. While this has sometimes led to optimistic accounts of positive deindustrialization and convergence between North and South in recent years, previous chapters have suggested that there are good grounds for questioning such upbeat scenarios. What we have instead seen is a global capitalism characterized by relatively low growth, especially since the global financial crisis, high profits, low-paid insecure jobs in the North and South, and new forms of subordination through global value chains. We have seen a backlash to this in the form of populism, largely of the right, but also including projects of the left that betray nothing much more than a nostalgia for the so-called Golden Age of manufacturing capitalism. Levelling up in Britain can be considered another example of politics through spectacle as it is not based on a serious commitment to dealing with the issue of regional uneven development. Universal basic income and especially the Green New Deal can be considered more serious attempts to deal with questions around "lousy jobs", low wages and economic insecurity, and in the case of the latter in particular, the most pressing question of environmental sustainability. While there remain difficult strategic and political questions around these issues, these strategies remain more serious than the populist reaction to deindustrialization, neoliberalism and globalization.

CHAPTER 9

CONCLUSION

This book has focused on deindustrialization. In doing so, it has examined in some depth the economic arguments around deindustrialization, and the claims made in terms of whether or not it has caused certain other things to happen. While providing evidence to support or reject particular views (or indeed combine both), it has taken these debates seriously. The first half of the book explored three key accounts of deindustrialization. First, the argument that it does not matter as the world moves to a post-industrial service economy in the Global North and (eventually) higher end manufacturing in the Global South. Second, there was the argument that deindustrialization in the Global North was a problem as it led to lower standards and a race to the bottom, as capital moved to the South where labour was cheaper. This was the "left" version of the relocation and/or import competition argument. The "right" version argued that deindustrialization reflected the "theft" of jobs by the South, due to cheating through unfair trade agreements, currency manipulation, or post-national corporate elites relocating investment. Third, there was the argument that deindustrialization in the North was a product of technological change rather than "stolen" or relocated jobs, and this fed into debates around automation and longer-term threats to jobs.

The first half of the book demonstrated the strengths and weaknesses of these perspectives, but argued that all were prone to exaggeration from trends in particular sectors, and were far from convincing about what was happening in the Global South. The broad arguments made were essentially: (1) the first position was far too optimistic when it came to the "replacement" jobs for those lost in the manufacturing sector, and most new jobs were lower paid and more insecure; (2) it also failed to see that intense competition in the Global South was hindering upgrading and in fact stalled industrialization or even premature deindustrialization was taking place there; (3) the second position does point to certain labour-intensive sectors such as clothing and textiles or parts of electronics where import competition and/or relocation has occurred; (4) this reflects the rise of global value chains and the fragmentation of manufacturing production (which also feeds into the fact of stalled industrialization); (5) but at the same time it is mistaken to reduce deindustrialization in the so-called advanced economies to the rise of the South, because at aggregate level productivity and output has continued to increase in the Global North, albeit with less workers; (6) furthermore, the defeat of labour in the North is not restricted to manufacturing but applies to non-tradeable sectors, which suggests that slow wage rises, stagnant wages and reduced benefits such as pensions has other causes; (7) at the same time, there have been specific periods as well as sectors where deindustrialization has been rapid, such as Britain in 1980–82, and the so-called China shock in the US in 2000–02, which have had wider implications; (8) given the significance of point (5), it is clear that technological change and productivity increases have had some impact on manufacturing employment, in both the Global North and South; (9) but we need to treat this argument with some caution, because productivity and output increases have slowed down since the 1970s, and we have seen a shift away from relatively well-paid and secure manufacturing jobs in the Global North, to more insecure service jobs, irrespective of debates over automation, which brings us back to point (1).

The discussion in the first half of the book also showed how different positions on the deindustrialization debate influenced different political approaches to deal with it. These reflect the wider changes that have taken place within global capitalism from the 1970s onwards. The changes within capitalism and the political responses to deindustrialization were discussed in more depth in the second half of the book. In terms of changes within global capitalism, we highlighted the growing importance of finance and asset ownership, global imbalances with the rise of China in particular, and the rise of global production networks. While it was accepted that – even with the rise of China – productivity and output increases have slowed down since the 1970s, it is mistaken to see this in terms of a long crisis of capitalism. Increased inequality, shareholder value maximization, asset ownership (for some), the rise of China, containerization and the use of global value chains all reflect a dynamic restructuring of capitalism (and one in which the marketized state has come to play a more central role in innovation, despite pro-free market rhetoric). Nonetheless it is also one that is also prone to crisis, and indeed we have seen a period of crisis management through central bank interventions since 2008, which has undermined – but not reversed – globalization. In many respects this is a crisis of neoliberalism, but without any clear replacement for it. The crisis has numerous manifestations, including rising geopolitical tensions, the rise of populism and debates around uneven regional development and the need for levelling up. In each of these cases it was shown how it would be mistaken to claim that deindustrialization *caused* these things to happen, but at the same time it was shown how a focus on deindustrialization can help us to understand them. For example, China's rise cannot be understood without understanding its role in global value chains and its attempts to climb the value chain ladder, contemporary populism cannot be understood without some understanding of the decline of manufacturing employment (but also how this is more nuanced than populists claim), and levelling up debates in Britain cannot be understood without some understanding of the negative deindustrialization of the early 1980s and austerity in the 2010s. Finally, we examined two current debates – around universal basic income and a Green New Deal – where deindustrialization helps us to understand the context for these becoming increasingly influential. In particular, UBI may pre-date it, but the debate has a greater resonance given current concerns over automation and fears of jobless futures. Similarly, while debates over a Green New Deal are ones that reflect the global environmental crisis, they are also ones that explicitly attempt to combine that with the fact that the world faces a crisis of jobs, both in terms of those offering relatively low wages and economic insecurity, and those that do not even offer this. Seen in this way, deindustrialization is best seen as a useful way into understanding some of the major social, economic and political issues of our time. It is not however, a substitute for understanding these issues, and too often deindustrialization, seen in isolation, is an excuse to propagate reactionary political agendas that are neither feasible nor desirable.

REFERENCES

Acemoglu, D. 2021. "AI's future does not have to be dystopian". *Boston Review*, 20 May. https://www.bostonreview.net/forum/ais-future-doesnt-have-to-be-dystopian/.

Acemoglu, D. *et al.* 2016. "Import competition and the great employment sag of the 2000s". *Journal of Labor Economics* 34(S1): 5141–98.

Acemoglu, D. & S. Johnson 2023. *Power and Progress.* London: Basic.

Adkins, L., M. Cooper & M. Konings 2020. *The Asset Economy.* Cambridge: Polity.

Akyuz, Y. 2012. "The staggering rise of the South?" Geneva: South Centre Research Paper No. 44, 1–54.

Albertson, K. & P. Stepney 2019. "1979 and all that: a 40-year reassessment of Margaret Thatcher's legacy on her own terms". *Cambridge Journal of Economics* 44(2): 319–42.

AmCham China 2018. *China Business Climate Survey Report 2018.* Beijing: AmCham China.

AmCham China 2019. *China Business Climate Survey Report 2019.* Beijing: AmCham China.

Amin, S. 1976. *Unequal Development.* New York: Monthly Review Press.

Amsden, A. 1989. *Asia's Next Giant.* Oxford: Oxford University Press.

Anderson, P. 1964. "The origins of the present crisis". *New Left Review* I/23: 26–53.

Appelbaum, R. *et al.* 2018. *Innovation in China.* Cambridge: Polity.

Arrighi, G. 1994. *The Long Twentieth Century.* London: Verso.

Arrighi, G. 2007. *Adam Smith in Beijing.* London: Verso.

Arrighi, G. & J. Moore 2001. "Capitalist development in world historical perspective". In R. Albritton (ed.), *Phases of Capitalist Development*, 56–75. Basingstoke: Palgrave Macmillan.

Aston, T. & C. Philpin (eds) 1987. *The Brenner Debate: Agrarian Class Structure and Economic Development in Pre-Industrial Europe.* Cambridge: Cambridge University Press.

Athukorala, P. 1993. "Manufactured exports from developing countries and their terms of trade: a re-examination of the Sarkar-Singer thesis". *World Development* 21(10): 1607–13.

Autor, D., D. Dorn & G. Harrison 2016. "The China shock: learning from labor market adjustment to large changes in trade". NBER Working Paper 21906.

Bacon, R. & W. Eltis 1978. *Britain's Economic Problem: Too Few Producers.* London: Macmillan.

Bairoch, P. 1993. *Economics and World History*. Brighton: Harvester-Wheatsheaf.

Baker, D. 2016. *Rigged: How Globalization and the Rules of the Modern Economy Were Structured to Make the Rich Richer*. Washington, DC: Center for Economic Policy Research.

Barbrook, R. & A. Cameron 1996. "The Californian ideology". *Science as Culture* 6(1): 44–72.

Barnett, T. 2005. *The Pentagon's New Map*. Berkeley, CA: Berkley.

Bastani, A. 2020. *Fully Automated Luxury Communism*. London: Verso.

Battistoni, A. 2023. "The lithium problem: an interview with Thea Riofrancos". *Dissent*, Spring. https://www.dissentmagazine.org/article/the-lithium-problem.

Bauer, P. 1971. *Dissent on Development*. London: Weidenfeld & Nicholson.

Bayer, P. & K. Charles 2016. "Divergent paths: structural change, economic rank, and the evolution of black–white earnings differences, 1940–2014". Washington: NBER Working Paper No. 22797.

Beauchamp, Z. 2023. "The far left and far right agree on Donald Trump's legacy: they are both wrong". *Vox*, 14 April. https://www.vox.com/23677654/trump-foreign-policy-revisionist-history-dove-anti-imperial.

Beattie, A. 2023. "Insular India's exporters will struggle to fill China's shoes". *Financial Times*, 2 March. https://www.ft.com/content/6b5cee30-3e30-4208-a5ed-fabf27a25cce.

Becker, D. & R. Sklar 1987. "Why postimperialism?" In D. Becker *et al.* (eds), *Postimperialism: International Capitalism and Development in the Late Twentieth Century*, 1–18. Boulder, CO: Lynne Rienner.

Becker, G. 1976. *The Economic Approach to Human Behaviour*. Chicago, IL: University of Chicago Press.

Bel, G. 2010. "Against the mainstream: Nazi privatization in 1930s Germany". *Economic History Review* 63(1): 34–55.

Bell, D. 1976. *The Cultural Contradictions of Capitalism*. New York: Basic.

Bell, D. 2016. *Reordering the World*. Princeton, NJ: Princeton University Press.

Bellamy Foster, J. 2003. "The new age of imperialism". *Monthly Review* 55(3). https://monthlyreview.org/2003/07/01/the-new-age-of-imperialism/.

Benanav, A. 2016. "Precarity rising". www.viewpointmag.com/2015/06/15/precarity-rising/.

Benanav, A. 2020a. *Automation and the Future of Work*. London: Verso.

Benanav, A. 2020b. "World asymmetries". *New Left Review* II/125: 138–49.

Benanav, A. 2023a. "The revolution will not be brought to you by ChatGPT". *New Statesman*, 11 April. https://www.newstatesman.com/ideas/2023/04/revolution-brought-chatgpt-artificial-intelligence.

Benanav, A. 2023b. "A dissipating glut?". *New Left Review* II/140–41: 53–81.

Bennett, J. 2016. *A Time for Audacity*. https://www.amazon.co.uk/Time-Audacity-Brexit-Created-CANZUK-ebook/dp/B01H4U7FAQ.

Benoist, A. de 2017. *View from the Right Vol. 1*. Budapest: Arktos.

Bhambra, G. 2017. "Brexit, Trump, and 'methodological whiteness': on the misrecognition of race and class". *British Journal of Sociology* 68(1): 214–32.

Birch, K. 2015. *We Have Never Been Neoliberal*. London: Zero.

Blackaby, F. (ed.) 1977. *De-Industrialisation.* London: Heinemann Educational.
Blair, T. 2000. "Labour Party Conference speech". http://www.britishpoliticalspeech.org/speech-archive.htm?speech=206.
Blair, T. & G. Schroeder 1999. *Europe: The Third Way.* London: Labour Party.
Blanchflower, D. 2019. *Not Working: Where Have All the Good Jobs Gone?* Princeton, NJ: Princeton University Press.
Bloomfield, J. 2020. "Progressive politics in a changing world: challenging the fallacies of Blue Labour". *Political Quarterly* 91(1): 89–97.
Bloomfield, J & F. Steward 2020. "The politics of the Green New Deal". *Political Quarterly* 91(4): 770–79.
Blyth, M. 2013. *Austerity.* Oxford: Oxford University Press.
Boggs, J. 2009. *The American Revolution.* New York: Monthly Review Press.
Bork, R. 1978. *The Anti-Trust Paradox.* Chicago, IL: University of Chicago Press.
Bounds, A. 2021. "Government criticised over design of levelling up funds". *Financial Times,* 11 March 11. https://www.ft.com/content/3a02454f-ee90-4b19-9fef-2e2c3d98b234.
Bounds, A. & A. Smith 2021. "Levelling Up fund bias in favour of Tory seats 'pretty blatant'". *Financial Times,* 5 March. https://www.ft.com/content/d485da2a-5778-45ae-9fa8-ca024bc8bbcf.
Bradford DeLong, J. 2017a. "NAFTA and other trade deals have not gutted American manufacturing". Vox. https://www.vox.com/the-big-idea/2017/1/24/14363148/trade-deals-nafta-wto-china-job-loss-trump.
Bradford DeLong, J. 2017b. "Grasping reality on typepad". https://www.bradford-delong.com/2017/05/delong-the-future-of-work-automation-and-labor-inclusive-ai-technology-and-policy-for-a-diverse-human-future-1.html.
Brenner, R. 1977. "The origins of capitalist development". *New Left Review* I/104: 25–92.
Brenner, R. 1998. "The economics of global turbulence". *New Left Review* I/229: 1–265.
Brenner, R. 2002. *The Boom and the Bubble.* London: Verso.
Brenner, R. 2006 *The Economics of Global Turbulence.* London: Verso.
Brenner, R. 2020. "Escalating plunder". *New Left Review* II/123: 5–24.
Brynjolfsson, E. & L. Hitt 2003. "Computing productivity: firm level evidence". MIT Working Paper 4210-01.
Brynjolfsson, E. & A. McAfee 2014. *The Second Machine Age.* New York: Norton.
Buchanan, J. & G. Tullock 1962. *The Calculus of Consent.* Ann Arbor, MI: University of Michigan Press.
Buchanan, P. 1992. "Republican National Convention Speech". http://buchanan.org/blog/1992-republican-national-convention-speech-148.
Buchanan, P. 1994. "The isolationist myth". http://buchanan.org/blog/the-isolationist-myth-165.
Buchanan, P. 1998. *The Great Betrayal.* New York: Little Brown.
Buchanan, P. 1999. *A Republic not an Empire.* Washington: Regnery.
Buchanan, P. 2002. *The Death of the West.* New York: St Martin's Press.
Buchanan, P. 2003. "Death of manufacturing". *American Conservative,* 11 April.
Buchanan, P. 2004. *Where the Right went Wrong.* New York: Thomas Dunne.

Buchanan, P. 2011. *Suicide of a Superpower*. New York: Thomas Dunne.
Buchanan, P. 2016. "Trump: middle America's messenger". *American Conservative*, 23 February.
Burawoy, M. 2010. "From Polanyi to Polyanna". *Global Labor Journal* 1(2): 301–13.
Burbach, R. & B. Robinson 1999. "The *fin de siecle* debate: globalization as epochal shift". *Science and Society* 63(1): 10–39.
Burnham, J. 1972. *The Managerial Revolution*. New York: Praeger.
Burnham, J. 2014. *Suicide of the West*. New York: Encounter.
Burnham, P. 2001. "New Labour and the politics of depoliticisation". *British Journal of Politics and International Relations* 3(2): 127–49.
Butler, P. 2015. "Tory MPs cheer George Osborne's climbdown on tax credits". *The Guardian*, 25 November. https://www.theguardian.com/money/2015/nov/25/tory-mps-cheer-george-osborne-climbdown-tax-credit-cuts.
Calhoun, C. & B. Fong 2022. "Introduction". In C. Calhoun & B. Fong (eds), *The Green New Deal and the Future of Work*, 1–17. New York: Columbia University Press.
Caliendo, L., M. Dvorkin & F. Parro 2019. "Trade and labor market dynamics: general equilibrium analysis of the China trade shock". *Econometrica* 87: 741–835.
Callinicos, A. 2023. *The New Age of Catastrophe*. Cambridge: Polity.
Cambridge Political Economy Group 1975. *Britain's Economic Crisis*. Nottingham: Spokesman.
Campling, L. & A. Colas 2021. *Capitalism and the Sea*. London: Verso.
Carr, E. 2001. *The Twenty Years' Crisis, 1919–1939*. Basingstoke: Palgrave Macmillan.
Castells, M. 1996. *The Rise of the Network Society*. Oxford: Blackwell.
Cebul, B. 2019. "Supply-side liberalism: fiscal crisis, post-industrial policy, and the rise of the New Democrats". *Modern American History* 2(2): 139–64.
Chait, J. 2021. "Why Glenn Greenwald says Tucker Carlson is a true socialist". *National Interest*, 4 March. https://nymag.com/intelligencer/2021/03/why-glenn-greenwald-says-tucker-carlson-is-a-true-socialist.html.
Chan, J., M. Selden & P. Ngai 2020. *Dying for an iPhone*. London: Pluto.
Chang, H.-J. 2002. *Kicking Away the Ladder*. London: Anthem.
Chang, H.-J. 2007. *Bad Samaritans*. London: Random House.
Charnock, G. & G. Starosta 2016. "Introduction". In G. Charnock & G. Starosta (eds), *The New International Division of Labour*, 1–22. Basingstoke: Palgrave Macmillan.
Christophers, B. 2018. *The New Enclosure*. London: Verso.
Christophers, B. 2020. *Rentier Capitalism*. London: Verso.
Christophers, B. 2023. *Our Lives in their Portfolios*. London: Verso.
Clarke, S. 1999. "Capitalist competition and the tendency to overproduction". *Historical Materialism* 4(1): 57–72.
Cloward, R. & F. Fox Piven 1966. "The weight of the poor". *The Nation*, 2 May. https://web.archive.org/web/20111124045536/http://www.commondreams.org/headline/2010/03/24-4.
Coase, R. 1937. "The nature of the firm". *Economica* 4(16): 386–405.
Coase, R. 1960. "The problem of social cost". *Journal of Law and Economics* 3(1): 1–44.
Coates, D. 2018. *Flawed Capitalism*. Newcastle upon Tyne: Agenda.
Collier, P. 2008. *The Bottom Billion*. Oxford: Oxford University Press.

Conservative Party 2019. Conservative Party Manifesto 2019. https://www.conservatives.com/our-plan/conservative-party-manifesto-2019.

Cooper, R. 2002. "Why we still need empires". *The Observer*, 7 April.

Corden, W. & J. Neary 1982. "Booming sector and deindustrialisation in a small open economy". *Economic Journal* 92/368: 825–48.

Crafts, N. 1997. "Some dimensions of the 'Quality of Life' during the British industrial revolution". *Economic History Review* 50(4): 617–39.

Crerar, P. 2023. "Rishi Sunak constituency bid raises fears of 'levelling up' favouritism". *The Guardian*, 18 January. https://www.theguardian.com/politics/2023/jan/18/rishi-sunak-constituency-bid-raises-fears-of-levelling-up-favouritism.

Crouch, C. 2009. "Privatised Keynesianism". *British Journal of Politics and International Relations* 11(3): 382–99.

Crouch, C. 2012. *The Strange Non-Death of Neoliberalism.* Cambridge: Polity.

Danielli, S. *et al.* 2021. "Economic interventions to ameliorate the impact of COVID-19 on the economy and health: an international comparison". *Journal of Public Health* 43(1): 42–6.

Dardot, P. & C. Laval 2014. *The New Way of the World.* London: Verso.

Davies, W. 2014. *The Limits of Neoliberalism.* London: Sage.

Davies, W. 2016. "Brexit will make things worse. Is that why people voted for it?". *Washington Post*, 1 July.

Daviron, B. & S. Ponte 2005. *The Coffee Paradox.* London: Zed.

Davis, B. & L. Wei 2020. *Superpower Slowdown.* New York: Harper Business.

Davis, M. 2001. *Late Victorian Holocausts.* London: Verso.

Davis, M. 2004. *Planet of Slums.* London: Verso.

Davis, M. 2017. "The great God trump and the white working class". Jacobin. https://www.jacobinmag.com/2017/02/the-great-god-trump-and-the-white-working-class.

Dedrick, J., K. Kraemer & J. Linden 2010. "Who profits from innovation in global value chains?". *Industrial and Corporate Change* 19(1): 81–116.

Deudney, D. & J. Ikenberry 1999. "The nature and sources of liberal international order". *Review of International Studies* 25(2): 179–96.

Diao, X. & M. McMillan 2018. "Toward an understanding of economic growth in Africa: a reinterpretation of the Lewis model". *World Development* 109: 511–22.

Dicken, P. 2014. *Global Shift.* London: Sage.

Dobb, M. 1976. "A reply". In R. Hilton (ed.), *The Transition from Feudalism to Capitalism*, 57–67. London: Verso.

Dorn, D. & P. Levell 2021. *Trade and Inequality in Europe and the US.* London: Institute for Fiscal Studies.

Drolet, J. 2011. *American Neoconservatism.* New York: Columbia University Press.

Dugin, A. 2009. *The Fourth Political Theory.* Budapest: Arktos.

Durand, C. 2017. *Fictitious Capital.* London: Verso.

Durand, C. 2023. "Hollow states". Sidecar, 15 May. https://newleftreview.org/sidecar/posts/hollow-states.

Easterly, W. 2014. *The Tyranny of Experts.* New York: Basic.

Eatwell, R. & M. Goodwin 2018. *National Populism: The Revolt against Liberal Democracy.* London: Pelican.

Economist 1977. "The Dutch Disease". *The Economist*, 26 November, 82–3.

Economists for Brexit 2016. "The economy after Brexit". http://issuu.com/efbkl/docs/economists_for_brexit_-_the_economy/1?e=24629146/35248609.

Edgerton, D. 2018. *The Rise and Fall of the British Nation.* London: Allen Lane.

Edin, K. & H. Schaefer 2015. *$2 a Day.* New York: Houghton Mifflin.

Edwards, C. 1992. "Industrialization in South Korea". In T. Hewitt, H. Johnson & D. Wields (eds), *Industrialization and Development*, 97–127. Oxford: Oxford University Press.

Ehrenreich, B. & J. Ehrenreich 1977. "The professional managerial class". *Radical America* 11(2): 7–33.

Eichengreen, B. & H. Tong 2004. "The impact of China on the exports of other Asian countries". Washington, DC: NBER Working Paper No. 10768.

Eloundou, T. *et al.* 2023. "GPTs are GPTs: an early look at the labor market impact of large language models". Open AI, Open Research, University of Pennsylvania. https://arxiv.org/pdf/2303.10130.pdf.

Enenkel, K. 2021. "What can German reunification teach the UK about levelling up". https://www.centreforcities.org/blog/what-can-german-reunification-teach-the-uk-about-levelling-up/.

Erken, H. & M. Tulen 2017. "US global value chain integration: a major impediment for Trump". https://economics.rabobank.com/publications/2017/june/us-global-value-chain-integration-trump-protectionist-trade/.

Erturk, I. *et al.* 2012. "Accounting for national success and failure: rethinking the UK case". *Accounting Forum* 36(1): 5–17.

Featherstone, D. 2012. *Solidarity.* London: Zed.

Feenstra, R. & A. Sasahara 2017. "The 'China Shock': exports and US employment: a global input-output analysis". NBER Working paper 24022.

Feffer, J. 2021. *Right Across the World.* London: Pluto.

Feldstein, M. 2019. "Underestimating the real growth of GDP, personal income and productivity". In D. Adler & L. Siegel (eds), *The Productivity Puzzle*, 50–73. https://www.cfainstitute.org/-/media/documents/book/rf-publication/2019/the-productivity-puzzle.ashx.

Ferguson, J. 2006. *Dark Shadows.* Durham, NC: Duke University Press.

Ferguson, J. 2015. *Give a Man a Fish.* Durham, NC: Duke University Press.

Ferguson, N. 2004. *Colossus.* London: Allen Lane.

Ferguson, N. & M. Schularik 2007. "Chimerica and the global asset market boom". *International Finance* 10(3): 215–39.

Fine, B., C. Lapavitsas & D. Milonakis 1999. "Addressing the world economy: two steps back". *Capital & Class* 23(1): 47–90.

Finlayson, A. 2003. *Making Sense of New Labour.* London: Lawrence & Wishart.

Flip Chart Rick 2021. "Labour's problem is not the Red Wall – it's the Grey Wall". https://flipchartfairytales.wordpress.com/2021/05/21/labours-problem-is-not-the-working-class-its-the-grey-wall/.

Florida, R. 2002. *The Rise of the Creative Class.* New York: Basic.

Ford, M. 2015. *Rise of the Robots.* Oxford: Oneworld.

Foucault, M. 2008. *The Birth of Biopolitics.* Basingstoke: Palgrave Macmillan.

Francis, S. 1983. "Message from MARs". In G. Schneider (ed.), *Conservatism in America since 1930*, 300–17. New York: New York University Press.

Francis, S. 1992. "Nationalism, old and new". *Chronicles*, 18 June.
Francis, S. 1994. *Beautiful Losers.* Columbia, MO: University of Missouri Press.
Francis, S. 2000. "Capitalism: the enemy". *Chronicles*, 24 August. http://www.chroniclesmagazine.org/2000/August/24/8/magazine/article/10828498/.
Francis, S. 2004. "Why immigrants kill". VDare, 29 November. http://www.vdare.com/francis/041129_kil.htm.
Francis, S. 2014. "Outsourcing: the economic equivalent of ethnic cleansing". Vdare. http://www.vdare.com/articles/outsourcing-the-economic-equivalent-of-ethnic-cleansing.
Francis, S. 2016. *Leviathan and its Enemies.* New York: Radix.
Frank. A. 1966. "The development of underdevelopment". *Monthly Review* 18(4): 45–58.
Frank, A. 1969. *Capitalism and Underdevelopment in Latin America*. New York: Monthly Review Press.
Frank, A. 1984. *Critique and Anti-Critique.* Basingstoke: Macmillan.
Frank, T. 2004. *What's the Matter with America?* London: Secker.
Frey, C. & M. Osborne 2013. "The future of employment". http://www.oxfordmartin.ox.ac.uk/downloads/academic/The_Future_of_Employment.pdf.
Friedman, M. 1970. "The social responsibility of business is to increase profits". *New York Times Magazine*, 13 September.
Friedman, M. 1962. *Capitalism and Freedom.* Chicago, IL: University of Chicago Press.
Friedman, T. 2005. *The World is Flat.* London: Penguin.
Friedman, T. 2007. "The power of green". *New York Times Magazine*, 15 April.
Frobel, F., J. Heinrichs & O. Kreye 1980. *The New International Division of Labour.* Cambridge: Cambridge University Press.
Furtado, C. 1964. *Development and Underdevelopment.* Berkeley, CA: University of California Press.
Furtado, C. 1965. "Development and stagnation in Latin America: a structuralist approach". *Studies in Comparative International Development* 1: 159–75.
Gabor, D. 2021. "Private finance won't decarbonise our economies, but the big green state can". *The Guardian*, 4 June. https://www.theguardian.com/commentisfree/2021/jun/04/private-finance-decarbonise-economies-green-state.
Gallardo-Albarran, D. & H. de Jong 2021. "Optimism or pessimism? A composite view on English living standards during the Industrial Revolution". *European Review of Economic History* 25(1): 1–19.
Gamble, A. 1994. *Britain in Decline.* Fourth edition. Basingstoke: Macmillan Press.
Garavini, G. 2022. "Thatcher's North Sea: the return of cheap oil and the 'neo-liberalisation' of European energy". *Contemporary European History*, First View, 1–16.
Geary, F. & T. Stark 2018. *150 Years of GDP.* London: Routledge.
Gereffi, G. 2018. *Global Value Chains and Development.* Cambridge: Cambridge University Press.
Gereffi, G. & M. Korzeniewicz (eds) 1994. *Commodity Chains and Global Capitalism.* Westport, CT: Praeger.
Germain, R. 2009. *Global Politics and Financial Governance.* Basingstoke: Palgrave Macmillan.
Germann, J. 2021. *Unwitting Architect: German Primacy and the Origins of Neoliberalism.* Stanford, CA: Stanford University Press.

Gerstle, G. 2022. *The Rise and Fall of the Neoliberal Order.* New York: Oxford University Press.

Ghitza, Y. & J. Robinson 2021. "What happened in 2020?". https://catalist.us/wh-national/.

Giddens, A. 1998. *The Third Way.* Cambridge: Polity.

Giddens, A. 1999. *Runaway World.* Cambridge: Polity.

Giddens, A. 2000. *The Third Way and its Critics.* Cambridge: Polity.

Giddens, A. 2002. *Which Way for New Labour?* Cambridge: Polity.

Gilbert, J. & A. Williams 2022. *Hegemony Now.* London: Verso.

Gindin, S. 2000. "Turning points and starting points: Brenner, left turbulence and class politics". In L. Panitch & C. Leys (eds), *The Socialist Register 2001*, 343–66. London: Merlin.

Glasman, M. 2020. "The coronavirus crisis has sounded the death knell of globalisation". *New Statesman.* https://www.newstatesman.com/long-reads/2020/04/coronavirus-crisis-has-sounded-death-knell-liberal-globalisation.

Goodhart, D. 2017. *The Road to Somewhere.* London: Hurst.

Goodwin, M. 2023a. *Values, Voices and Virtue.* London: Penguin.

Goodwin, M. 2023b. "How Britain came apart Part 1: The rise of hyper globalisation". https://mattgoodwin.substack.com/p/how-britain-came-apart.

Goodwin, M. 2023c. "Does Britain need a new party?". https://mattgoodwin.substack.com/p/does-britain-need-a-new-party.

Goos, M. & A. Manning 2007. "Lousy and lovely jobs: the rising polarization of work in Britain". *Review of Economics and Statistics* 89(1): 118–33.

Gordon, D. 1988. "The global economy: new edifice or crumbling foundations". *New Left Review* I/ 168: 24–65.

Gore, A. 1999. "Remarks of the vice-president". www.govinfo.library.unt.edu.

Gorz, A. 1987. *Farewell to the Working Class.* London: Pluto.

Gottfried, P. 2001. *After Liberalism: Mass Democracy in the Managerial State.* Princeton, NJ: Princeton University Press.

Gourinchas, P.-O. & H. Rey 2005. "From world banker to world venture capitalist: US external adjustment and the exorbitant privilege". http://socrates.berkeley.edu/~pog/academic/exorbitant/exorb_privilege_0804.pdfG.

Green, J. 2019. *Is Globalization Over?* Cambridge: Polity.

Greenwald, G. 2023. "System update: Marjorie Taylor Greene on Ukraine". Podcast. https://podcasts.apple.com/sk/podcast/marjorie-taylor-greene-on-ukraine-speakership-fallout/id1669610956?i=1000597791031.

Gronigen Growth and Development Centre 2014. Sector Database. https://www.rug.nl/ggdc/structuralchange/previous-sector-database/10-sector-2014?lang=en (accessed 08/02/23).

Grossman, G. & E. Helpman 1991. *Innovation and Growth in the Global Economy.* Cambridge, MA: MIT Press.

Guilford, G. 2016. "Everything we thought we knew about trade is wrong". https://qz.com/840973/everything-we-thought-we-knew-about-free-trade-is-wrong/.

Guinan, J. & M. O'Neill 2021. "The Third Way may have worked for New Labour, but it is impossible now". *The Guardian*, 13 May. https://www.theguardian.com/commentisfree/2021/may/13/third-way-new-labour-tony-blair-new-vision.

Gupta Barnes, S. 2021. "Waking the sleeping giant: poor and low income voters in the 2020 election". Poor People's Campaign. https://www.poorpeoplescampaign.org/wp-content/uploads/2022/09/PPC_LIV_Report.pdf.

Hammond, S. & A. Jain 2020. "Op-ed: Deindustrialization isn't (just) a white working class problem". https://www.niskanencenter.org/op-ed-deindustrialization-isnt-just-a-white-working-class-problem-2/.

Hanlon, J., A. Barrientos & D. Hulme 2010. *Just Give Money to the Poor.* Boulder, CO: Lynne Rienner.

Harding, V. 2023. "Beware the squirrel". https://samf.substack.com/p/beware-the-squirrel.

Harris, J. 2020. "Modern, multicultural and surprisingly liberal: this is the real 'red wall'". *The Guardian*, 4 October. https://www.theguardian.com/commentisfree/2020/oct/04/red-wall-labour-heartlands-britain.

Harriss, J. 2021. "Returning to the 'Great Transformation'". In T. Allen & A. Thomas (eds), *Poverty and Development in the Twenty-First Century*, 564–84. Oxford: Oxford University Press.

Harris, N. 1987. *The End of the Third World.* London: Penguin.

Hausmann, R. *et al.* 2011. *The Atlas of Economic Complexity.* Hollis, NH: Puritan Press.

Hay, C. 2013. *The Failure of the Anglo-Liberal Growth Model.* Basingstoke: Palgrave Macmillan.

Hay, C. & M. Watson 1999. "Globalisation: sceptical notes on the 1999 Reith Lectures". *Political Quarterly* 70(4): 418–25.

Hay, C. & M. Watson 2003. "The discourse of globalisation and the logic of no alternative". *Policy and Politics* 30(4): 289–305.

Hayek, F. 1967. *Studies in Philosophy, Politics and Economics.* Chicago, IL: University of Chicago Press.

Hayek, F. 2001. *The Road to Serfdom.* London: Routledge.

Hayek, F. 2006. *The Constitution of Liberty.* London: Routledge.

Hayek, F. 2013. *Law, Legislation and Liberty.* London: Routledge.

Hazeldine, T. 2020. *The Northern Question* London: Verso.

Heer, J. 2023. "The surprisingly durable myth of Donald Trump. Anti-Imperialist". *The Nation*, 7 April. https://www.thenation.com/article/politics/trump-anti-imperialist/.

Held, D. & A. McGrew 2007. *Globalization/Anti-Globalization.* Cambridge: Polity.

Held, D. *et al.* 1999. *Global Transformations.* Cambridge: Polity.

Helleiner, E. 1994. *States and the Re-emergence of Global Finance.* Ithaca, NY: Cornell University Press.

Heller, H. 2015. "Authoritarian liberalism". *European Law Journal* 21(3): 295–301.

Henwood, D. 2003. *The New Economy.* New York: New Press.

Herendorff, R. Rogerson & A. Valentinyi 2014. "Growth and structural transformation". In P. Aghion & S. Durlauf (eds), *Handbook of Economic Growth, Vol. 2*, 855–941. Amsterdam: Elsevier.

Hicks, M. & S. Devaraj 2015 "The myth and the reality of manufacturing in America". Ball State University Center for Business and Economic Research.

Hilton, R. (ed.) 1976. *The Transition from Feudalism to Capitalism.* London: Verso.

Hindmoor, A. 2018. *What's Left Now?* Oxford: Oxford University Press.

Hirst, P., G. Thompson & S. Bromley 2009. *Globalization in Question*. Third edn. Cambridge: Polity.

Hobsbawm, E. 1999. *Industry and Empire*. London: Penguin.

Hobson, J. 2018. *Imperialism: A Study*. London: Franklin Classics.

Hochschild, A. 2016. *Strangers in their Own Land*. New York: New Press.

Hohmann, J. 2016. "The Daily 202: The Reagan Democrats are no longer Democrats. Will they ever be again?". *Washington Post*, 11 November.

Hopkins, T. & I. Wallerstein 1986. "Commodity chains in the world economy prior to 1800". *Review* 10(1): 157–70.

Houseman, S. 2018. "Understanding the decline of US manufacturing employment". Upjohn Institute Working Paper 18-287.

Hung, H.-F. 2009. "America's head servant?". *New Left Review* II/64: 97–108.

Hung, H.-F. 2022. *Clash of Empires*. Cambridge: Cambridge University Press.

Huntington, S. 1957. "Conservatism as an ideology". *American Political Science Review* 51(2): 454–73.

Huntington, S. 2004. *Who are We?* New York: Simon & Schuster.

IMF 2023. Commodity Prices Indices. https://www.imf.org/en/Research/commodity-prices (accessed 14/04/2023).

Ikenberry, J. 2007. *Liberal Order and Imperial Ambition*. Cambridge: Polity.

Independent International Commission on Kosovo 2000. *Kosovo Report*. New York: Oxford University Press.

IPCC 2021. *Climate Change 2021*. Geneva: IPCC.

Jager, A. & D. Zamora Vargas 2022. "Foreword". In W. Benn Michaels & A. Reed (eds), *No Politics but Class Politics*, 11–23. London: Eris.

Jager, A. & D. Zamora Vargas 2023. *Welfare for Markets*. Chicago, IL: University of Chicago Press.

Jenkins, R. 1992. "Industrialization and the global economy". In T. Hewitt, D. Wield & H. Johnson (eds), *Industrialization and Development*, 13–40. Oxford: Oxford University Press.

Jennings, W., L. McKay & G. Stoker 2021. "The politics of Levelling Up". *Political Quarterly* 92(2): 302–11.

Johnson, G. 2019 "National populism is here to stay". www.counter-currents.com/2019/07/national-populism-is-here-to-stay-2/.

Johnson, P. 1980. *The Recovery of Freedom*. Oxford: Blackwell.

Johnson, R. 2020. *The End of the Second Reconstruction*. Cambridge: Polity.

Jones, L. & S. Hameiri 2020. *Fractured China*. Cambridge: Cambridge University Press.

Jones, L. & J. Zeng 2019. "Understanding China's Belt and Road Initiative: Beyond 'Grand Strategy' to a state transformation analysis". *Third World Quarterly* 40(8): 1415–39.

Kabeer, N. 2000. *The Power to Choose*. London: Verso.

Kaldor, N. 1967. *Strategic Factors in Economic Development*. Ithaca, NY: Cornell University Press.

Kaldor, N. 1978. *Causes of the Slow Rate of Economic Growth in the United Kingdom*. Cambridge: Cambridge University Press.

Kalecki, M. 1943. "Political aspects of full employment". *Political Quarterly* 14(4): 322–30.

Kaplinsky, R. 2005. *Globalization, Poverty and Inequality*. Cambridge: Polity.

Kaplinsky, R. & A. Santos-Paulinho 2005. "Innovation and competitiveness: trends in unit prices in global trade". *Oxford Development Studies* 33(3/4): 333–55.

Katznelson, I. 2014. *Fear Itself.* New York: Liveright.

Keen, S. 2017. "Ricardo's vice and the virtues of industrial diversity". *American Affairs* 1(3). https://americanaffairsjournal.org/2017/08/ricardos-vice-virtues-industrial-diversity/.

Keller, M. & F. Block 2023. "The new levers of state power". *Catalyst* 7(1): 8–43.

Kiely, R. 1995. *Sociology and Development.* London: UCL Press.

Kiely, R. 1998. *Industrialization and Development: A Comparative Analysis.* London: UCL Press.

Kiely, R. 2003. "The race to the bottom and international labor solidarity". *Review* 26(1): 67–88.

Kiely, R. 2007. *The New Political Economy of Development.* Basingstoke: Palgrave Macmillan.

Kiely, R. 2008. "Poverty through 'insufficient exploitation and/or globalization?': globalized production and new dualist fallacies". *Globalizations* 5(3): 419–32.

Kiely, R. 2010. *Rethinking Imperialism.* Basingstoke: Palgrave Macmillan.

Kiely, R. 2015. *The BRICs, US Decline and Global Transformations.* Basingstoke: Palgrave Macmillan.

Kiely, R. 2018. *The Neoliberal Paradox.* Cheltenham: Elgar.

Kiely, R. 2020. *The Conservative Challenge to Globalization.* Newcastle upon Tyne: Agenda.

Kilibarda K. & D. Roithmayr 2016. "The myth of the Rustbelt Revolt". http://www.slate.com/articles/news_and_politics/politics/2016/12/the_myth_of_the_rust_belt_revolt.html.

Kitching, G. 1982. *Development and Underdevelopment in Historical Perspective.* London: Methuen.

Kitching, G. 2001. *Seeking Social Justice through Globalization.* Philadelphia, PA: Pennsylvania State University Press.

Klein, M. & M. Pettis 2020. *Trade Wars are Class Wars.* New Haven, CT: Yale University Press.

Kletzer L. 2001. *Job Losses from Imports.* Washington, DC: Peterson Institute for International Economics.

Kotkin, J. 2020. *The Coming of Neo-Feudalism.* New York: Encounter.

Kozul Wright, R. & P. Rayment 2004. "Globalization reloaded: an UNCTAD perspective". UNCTAD Discussion Papers no.167, 1–50.

Kristol, I. 1970. "'When virtue loses her loveliness': some reflections on capitalism and the 'free society'". *The Public Interest* 21(Fall): 3–15.

Krueger, A. 1974. "The political economy of the rent seeking society". *American Economic Review* 64(3): 291–303.

Krugman, P. 1986. *Strategic Trade Policy and the New International Economics.* Cambridge, MA: MIT Press.

Kuznets, S. 1955. "Economic growth and income inequality". *American Economic Review* 45(1): 1–28.

Lal, D. 1983. *The Poverty of Development Economics.* London: Institute of Economic Affairs.

Lal, D. 2004. *In Praise of Empires.* London: Palgrave Macmillan.
Lal, D. 2008. *Reviving the Invisible Hand.* Princeton, NJ: Princeton University Press.
Lamp, N. 2018. "How should we think about the winners and losers from globalization?" Queens University Legal Research Paper No. 2018/102.
Langley, P. 2008. *The Everyday Life of Global Finance.* Oxford: Oxford University Press.
Lasch, C. 1979. *The Culture of Narcissism.* New York: Norton.
Lasch, C. 1996. *The Revolt of the Elites.* New York: Norton.
Lawrence, R. 2020. "Trade surplus or deficit? Neither matters for changes in manufacturing employment shares". Pietersen Institute for International economics Working Paper 20–15.
Lawson. C. 2020. "Making sense of the ruins: the historiography of deindustrialisation and its continued relevance in neoliberal times". *History Compass* 18(8): 126–45.
Lazonick, W. & M. O'Sullivan 2000. "Maximizing shareholder value: a new ideology for corporate governance". *Economy and Society* 29(1): 13–35.
Lazzarato, M. 2012. *The Making of the Indebted Man.* Cambridge, MA: MIT Press.
Lenin, V. 1977 [1916]. "Imperialism: The Highest Stage of Capitalism". In *Selected Works.* Moscow: Progress Publishers.
Lenin, V. 2003. "Introduction". In N. Bukharin, *Imperialism and World Economy*, 9–13. London: Bookmarks.
Levelling Up Campaign 2023. "What is Levelling Up". https://levellingup.campaign.gov.uk/what-is-levelling-up/.
Lewis, P. *et al.* 2018. "Revealed: the rise and rise of populist rhetoric". *The Guardian*, 6 March. https://www.theguardian.com/world/ng-interactive/2019/mar/06/revealed-the-rise-and-rise-of-populist-rhetoric.
Lewis, W. 1954. "Economic development with unlimited supplies of labour". *The Manchester School* 22(2): 139–91.
Lind, M. 1996. *The Next American Nation.* New York: Simon & Schuster.
Lis, J. 2017. "To the Commonwealth, 'Global Britain' sounds like nostalgia for something else". *New Statesman.* www.newstatesman.com/politics/staggers/2017/02/commonwealth-globalbritain-sounds-nostalgia-something-else.
Liu, C. 2021. *Virtue Hoarders.* Minneapolis, MN: University of Minnesota Press.
Lloyd, J. 2000. "The anglosphere project". *New Statesman*, 13 March.
Lowrey, A. 2018. "Trump's 'smart tariffs' don't make economic sense". *The Atlantic*, 1 March.
Mackintosh, M. 2004. "Gaining from trade". In S. Bromley, M. Mackintosh & W. Brown (eds), *Making the International*, 33–72. London: Pluto.
Macklin, G. 2020. *Failed Fuhrers.* London: Routledge.
Maddison, A. 2001. *The World Economy: Historical Statistics.* Paris: OECD.
Makin-Waite, M. 2021. *On Burnley Road: Class, Race and Politics in an English Town.* London: Lawrence & Wishart.
Maizels, A., T. Palaskas & T. Crowe 1998. "The Prebisch Singer hypothesis revisited". In D. Sapford & J. Chen (eds), *Development Economics and Policy*, 95–110. Basingstoke: Palgrave Macmillan.
Malik, K. 2021. "It's too easy to lapse into stereotypes when we talk about 'Red Wall' seats". *The Observer*, 3 January. https://www.theguardian.com/commentisfree/2021/jan/03/its-too-easy-to-lapse-into-stereotypes-when-we-talk-about-red-wall-seats.

Malm, A. 2016. *Fossil Capital.* London: Verso.
Marazzi, C. 2010. *The Violence of Financial Capitalism.* Los Angeles, CA: Semiotexte.
Marcuse, H. 2002. *One Dimensional Man.* London: Routledge.
Mason, J. 2023. "Yes, socialists should support industrial policy and a Green New Deal". *Jacobin,* 6 April. https://jacobin.com/2023/04/svb-dylan-riley-green-new-deal-capitalism-socialism.
Mason, P. 2009. *Meltdown.* London: Verso.
Mazower, M. 2001. *Dark Continent.* Harmondsworth: Penguin.
Mazower, M. 2008. *Hitler's Empire.* Harmondsworth: Penguin.
Mazzucato, M. 2020. "We socialize bailouts. We should socialize successes too". *New York Times,* 1 July. https://www.nytimes.com/2020/07/01/opinion/inequality-goverment-bailout.html.
McGee, P. 2023. "What it would take for Apple to disentangle itself from China". *Financial Times,* 18 January. https://www.ft.com/content/74f7e284-c047-4cc4-9b7a-408d40611bfa.
McGeever J. 2023. "China slips away from Treasuries but sticks with dollar bonds". Reuters. https://www.reuters.com/markets/asia/china-slips-away-treasuries-sticks-with-dollar-bonds-2023-02-22/.
McKinsey Global Institute 2017. "Jobs lost, jobs gained". https://www.mckinsey.com/~/media/BAB489A30B724BECB5DEDC41E9BB9FAC.ashx.
Meadway, J. 2023a. "Bank bailouts aren't the start of another global crisis, but they should have us worried". https://novaramedia.com/2023/03/17/bank-bailouts-arent-the-start-of-another-global-crisis-but-they-should-still-have-us-worried/.
Meadway, J. 2023b. "Labour must seize the interventionist moment" *New Statesman,* 14 February. https://www.newstatesman.com/comment/2023/02/labour-must-seize-interventionist-moment-globalisation.
Mearsheimer, J. 2001. *The Tragedy of Great Power Politics.* New York: Norton.
Mearsheimer, J. 2006. "China's unpeaceful rise". *Current History* (April): 160–2.
Meek, J. 2019. *Dreams of Leaving and Remaining.* London: Verso.
Michaels, W. Benn 2016. *The Trouble with Diversity: How we Learned to Love Identity and Ignore Inequality.* New York: Picador.
Milberg, W. & D. Winkler 2013. *Outsourcing Economics.* Cambridge: Cambridge University Press.
Milburn, K. 2019. *Generation Left.* Cambridge: Polity.
Milman, O. 2018. "Donald Trump tariffs on panels will cost US solar industry thousands of jobs". *The Guardian,* 24 January.
Min, D. 2011. *Why Wallison is Wrong about the Genesis of the US Housing Crisis.* Washington, DC: Center for American Progress.
Minford, P. 2016. *From Project Fear to Project Prosperity.* London: Economists for Free Trade.
Mirowski, P. 2013. *Never Let a Serious Crisis Go to Waste.* London: Verso.
Mohun, S. 2012. "Rate of profit and crisis in the US economy: a class approach". In T. Michl, A. Rezai & L. Taylor (eds), *Social Fairness and Economics: Economic Essays in the Spirit of Duncan Foley,* 171–98. Abingdon: Routledge.
Moody, K. 2017. *On New Terrain.* Chicago, IL: Haymarket.
Morozov, E. 2022. "Critique of techno feudal reason". *New Left Review* II/133/4: 89–126.

Moser, C. 1978. "Informal sector or petty commodity production: dualism or dependence in urban development". *World Development* 6(9/10): 1041–64.

Motopu, C. 2021. "The PMC meets the Tucker Carlson left". https://libcom.org/article/pmc-meets-tucker-carlson-left.

Mount, F. 2012. *The New Few, or, A Very British Oligarchy.* London: Simon & Schuster.

Moynihan, D. 1965. *The Negro Family.* Washington, DC: Department of Labor.

Muller, J.-W. 2016. *What is Populism?* Philadelphia, PA: University of Pennsylvania Press.

Murray, C. 2012. *Coming Apart.* New York: Crown.

Murray, C. 2016. *In Our Hands* Washington, DC: American Enterprise Institute.

Nachtwey, O. 2016. *Germany's Hidden Crisis.* London: Verso.

Navarro, P. & G. Autry 2011. *Death by China.* New York: Prentice Hill.

Negri, A. 1991. *Marx Beyond Marx.* New York: Autonomedia.

Nelson, F. 2016. "Of course Britain is open for business: that was the point of Brexit". *Spectator* blog. https://blogs.spectator.co.uk/2016/07/course-britain-open-business-point-brexit/.

New Economy Brief 2023. "Interest rate rises, choices and consequences". https://www.neweconomybrief.net/the-digest/interest-rate-rises-choices-and-consequences.

Nickell, S. & J. Saleheen 2015. "The impact of immigration on occupational wages: the evidence from Britain". Bank of England Staff Working Paper, No. 574.

Nolan, P. 2001. *China and the Global Economy.* Basingstoke: Palgrave Macmillan.

NSS 2002. "The National Security Strategy of the United States of America". www.whitehouse.gov/nsc/nss.html.

Office of the US Trade Representative 2017. *2017 Trade Policy Agenda and 2016 Annual Report.* https://ustr.gov/sites/default/files/files/reports/2017/AnnualReport/AnnualReport2017.pdf.

Ohlin, B. 1933. *Inter-Regional and International Trade.* Cambridge, MA: Harvard University Press.

Ohmae, K. 1995. *Borderless World.* Cambridge, MA: Harvard University Press.

Oks, D. & H. Williams 2022. "The long, slow death of global development". *American Affairs* 6(4). https://americanaffairsjournal.org/2022/11/the-long-slow-death-of-global-development/.

O'Meara, M. 2013. *New Culture, New Right.* Budapest: Arktos.

ONS 2019. "Housing affordability in England and Wales, 2018". https://www.ons.gov.uk/peoplepopulationandcommunity/housing/bulletins/housingaffordabilityinenglandandwales/2018.

ONS 2020. "Living longer: changes in housing tenure over time". https://www.ons.gov.uk/peoplepopulationandcommunity/birthsdeathsandmarriages/ageing/articles/livinglonger/changesinhousingtenureovertime#what-would-be-the-implications-of-an-increase-in-older-people-renting-privately.

Ozkirimli, U. 2023. *Cancelled.* Cambridge: Polity.

Pabst, A. 2023. "Why universities are making us stupid". *New Statesman,* 8 March.

Palan, R., R. Murphy & C. Chavagneux 2010. *Tax Havens.* Ithaca, NY: Cornell University Press.

Palma, J. 2005. "Four sources of 'de-industrialisation' and a new concept of the 'Dutch disease'". In J. Ocampo (ed.), *Beyond Reforms: Structural Dynamics and Macroeconomic Vulnerability*, 71–116. Palo Alto, CA: Stanford University Press.
Palma, J. 2008. "De-industrialization, 'premature' de-industrialization and the Dutch disease". In S. Durlauf & L. Blume (eds), *The New Palgrave Dictionary of Economics*, 1297–306. Basingstoke: Palgrave Macmillan.
Palma, G. 2009. "The revenge of the market on the rentiers: why neo-liberal reports of the end of history turned out to be premature". *Cambridge Journal of Economics* 33(4): 829–69.
Palmer, D. 2021. "America's trade gap spared under Trump, final figures show". Politico. https://www.politico.com/news/2021/02/05/2020-trade-figures-trump-failure-deficit-466116.
Panitch, L. & S. Gindin 2010. "Capitalist crises and the crisis this time". In L. Panitch, G. Albo & V. Chibber (eds), *The Socialist Register 2011*, 1–20. London: Merlin.
Panitch, L. & S. Gindin 2012. *The Making of Global Capitalism*. London, Verso.
Parenti, C. 2023. "Trump's real crime is opposing empire". CompactMag, 7 April. https://compactmag.com/article/trump-s-real-crime-is-opposing-empire.
Parijs, P. van & Y. Vanderborght 2017. *Basic Income*. Cambridge, MA: Harvard University Press.
Partington, R. 2020. "Home ownership among people aged 34–44 has plunged – ONS". *The Guardian*, 10 February.
Paul, H. 2020. "Can we go green without plundering the Global South?". https://novaramedia.com/2020/12/01/can-we-go-green-without-plundering-the-global-south/.
Payne, C. 2012. *The Consumer, Credit and Neoliberalism*. London: Routledge.
Pepper, D. 2002. *Modern Environmentalism*. London: Routledge.
Petroff, A. 2018. "Tariffs aren't the biggest problem for American exporters". https://money.cnn.com/2018/06/07/news/economy/trump-tariffs-trade-us-eu/index.html.
Piketty, T. 2014. *Capital in the Twenty-First Century*. Cambridge, MA: Harvard University Press.
Pinker, S. 2018. *Enlightenment Now*. London: Penguin.
Polanyi, K. 2001. *The Great Transformation*. Boston, MA: Beacon Press.
Powell, E. 1971. *Common Market: The Case Against*. Tadworth: Elliot Right Way Books.
Prebisch, R. 1959. "Commercial policy in the underdeveloped countries". *American Economic Review* 44: 251–73.
Progressive Economy Forum 2022. "The economic mainstream is getting inflation wrong". https://progressiveeconomyforum.com/blog/the-economic-mainstream-is-getting-inflation-wrong/.
Reid, C. 2019. "Brexit to destroy UK car manufacturing, lead to cheaper imported cars, increase traffic congestion". Forbes. https://www.forbes.com/sites/carltonreid/2019/01/28/brexit-to-destroy-u-k-car-manufacturing-lead-to-cheaper-imported-cars-increase-traffic-congestion/?sh=33edf47c5c4b.
Reinert, E. 2007. *How Rich Countries got Rich and Why Poor Countries Stay Poor*. London: Constable.
Ricardo, D. 2004 [1817]. *On the Principles of Political Economy and Taxation*. Whitefish, MT: Kessinger Publishing.

Ridley, M. 2010. *The Rational Optimist.* London: Fourth Estate.

Rifkin, J. 1995. *The End of Work.* New York: Putnam.

Riley, D. 2023. "Drowning in deposits". *Sidecar,* 4 April. https://newleftreview.org/sidecar/posts/drowning-in-deposits.

Riley, D. & R. Brenner 2022. "Seven theses on American politics". *New Left Review* II/138: 5–28.

Roberts, A. 2016. "CANZUK: after Brexit, Canada, Australia, New Zealand and Britain can unite as a pillar of western civilisation". *Daily Telegraph,* 13 September.

Robinson, B. 2004. *A Theory of Global Capitalism.* Baltimore, MD: Johns Hopkins University Press.

Rodrik, D. 2001. *The Global Governance of Trade as if Development Really Mattered.* Geneva: United Nations Development Programme.

Rodrik, D. 2002. "Comments on 'Trade, Growth and Poverty' by D. Dollar and A. Kraay". www.ksghome.harvard.edu.

Rodrik, D. 2016. "Premature deindustrialization". *Journal of Economic Growth* 21(1): 1–33.

Roediger D. 2017. "Who's afraid of the white working class? On Joan Williams' 'White Working Class: Overcoming Class Cluelessness in America'". *Los Angeles Review of Books,* 17 May.

Ropke, W. 2009. *The Social Crisis of Our Time.* New Brunswick, NJ: Transaction.

Rose, S. 2018. *Is Foreign Trade the Cause of Manufacturing Job Losses?* Washington: Urban Institute.

Rosenberg, J. & C. Boyle 2019. "Understanding 2016: China, Brexit and Trump in the history of uneven and combined development". *Journal of Historical Sociology* 32(1): 32–58.

Rosenstein-Rodan, P. 1943. "The problems of industrialisation of Eastern and South-Eastern Europe". *Economic Journal* 53(210/11): 202–11.

Roser, M. 2014. "Income inequality". https://ourworldindata.org/income-inequality.

Rostow, W. 1960. *The Stages of Economic Growth.* Cambridge: Cambridge University Press.

Rothfeder, J. 2016. "Why Donald Trump is wrong about manufacturing jobs and China". *The New Yorker,* 14 March.

Rowthorn, R. 2001 "Replicating the experience of the NIEs on a large scale". In K. Jomo & S. Nagaraj (eds), *Globalization Versus Development,* 85–112. Basingstoke: Palgrave Macmillan.

Rowthorn, R. & K. Coutts 2004. "De-industrialization and the balance of payments in advanced economies". UNCTAD Discussion Papers No.170.

Rowthorn, R. & K. Coutts 2013. "Deindustrialisation and the balance of payments in advanced countries". University of Cambridge Centre for Business Research Working Paper No.453. www.cbr.cam.ac.uk/fileadmin/user_upload/centre-for-business-research/downloads/working-papers/wp453.pdf.

Rowthorn, R. & R. Ramaswamy 1999. "Growth, trade and deindustrialization". IMF Staff Papers 46(1): 18–41.

Rowthorn, R. & J. Wells 1987. *Deindustrialization and Foreign Trade.* Cambridge: Cambridge University Press.

Runciman, D. 2005. *The Politics of Good Intentions.* Princeton, NJ: Princeton University Press.

Rushe, D. 2017. "Trump's growth problem: jobs boost masks trouble ahead for US economy". *The Guardian*, 9 July. https://www.theguardian.com/business/2017/jul/09/us-economy-trump-growth-wages.

Rutherford, J. 2023. "The new class war: interview with Michael Lind". *New Statesman*, 7 January. https://www.newstatesman.com/ideas/2023/01/us-political-analyst-michael-lind-interview-new-class-war.

Sachs, J. 2005. *The End of Poverty: How We Can Make It Happen in Our Lifetime.* London: Penguin.

Sachs, W. (ed.) 1992. *The Development Dictionary.* London: Zed.

SAIIA 2022. "Brics and the Russia–Ukraine war: a global rebalance?". https://saiia.org.za/research/a-global-rebalance/.

Sampson, T. *et al.* 2016. *Economists for Brexit: A Critique*. London: LSE Centre for Economic Performance.

Sarkar, P. & H. Singer 1991. "Manufactured exports of developing countries and their terms of trade". *World Development* 19(4): 333–40.

Sayer, D. 1987. *The Violence of Abstraction.* Oxford: Blackwell.

Schickler, E. 2016. *Racial Re-alignment: The Transformation of American Liberalism, 1932–1965.* Princeton, NJ: Princeton University Press.

Schlogl, L. & A. Sumner 2020. *Disrupted Development and the Future of Inequality in the Age of Automation.* Basingstoke: Palgrave Macmillan.

Schofield, C. 2013. *Enoch Powell and the Making of Postcolonial Britain.* Cambridge: Cambridge University Press.

Schumpeter, J. 1954. *Capitalism, Socialism and Democracy*. Floyd, VA: Impact Books.

Schwab, C. 2016. *The Fourth Industrial Revolution.* London: Random House.

Schwartz, H. 2009. *Sub-Prime Nation.* Ithaca, NY: Cornell University Press.

Scott, R. 2017. "Growth in US–China trade deficit between 2001 and 2015 cost 3.4 million jobs". Washington, DC: Economic Policy Institute.

Scruton, R. 2005. "National interest and international law". In T. Cushman (ed.), *A Matter of Principle*, 95–105. Berkeley, CA: University of California Press.

Seers, D. 1979. "The meaning of development". In D. Lehmann (ed.), *The Meaning of Development*, 8–30. London: Routledge.

Selwyn, B. 2012. *Workers, State and Development in Brazil.* Manchester: Manchester University Press.

Selwyn, B. 2019. "Poverty chains and global capitalism". *Competition and Change* 23(1): 71–97.

Selwyn, B. & D. Leyden 2021. "Understanding development in a value chain world". https://socialistproject.ca/2021/05/understanding-development-global-value-chain-world/.

Selwyn, B. & D. Leyden 2022. "Oligopoly-driven development: the World Bank's Trading for Development in the Age of Global Value Chains in perspective". *Competition and Change* 26(2): 174–96.

Sender, J. & S. Smith 1985. *The Development of Capitalism in Africa.* London: Routledge.

Seymour, R. 2019. "What's the deal with the Green New Deal". https://mronline.org/2019/04/27/whats-the-deal-with-the-green-new-deal/.

Seymour, R. 2021. "Should the left abandon the Green New Deal?". *New Statesman*, 17 November. https://www.newstatesman.com/ideas/2021/11/should-the-left-abandon-the-green-new-deal.

Shafaeddin, S. 2005a. "Trade liberalization and economic reform in developing countries". UNCTAD Discussion Paper No.179.

Shafaeddin, S. 2005b. *Trade Policy at the Crossroads*. Basingstoke: Palgrave Macmillan.

Shaikh, A. (ed.) 2005. *Globalization and the Myths of Free Trade*. London: Routledge.

Simon, E. 2022. "Demystifying the link between higher education and liberal values: a within-sibship analysis of British individuals' attitudes from 1994–2020". *British Journal of Sociology* 73(5): 967–84.

Singer, H. 1950. "The distribution of gains from trade between investing and borrowing countries". *American Economic Review* 40: 473–85.

Singer, H. 1989. "The 1980s: a lost decade – development in reverse?" In H. Singer & S. Sharma (eds), *Growth and External Debt Management*, 46–56. Basingstoke: Macmillan.

Singh, A. 1977. "UK industry and the world economy: a case of de-industrialization?" In A. Jacquemin & H. de Jong (eds), *Welfare Aspects of Industrial Markets. Nijenrode Studies in Economics, Vol 2*, 183–214. Boston, MA: Springer.

Skidelsky, R. 1975. *Oswald Mosley*. London: Macmillan.

Slobodian, Q. 2018. "You live in Robert Lighthizer's world now". *Foreign Policy*, 6 August. https://foreignpolicy.com/2018/08/06/you-live-in-robert-lighthizers-world-now-trump-trade/.

Smith, A. 1981 [1776]. *Wealth of Nations*. Indianapolis, IN: Liberty Fund.

Smith, N. 2022. "Review: Trade Wars are Class Wars". https://noahpinion.substack.com/p/book-review-trade-wars-are-class.

Snooks, G. (ed.) 1994. *Was the Industrial Revolution Necessary?* London: Routledge.

Sobolewska, M. & R. Ford 2020. *Brexitland*. Cambridge: Cambridge University Press.

Soederberg, S. 2010. "Cannibalistic capitalism: the paradoxes of neoliberal pension reform". In L. Panitch & G. Albo (eds), *The Socialist Register 2011*, 224–41. London: Merlin.

Solow, R. 1987. "We'd better watch out". *New York Review of Books*, 12 July.

Spektorowski, A. 2003. "The new right: ethno-regionalism, ethno-pluralism and the emergence of a neo-fascist 'third way'". *Journal of Political Ideologies* 8(1): 111–30.

Srnicek, N. & A. Williams 2015. *Inventing the Future*. London: Verso.

Standing, G. 2011. *The Precariat*. London: Bloomsbury.

Starrs, S. 2013. "American economic power hasn't declined – it globalized! Summoning the data and taking globalization seriously". *International Studies Quarterly* 57(4): 817–30.

Starrs, S. 2014. "The chimera of global convergence". *New Left Review* II/87: 81–96.

Starrs, S. 2015. "China's rise is designed in America, assembled in China". *China's World* 2(2): 9–20.

Starrs, S. & J. Germann 2023. "Responding to the China challenge in techno-nationalism: divergence between Germany and the United States". *Development and Change* 52(5): 1122–46.

Statista 2023. "Volume of US import of trade goods from China, 1985–2022". https://www.statista.com/statistics/187675/volume-of-us-imports-of-trade-goods-from-china-since-1985/ (accessed 13/04/2023).

Stedman-Jones, D. 2018. "The neoliberal origins of the Third Way". In D. Cahill *et al.* (eds), *Sage Handbook of Neoliberalism*, 167–78. London: Sage.

Steinfeld, E. 2010. *Playing Our Game.* Cambridge: Cambridge University Press.

Streeck, W. 2014. *Buying Time.* London: Verso.

Strom, T. 2022. "Capital and cybernetics". *New Left Review* II/135: 23–41.

Sumner, A. 2016. *Global Poverty.* Oxford: Oxford University Press.

Sumner, A. 2020. *Deindustrialization, Distribution and Development.* Oxford: Oxford University Press.

Sunkel, O. 1966. "The structural background of development problems in Latin America". *Weltwirtschaftliches Archiv* 97(1): 22.

Sutcliffe, B. 1984. "Industry and underdevelopment re-examined". In R. Kaplinsky (ed.), *Third World Industrialisation in the 1980s*, 121–33. London: Routledge.

Sweezy, P. 1976. "A critique". In R. Hilton (ed.), *The Transition from Feudalism to Capitalism*, 33–56. London: Verso.

Talbot, C. 2016. "The myth of neoliberalism". https://colinrtalbot.wordpress.com/2016/08/31/the-myth-of-neoliberalism/.

Thiessen, M. 2016. "Why, despite his insults, the Chinese love Trump". Newsweek. http://www.newsweek.com/why-despite-his-insults-chinese-love-trump-465807.

Trading Economics 2018. "US balance of trade". https://tradingeconomics.com/united-states/balance-of-trade.

Thompson, E. 1965. "The peculiarities of the English". In R. Miliband & J. Savile (eds), *The Socialist Register 1965*, 311–62. London: Merlin.

Thompson, H. 2011. *China and the Mortgaging of Amer*ica. Basingstoke: Palgrave Macmillan.

Tomlinson, J. 2017. "De-industrialization not decline: a new meta-narrative for post-war British history". *Twentieth-Century British History* 27(1): 76–99.

Tomlinson, J. 2020. "De-industrialization: strengths and weaknesses as a key concept for understanding post-war British history". *Urban History* 47(2): 199–219.

Tomlinson, J. 2021. "Deindustrialisation and 'Thatcherism': moral economy and unintended consequences". *Contemporary British History* 35(4): 620–42.

Tooze, A. 2020. "China takes the climate stage". Social Europe. https://www.socialeurope.eu/china-takes-the-climate-stage.

Tooze, A. 2021a. *Shutdown.* London: Allen Lane.

Tooze, A. 2021b. "The first climate Kalecki moment". https://adamtooze.substack.com/p/chartbook-48-the-first-climate-kalecki.

Tooze, A. 2023a. "Defining polycrisis". https://adamtooze.com/2022/06/24/chartbook-130-defining-polycrisis-from-crisis-pictures-to-the-crisis-matrix/.

Tooze, A. 2023b. "Carbon Note 2: The "Western" energy transitions – the narcissism of small differences". https://adamtooze.substack.com/p/carbon-note-2-the-western-energy.

Toye, J. 1987. *Dilemmas of Development.* Oxford: Blackwell.

Trafecante, K. 2020. "The myth of the manufacturing job renaissance". https://edition.cnn.com/2020/02/08/economy/manufacturing-jobs/index.html.

Troise, D. 2019. "US companies tax windfall fuels record share buybacks". https://apnews.com/article/north-america-business-438fae12f9204b1fbd8e8b1985ae554f.

Trump, D. 2017. "The inaugural address". 20 January. www.whitehouse.gov/briefings-statements/the-inaugural-address/.

Tufecki, B. 2020. *The Socialist Ideas of the British Left's Alternative Economic Strategy.* Basingstoke: Palgrave Macmillan.

Turner, F. 2006. *From Counterculture to Cyberculture.* Chicago, IL: University of Chicago Press.

UNCTAD 1998. *World Investment Report 1998.* Geneva: UNCTAD.

UNCTAD 2002. *Trade and Development Report 2002.* Geneva: UNCTAD.

UNCTAD 2004. *The Least Developed Countries Report 2004* Geneva: UNCTAD.

UNCTAD 2004. *Trade and Development Report 2004.* Geneva: UNCTAD.

UNCTAD 2006. *Trade and Development Report 2006.* Geneva: UNCTAD.

UNCTAD 2007. *World Investment Report 2007.* Geneva: UNCTAD.

UNCTAD 2008. *Trade and Development Report 2008.* Geneva: UNCTAD.

UNCTAD 2010. *World Investment Report 2010.* Geneva: UNCTAD.

UNCTAD 2013. *World Investment Report 2013.* Geneva: UNCTAD.

UNCTAD 2015. *World Investment Report 2015.* Geneva: UNCTAD.

UNCTADStat 2022. Fact Sheet 9: Foreign Direct Investment. https://unctad.org/system/files/official-document/tdstat47_FS09_en.pdf.

UNIDO INDSTAT 2023. Industrial Statistics. https://stat.unido.org/.

UNSD 2023. National Accounts Database. https://unstats.un.org/unsd/snaama.

Urry, J. 2014. *Offshore.* Cambridge: Polity.

Voth, H. 2004. "Living standards and the urban environment". In R. Floud & P. Johnson (eds), *Cambridge Economic History of Modern Britain, Volume 1: Industrialisation, 1700–1860*, 268–94. Cambridge: Cambridge University Press.

Vu, K., N. Haraguchi & J. Amann 2021. "Deindustrialization in developed countries amid accelerated globalization: patterns, influencers, and policy insights". *Structural Change and Economic Dynamics* 59(C): 454–69.

Wacquant, L. 2009. *Punishing the Poor.* Durham, NC: Duke University Press.

Wade, R. 1990. *Governing the Market.* Princeton, NJ: Princeton University Press.

Wadsworth, J. 2017. "Immigration and the UK economy". LSE Centre for Economic Performance. http://cep.lse.ac.uk/pubs/download/ea039.pdf.

Wagner, A. & S. Starrs 2022. "Interview with Sean Starrs". https://join.substack.com/p/dominance.

Walker, M. 1979. "The National Front". In H. Drucker (ed.), *Multi-Party Britain*, 183–203. Basingstoke: Macmillan.

Walker, P. *et al.* 2021. "Tories accused of levelling up 'stitch up' over regional deprivation fund". *The Guardian*, 4 March. https://www.theguardian.com/politics/2021/mar/04/tories-accused-of-levelling-up-stitch-up-over-regional-deprivation-fund.

Wallerstein, I. 1974. *The Modern World System, Vol. 1.* New York: Academic Press.

Wallerstein, I. 1980. *The Modern World System, Vol. 2.* New York: Academic Press.

Wallison, P. 2009. "Cause and effect: government policy and the housing crisis". *Critical Review* 21(2/3): 365–76.

Wark, M. 2019. *Capital is Dead.* London: Verso.

Warren, B. 1980. *Imperialism: Pioneer of Capitalism.* London: Verso.

Weber, I. 2020. "Could the US and Chinese economies really 'decouple'?". *The Guardian*, 11 September. https://www.theguardian.com/commentisfree/2020/sep/11/us-china-global-economy-donald-trump.

Weber, I. 2021. *How China Escaped Shock Therapy.* London: Routledge.

Weiss, L. 2014. *America Inc?* Ithaca, NY: Cornell University Press.

Werner, M., J. Bair & V. Fernandez 2016. "Liking up to development? Global value chains and the making of a post-Washington Consensus". *Development and Change* 45(6): 1219–47.

Werner, M. & J. Bair 2019. "Global value chains and uneven development: a disarticulations perspective". In S. Ponte, G. Gereffi & G. Raj-Reichert (eds), *Handbook on Global Value Chains*, 83–198. Cheltenham: Elgar.

White, M. & A. Travis 2002. "Blunkett defends 'swamping' remark". *The Guardian*, 25 April. https://www.theguardian.com/politics/2002/apr/25/immigrationandpublicservices.immigration.

White House 2023. "Remarks by National Security Adviser Jake Sullivan on renewing American economic leadership at the Brookings Institution". https://www.whitehouse.gov/briefing-room/speeches-remarks/2023/04/27/remarks-by-national-security-advisor-jake-sullivan-on-renewing-american-economic-leadership-at-the-brookings-institution/.

Williams, J. 2014. "The political education of Walter Benn Michaels: an interview". *Symploke* 22(1/2): 337–59.

Williams, J. 2017. *White Working Class.* Cambridge, MA: Harvard Business Review Press.

Wilson, W. 1997. *When Work Disappears.* New York: Vintage.

Winant, G. 2021. *The Next Shift.* Cambridge, MA: Harvard University Press.

WMO 2023. "Past eight years confirmed to be the warmest on record". Press release, 12 January. https://public.wmo.int/en/media/press-release/past-eight-years-confirmed-be-eight-warmest-record#:~:text=The%20warmest%20eight%20years%20have,contributed%20to%20record%20global%20temperatures.

Wood, E. 1991. *The Pristine Culture of Capitalism.* London: Verso.

Wolf, M. 2023. "We must tackle the looming debt crisis before it is too late". *Financial Times*, 17 January.

Wood, A. 2017. "How globalisation affected manufacturing around the world". VoxEu. https://voxeu.org/article/how-globalisation-affected-manufacturing-around-world.

World Bank 1993. *The East Asian Miracle.* Oxford: Oxford University Press.

World Bank 1997. *World Development Report 1997.* Oxford: Oxford University Press.

World Bank 1999. *World Development Report 1999.* Oxford: Oxford University Press.

World Bank 2002. *Globalization, Growth and Poverty.* Oxford: Oxford University Press.

World Bank 2019. PovcalNet. Washington, DC: World Bank.

World Bank 2020. *World Development Report 2020.* Oxford: Oxford University Press.

World Bank 2023a. *Collapse and Recovery: How Covid-19 Eroded Human Capital and What to do About It.* Washington, DC: World Bank.

World Bank 2023b. "The global economic outlook in five charts". https://blogs.worldbank.org/developmenttalk/global-economic-outlook-five-charts-0.

Wright, E. 1985. *Classes.* London: Verso.

Younge, G. 2009. "When you watch the BNP on TV, remember Jack Straw started all this". *The Guardian*, 21 October. https://www.theguardian.com/commentisfree/2009/oct/21/jack-straw-bnp-griffin-hain.

Zhang, B. 2017. "Trump's 'America First' policies are catapulting Boeing into dangerous territory". Business Insider. http://uk.businessinsider.com/boeing-trump-administration-policies-effects-2017-2.

Zheng, Z. 2002. "China's terms of trade in world manufactures, 1993–2000". UNCTAD Discussion Paper No.161.

Zuboff, S. 2019. *The Age of Surveillance Capitalism*. New York: Profile.

INDEX